# DREAMSTREETS

## ART IN WILMINGTON 1970–1990

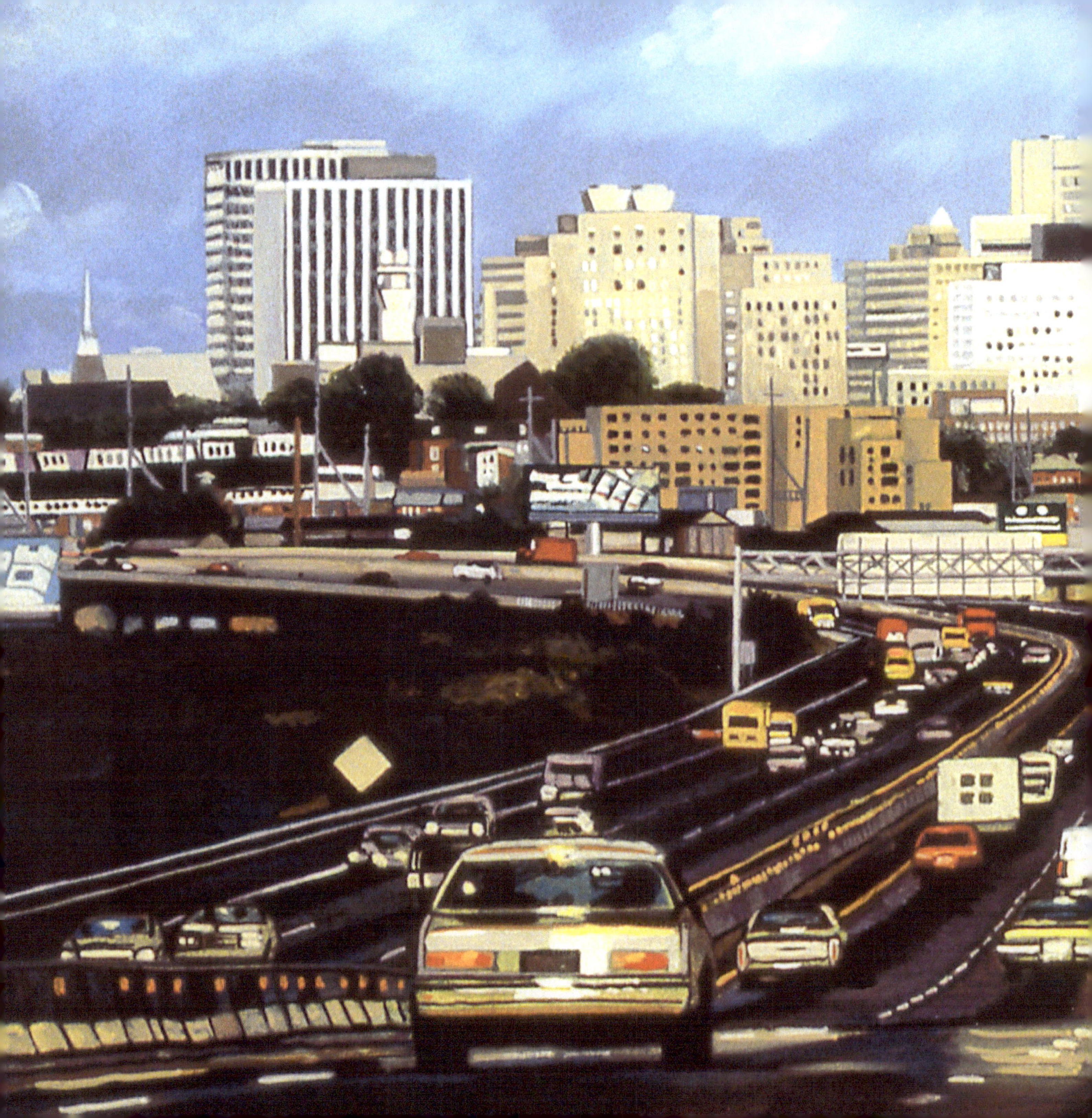

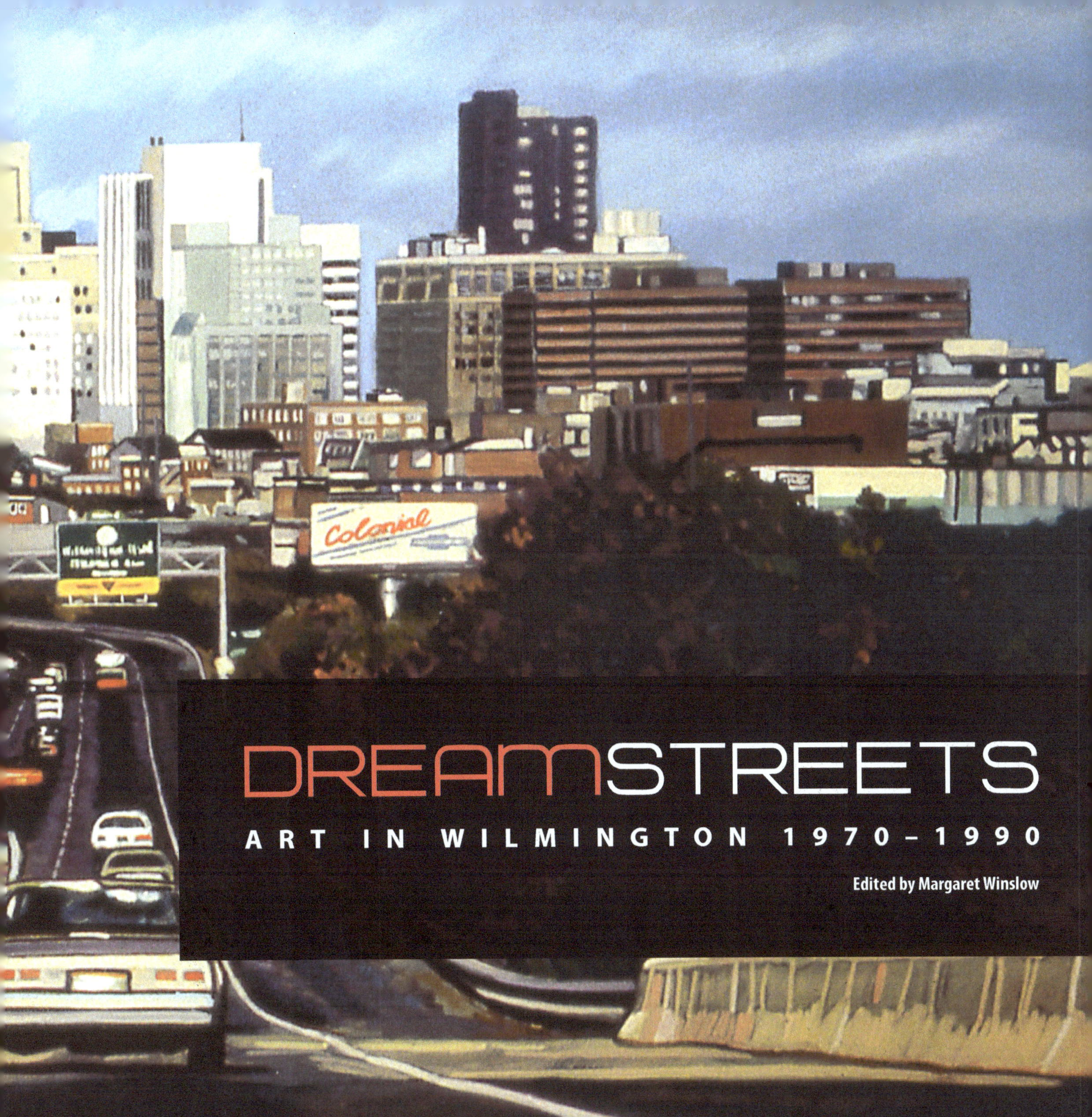
Colonial
DREAMSTREETS
ART IN WILMINGTON 1970–1990
Edited by Margaret Winslow

*Dream Streets: Art in Wilmington 1970–1990*



Published in conjunction with the exhibition
*Dream Streets: Art in Wilmington 1970–1990*
Organized by the Delaware Art Museum
June 27–September 27, 2015

*Dream Streets: Art in Wilmington 1970–1990* is made possible by DuPont and the Johannes R. and Betty P. Krahmer American Art Exhibition Fund. This exhibition is partially funded by a grant from the Delaware Humanities Forum, a state program of the National Endowment for the Humanities. Additional support is provided by grants from the Delaware Division of the Arts, a state agency dedicated to nurturing and supporting the arts in Delaware, in partnership with the National Endowment for the Arts.

Published by the Delaware Art Museum

Designed by Candice Kearns

Edited by Gretchen Dykstra
Library of Congress Control Number: 2015931775

ISBN 978-0-9960676-2-1

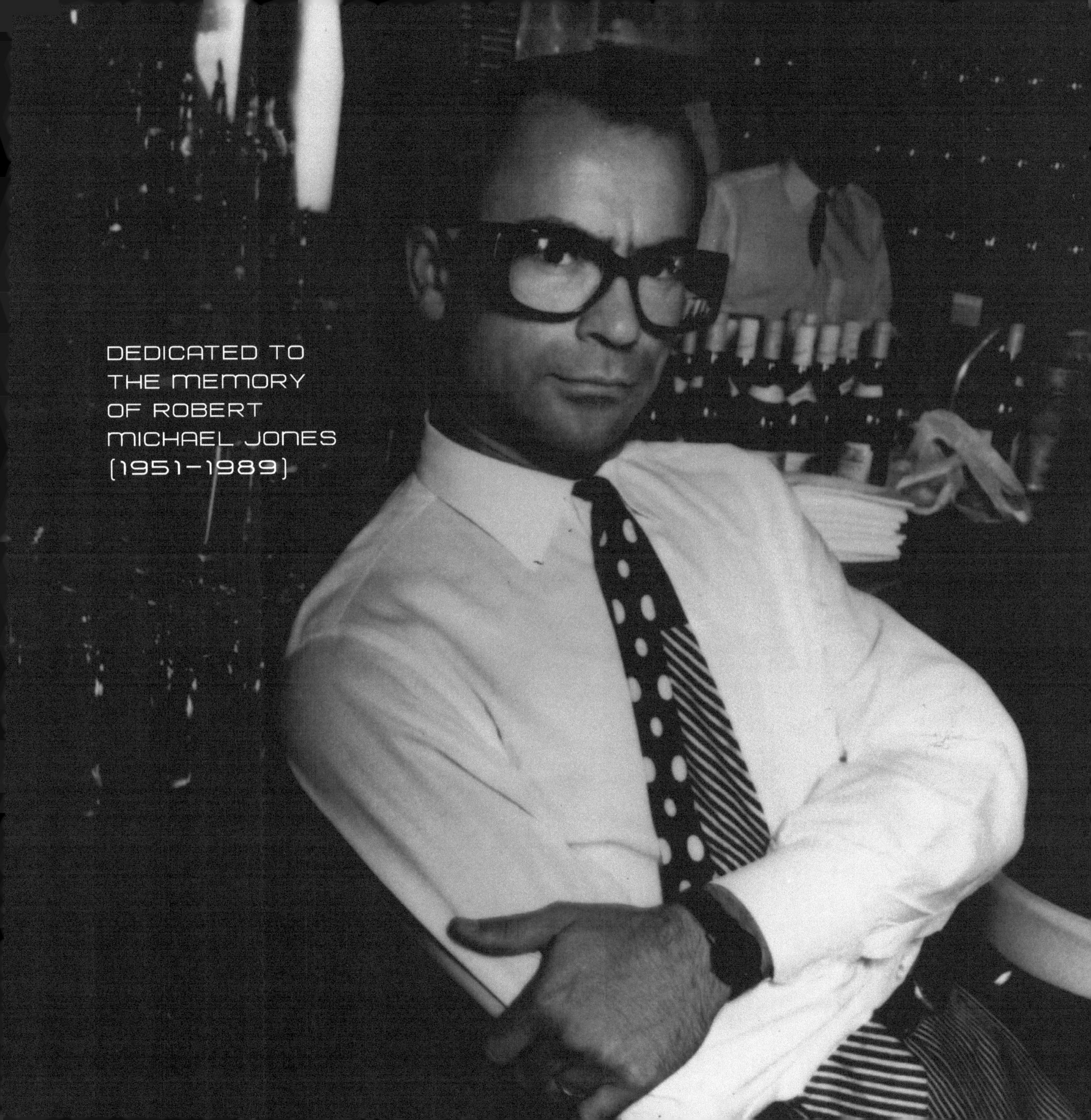
DEDICATED TO
THE MEMORY
OF ROBERT
MICHAEL JONES
(1951–1989)

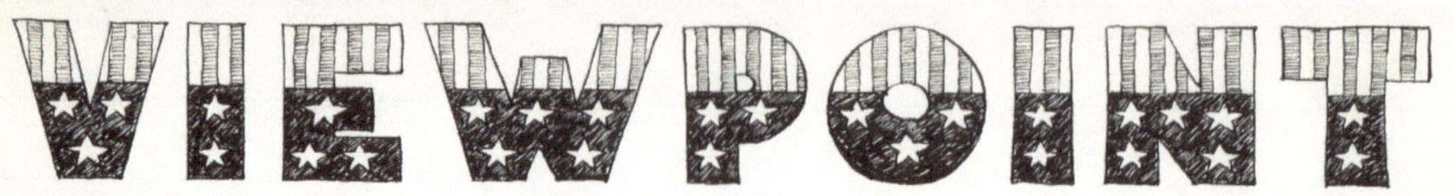


VOL. 2 NO. 2 University of Delaware NOVEMBER 1972

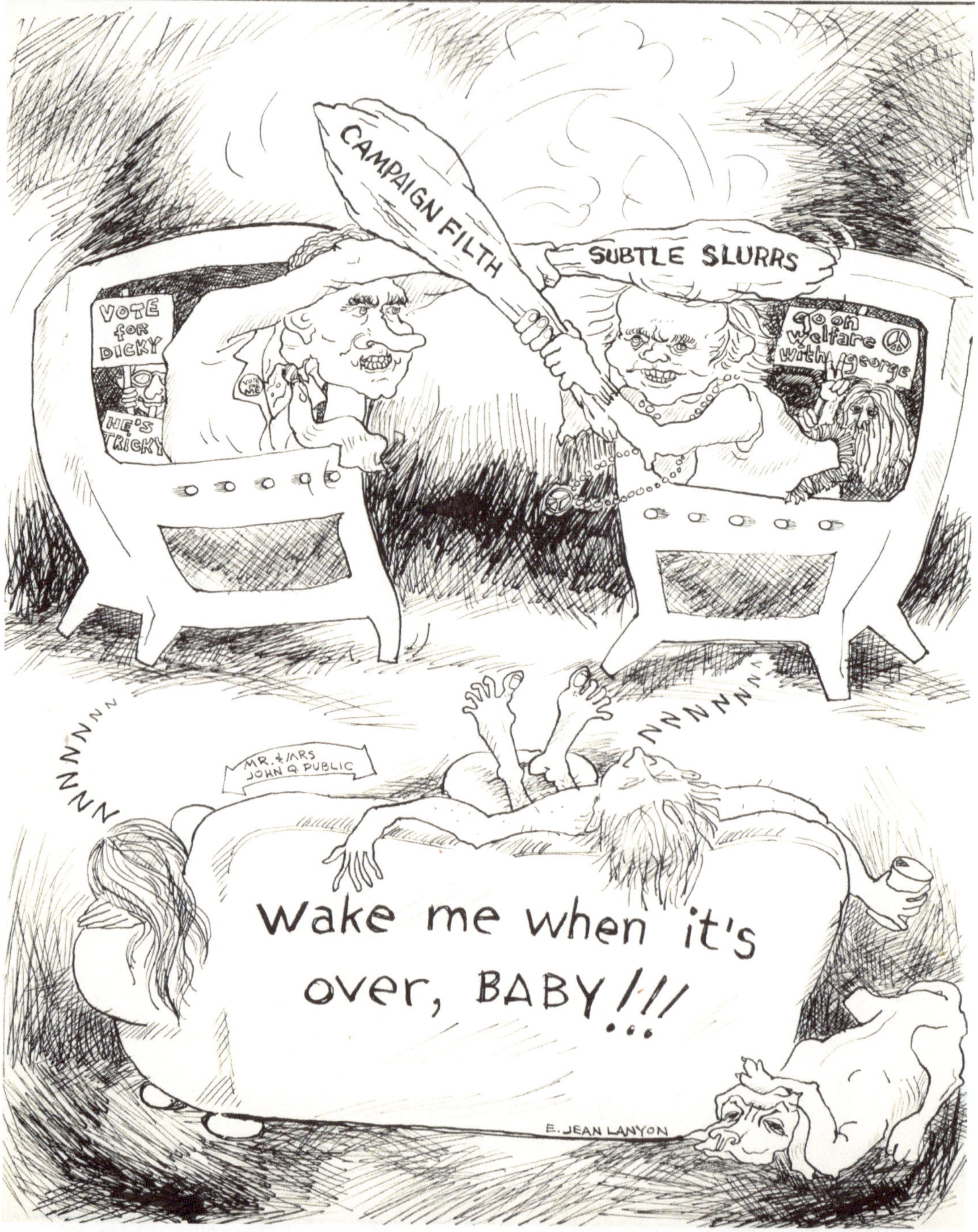

CAMPAIGN FILTH

SUBTLE SLURRS

VOTE for DICKY

HE'S TRICKY

go on welfare with george

NNNNNNN

NNNNNNN

MR. & MRS JOHN Q. PUBLIC

Wake me when it's over, BABY!!!

E. JEAN LANYON

# CONTENTS

# FOREWORD

The history of art is replete with cycles of intensive creativity, dormancy, and rebirth. It is with great pleasure that I introduce this compendium of essays, accompanying Margaret Winslow's brilliant reckoning of Wilmington in the politically tumultuous, free-spirited, exuberant decades of the 1970s and '80s. The project was conceived almost at the moment of Ms. Winslow's arrival as Assistant Curator of Contemporary Art at the Delaware Art Museum over five years ago. Fresh from graduate school and having re-engaged with the Wilmington community through her role in the New Wilmington Art Association, she developed a fascination with this earlier moment of intensive creativity in the region. As always, her sense of timing was auspicious, synchronizing with a newfound and widespread curiosity about this period in our national history of art.

Wilmington's rich role in these decades of artistic experimentation may come as a surprise to newcomers. But inhabitants of the city have historically shown a deep commitment to its cultural depth. The Delaware Art Museum was founded through the perseverance and support of those who understood the importance of Howard Pyle's contribution to the history of American illustration when, at his sudden death, they purchased the remaining works in his studio and established the Wilmington Society of Fine Arts. Since then, the Museum has continued to support and promote the wealth of aesthetic talent indigenous to the region. It is therefore a right and a good thing that this project celebrating this intensive interval of creativity should be undertaken with the advantage of a quarter century of hindsight, here, at the Delaware Art Museum.

Having lived through a good portion of these two decades, I look forward to a continuation of the conversation that this text will undoubtedly engender. What a long, strange trip it's been!

**Margaretta S. Frederick**
*Chief Curator and Annette Woolard-Provine Curator of the Bancroft Collection*



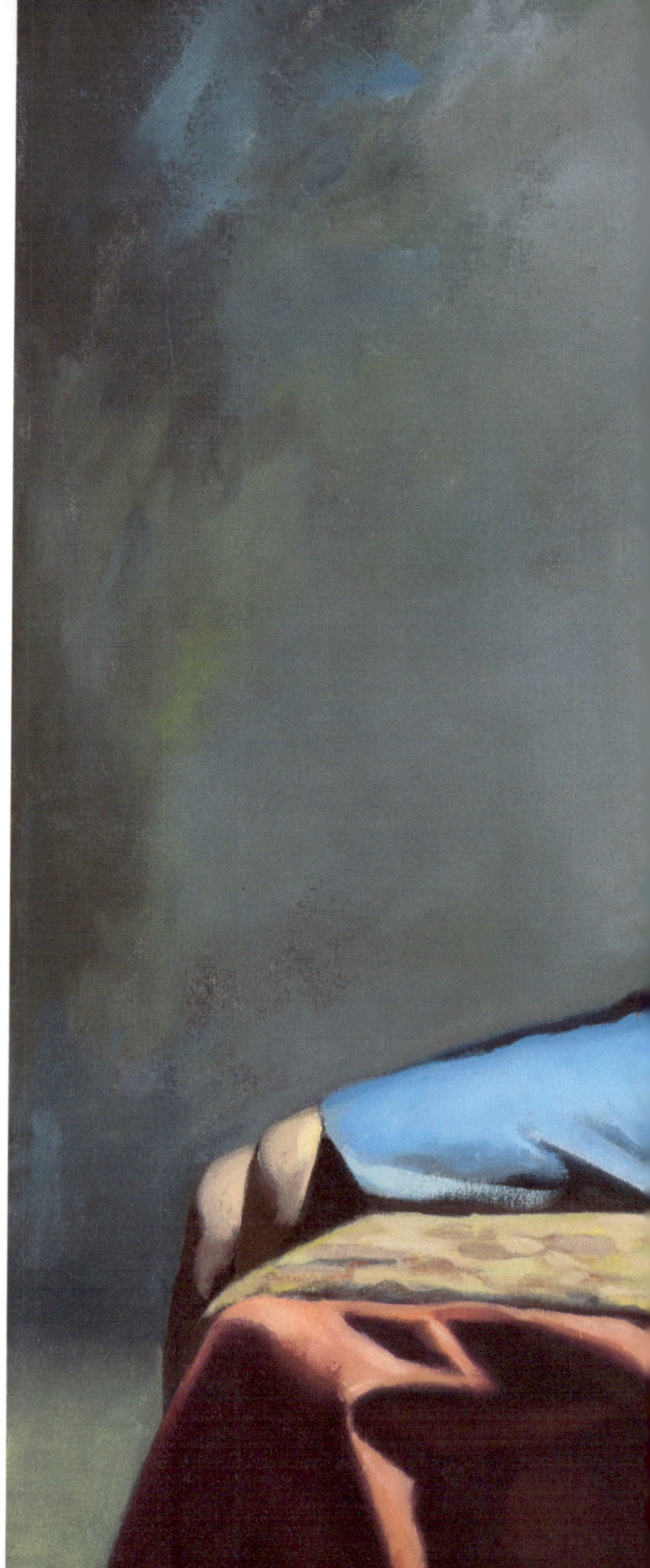

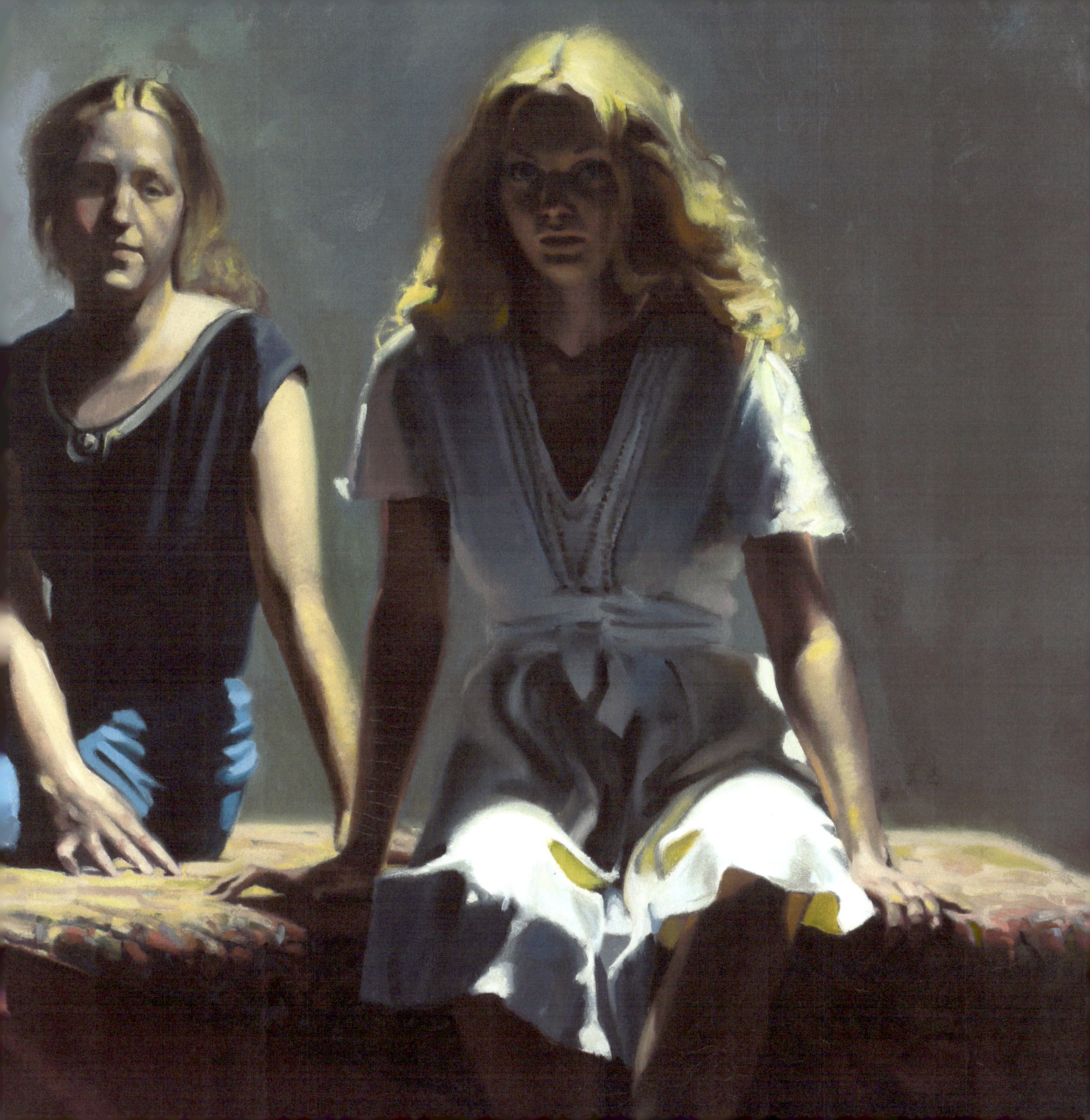

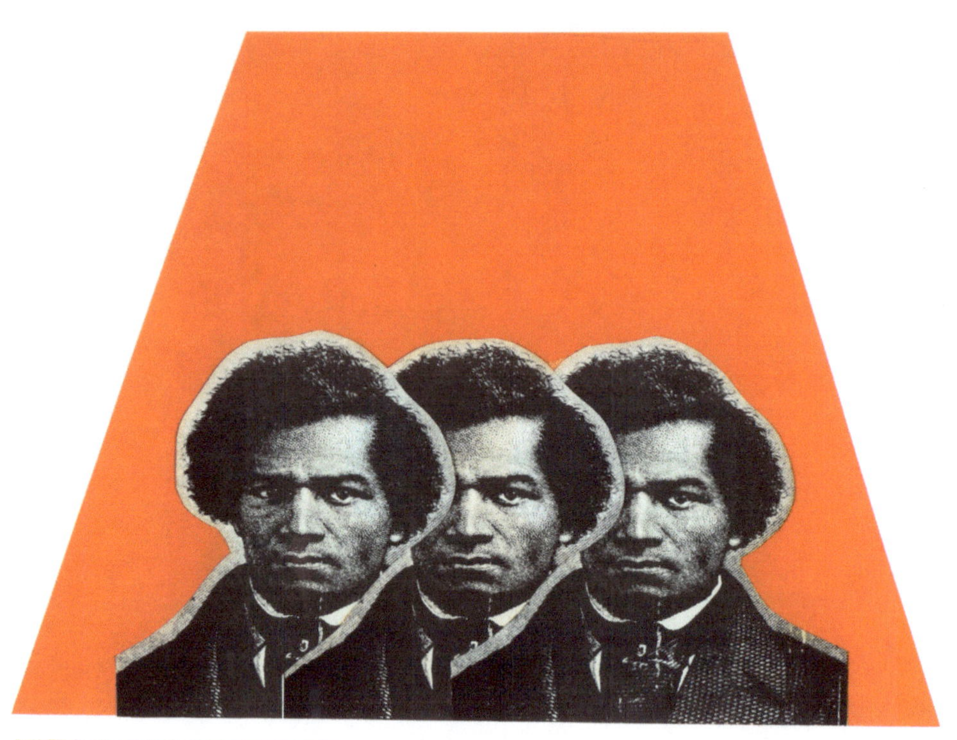

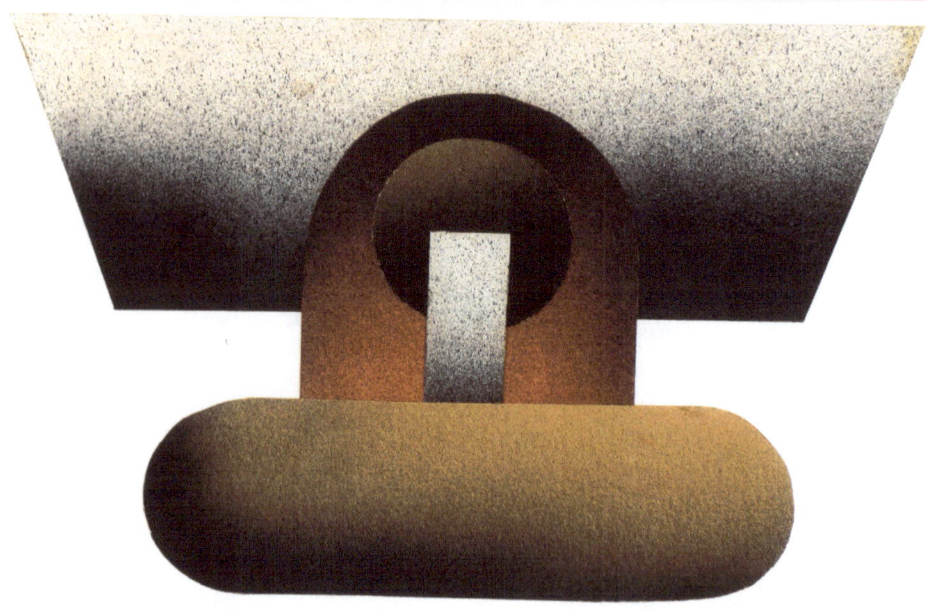

# PREFACE AND ACKNOWLEDGMENTS

This project originated with a chance tour of the Queen Theater in downtown Wilmington in 2009, just prior to the start of a major renovation project to create World Café Live at The Queen. On viewing the Fifth Street stairwell, I was met by bold, black graphics that repeated the word—*gallery*—up to the landing. My interest was immediately piqued, having not been familiar with any commercial art endeavors based in The Queen. A brief history of the building chronicles the construction as the Indian Queen Hotel in 1789, an upgrade to the first-class Clayton House hotel in 1871, and the subsequent conversion to a 2,000-seat movie theater in 1916. The last film shown was *House on Haunted Hill*, and following that April 1959 screening, the space was said to have remained dark and vacant for the next five decades. What this concise chronology omits is the infusion of energy into the second floor space of The Queen throughout the mid-to late 1970s.

On April 30, 1974, the Fifth Street Gallery opened its first show, and what followed through 1978 were regular exhibitions and events in the 3,000-square-foot gallery that brought artists, celebrities, and musicians into the city. Combined with the endeavors of nonprofit arts organizations and elected officials, Fifth Street Gallery helped advance efforts to create a centralized, creative community in downtown Wilmington. This publication traces the flourishing art scene during the two decades between the 1968 riots and the 1987 stock market crash and subsequent economic downturns of the late 1980s and the early 1990s—a time in which Wilmington experienced the establishment of arts and cultural organizations, such as the Delaware Center for the Contemporary Arts, Delaware Humanities Forum, and Delaware Theatre Company; new commercial art galleries; and dedicated federal funding for outreach programs. Within this encouraging climate, artists utilized collaborative, social practices to create spaces in which to share and grow the contemporary art community within and surrounding the city of Wilmington.

Countless individuals assisted with this project. Caitlin Davis served as curatorial intern, devoting over 3,500 hours between June 2011 and April 2012, tirelessly researching and connecting with numerous artists; her contribution is invaluable. 16 other contributors added their voices to this publication, enriching it with their recollections, and I thank each one of them for their memories. I would also like to thank Dr. Connie Cooper and Heather Isbell Schumacher at the Delaware Historical Society; Gretchen Dykstra for a well-edited text; Margaretta Frederick and Alice Hupfel for first answering my endless questions about the Fifth Street Gallery; the family of Robert Jones, especially Wendy Jones Donahoe, Kim Jones, and Don Gouge; Leah V. Kacanda in the City of Wilmington's Department of Planning and Development; Candice Kearns for a beautiful publication; Wesley Memeger, who kindly introduced me to many of the artists involved; and staff at *The News Journal*. 63 individuals consented to an interview for this project, and I am pleased that their oral histories will be preserved in the Museum's Helen Farr Sloan Library and Archives thanks, in part, to a grant from the Delaware Humanities Forum. And finally, I extend the greatest possible appreciation to the artists, lenders, and Delaware Art Museum staff and volunteers who made the related exhibition, *Dream Streets: Art in Wilmington 1970–1990* (June 27–September 27, 2015), possible. Keith Ragone produced a brilliant exhibition design, and registrars Amy Hussey and Erin Tohill Robin and preparators John Gibbons and Jonathan Scoff ensured a seamless installation.

My hope is that my earnest efforts to document this rich history will prompt others to examine the stories that may have been unintentionally excluded.

**Margaret Winslow**
*Associate Curator for Contemporary Art*

## HATS OFF TO THE SEVENTIES

**e. jean lanyon**
*Artist and Delaware Poet Laureate Emerita*

hats off!   hats off!   no more fedoras!
no more tiny hats with veils!
a restless wind is blowing,
the sixties are gone, flower children grown up.
a time of energy is happening,
a new indignation arises —
rebirth of the suffragettes into feminists,
a time to make new voices heard.

hats off!   hats off!
women once silenced breaking through
to recognition and rights,
artists, writers, scholars, leaders,
these women, these uppity women,
these wonderful uppity women
leading the way into the future.

hats off!   toss off the old hats!
welcome lighted floors and disco dance.
hats off to the new, to our country's birthday,
our bicentennial of freedom.
women opening paths, giving new strength
to civil rights,  to equal rights.
off with the old hats, on with the pant suits,
new voices in poetry and art, new songs to sing,
voices once silenced now heard.
hats off!   hats off!

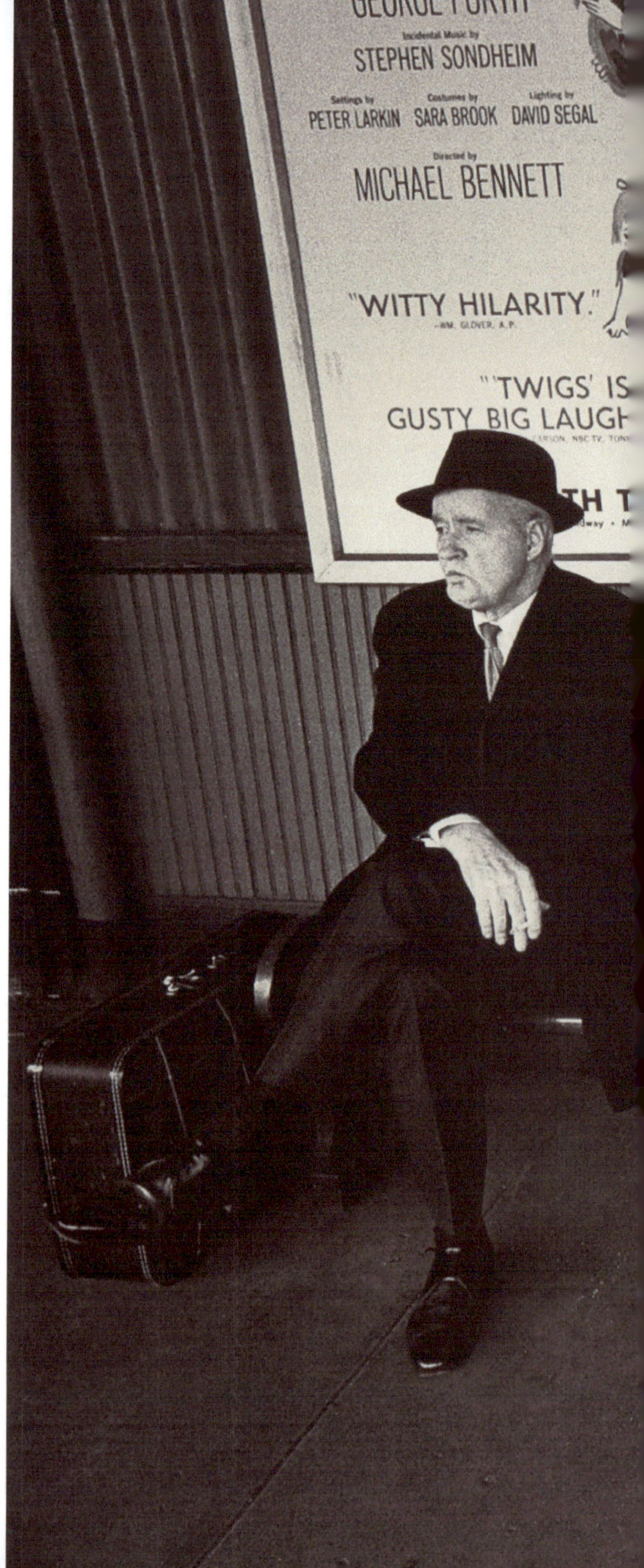

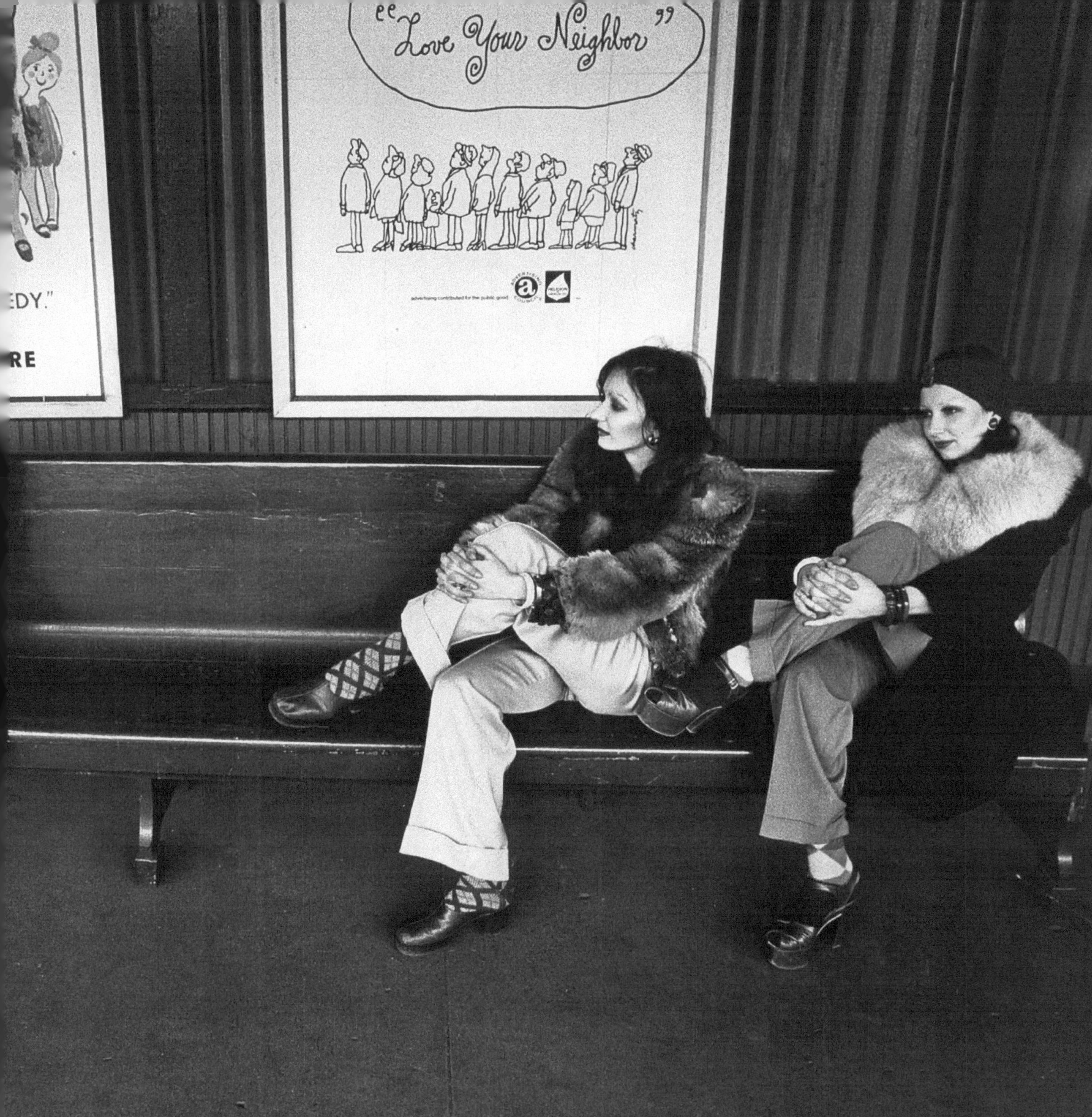

“Love Your Neighbor”
advertising contributed for the public good
EDY.”
RE

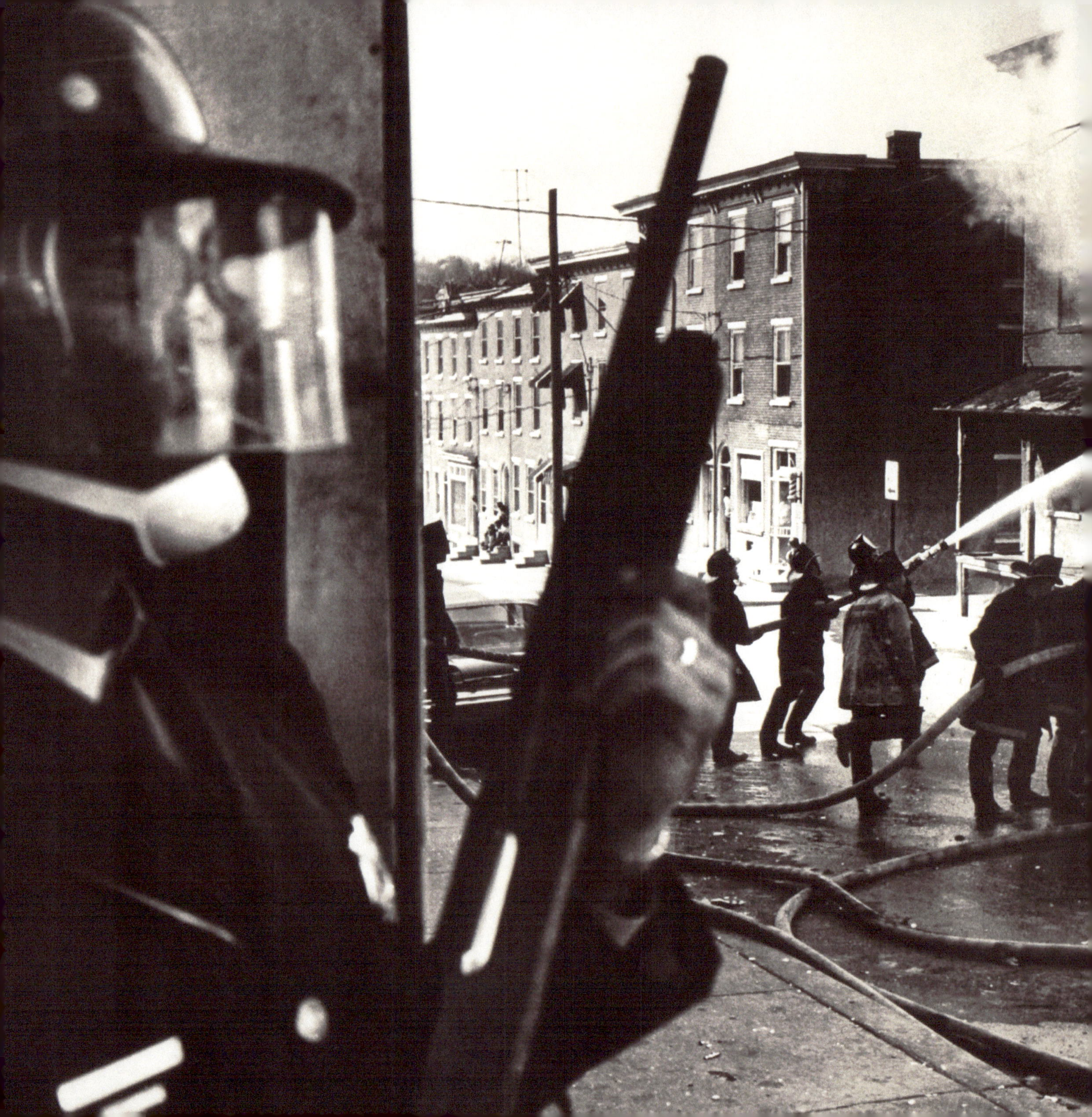

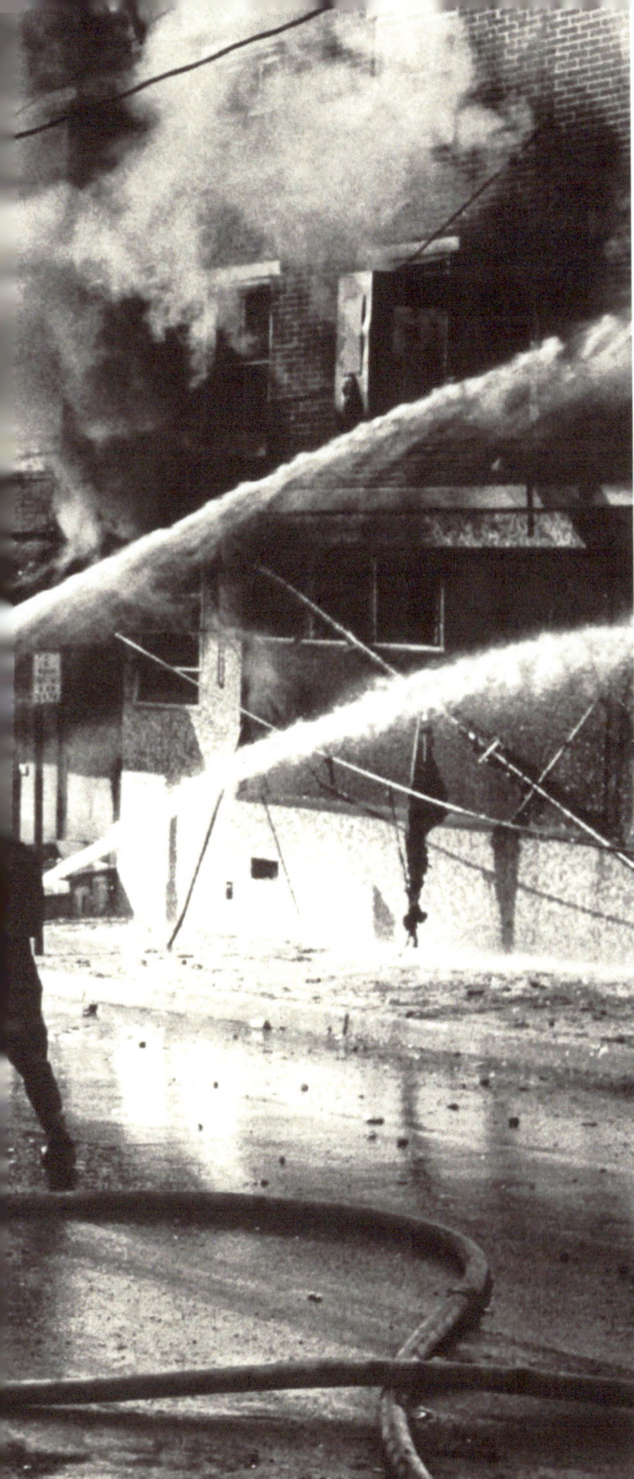

# DREAM STREETS

**Margaret Winslow**

Race riots erupted throughout the United States in the long, hot summer of 1967, but the assassination of Martin Luther King, Jr., on April 4, 1968, escalated the rioting as the country mourned the loss of the civil rights leader. Following the riots, National Guard troops occupied the city of Wilmington for nine months until the election of Governor Russell W. Peterson. Tensions from the prolonged military presence coupled with the flight of downtown residents created for some a culture of fear and uncertainty about venturing into the city. Such anxieties were mitigated through various solutions initiated by government agencies, nonprofit organizations, and private individuals. It was during this transitional moment, for both the city and the nation, that a burgeoning avant-garde arts scene found traction, resulting in the establishment of many of the cultural pillars that continue to support contemporary art in Wilmington.

In March 1969, the Delaware State Arts Council (DSAC) was established through an executive order, creating a dedicated body through which to distribute all funds received from the National Endowment for the Arts (NEA). Headed by Mrs. C. Douglass (Polly) Buck, Jr., the first initiative was a two-part exhibition installed in government offices downtown in August 1969. Nine paintings by Tua Hayes hung in the office of Mayor Harry G. Haskell, Jr., while five oils by Lulu Cooper were displayed Governor Peterson's Wilmington office at 704 Delaware Avenue. Shortly after, the DSAC was divided into subcommittees; Bruce St. John, director of the Delaware Art Center, was named head of the visual arts committee, and Dr. Thomas S. Watson from the University of Delaware's Department of Dramatic Arts and Speech led the performing arts committee.[1] By the fall of 1969, Craig A. Gilborn was hired as DSAC's executive director and grants were awarded to four nonprofit organizations throughout the state.

Two of DSAC's most visible programs in the early 1970s were ArtMobile and *Sculptures in the Square*. Presented in cooperation with the Wilmington Department of Parks and Recreation—and supported by Connecticut-based, large-scale sculpture fabricator Lippincott, Inc.—*Sculptures in the Square* was a temporary sculpture installation in Rodney Square during the summer of 1970. Wilmington's contemporary public art initiative took place concurrently with similar programs in New York City, Cincinnati, and other major US cities.[2] The two works on view—George Sugarman's *Square Spiral* (1968) and Bernard Rosenthal's *Cube in Seven Parts* (1967)—had been displayed the previous summer in Detroit's *Sculpture Downtown*. The presentation elicited excited public response, some critical, but as Bill Frank reported in the June 18, 1970, edition of the *Morning News*, Sugarman—who was on hand with Rosenthal for the installation—said, "First you pass it. Maybe you touch it. You can kick it, even hate it, O.K. Maybe you will love it…"[3]

ArtMobile was developed following a visit by DSAC members to the Virginia Museum of Fine Arts' Artmobile program in spring 1970. By January 1971, plans were announced to create Delaware's first mobile art gallery—housed in a converted moving van—to tour the state with fine art exhibitions. On April 13, 1971, the opening ceremony was held at Legislative Hall in Dover and the ribbon was cut for *Howard Pyle's Pupils*, a display of photographs of Pyle in his studio and 14 paintings by his students. Culled from the collections of the Delaware Art Museum, DuPont, and private lenders, the exhibition was visited by over 5,000 people within its first week on the road and was parked in Rodney Square in addition to other venues statewide. The program continued until 1980—despite the energy crisis at mid-decade—with a contemporary illustration exhibition, loans from the Philadelphia Museum of Art, and patent models and kitchen appliances from the Hagley Museum. The most popular traveling show, *Delaware Artists*, in 1977, included work by five sculptors and 17 painters statewide. It attracted 36,000 visitors.[4]

Happening at the same time as DSAC's public programs were outreach efforts that would create a physical arts presence in the heart of the city. Wilmington's first commercial art galleries had opened downtown in the late 19th century: the Yerger Brothers' Art Gallery was located at 419 Market Street, while the Fine Art Gallery opened at 604 Market Street (the latter showed, to great enthusiasm, Marceli Suchorowski's *Nana*, a painting of the heroine of Émile Zola's 1880 tale of the same name).[5] The Delaware Art Museum,

**PAT CROWE, *ART VAN*,** APRIL 17, 1972

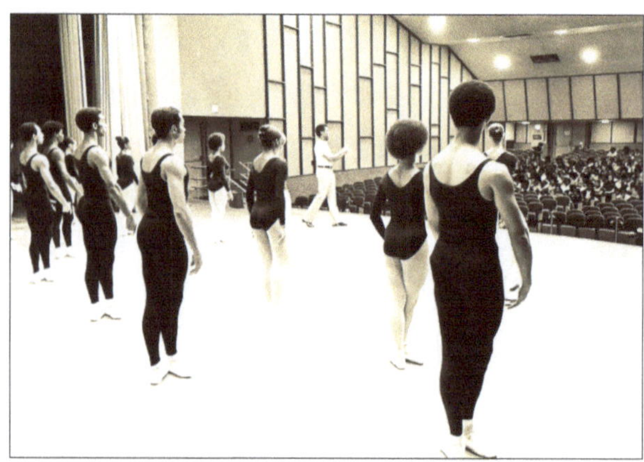

**RON DUBICK, *ART MITCHELL DANCE*,** OCTOBER 17, 1972

founded as the Wilmington Society of the Fine Arts in 1912, held its earliest exhibitions on Rodney Square, first in the Hotel DuPont and later in the Wilmington Free Library. The Museum's presence in downtown Wilmington was strengthened with the establishment of the Downtown Gallery in October 1970 during the renovation of the 1935 building.[6] Organized by the Women's Committee, the gallery—located in the former Bank of Delaware's Ninth and Market Street branch—featured monthly exhibitions of work from the permanent collection as well as loans from local artists and collectors. The program brought regional attention and acknowledgment of "Delaware's expanding art program."[7] Coordination of the space shifted to staff responsibility and changed hands multiple times in the 1970s.[8] Similar satellite galleries and outreach programs were established by museums throughout the country, including the Philadelphia Museum of Art's Department of Urban Outreach in 1970 and the Whitney Museum of American Art's Downtown Branch Museum in 1973. The Museum had supported the regional artist community with its annual exhibitions since its founding in 1912, but the Downtown Gallery reestablished the physical connection between the city center and the building on Kentmere Parkway.

In February 1972, the Museum—along with Wilmington's Department of Planning and Development, the Wilmington Housing Authority, and the Greater Wilmington Development Council—sponsored an exhibition in the Downtown Gallery of improvement plans for the city's central business district.[9] When the plans for a civic center and urban shopping area were scrapped soon after, then-mayor Harry G. Haskell, Jr., proposed the conversion of Market Street into a pedestrian mall.[10] However, it was not until Thomas C. Maloney defeated Haskell in the fall 1972 mayoral election and took office the next year that plans for the mall moved ahead. Simultaneous was the revitalization of the Grand Opera House, launched on December 22, 1971, with a joint gala for the centennial celebration of the Wilmington-based *News Journal* newspaper.[11] Following the gala, a nonprofit—Grand Opera

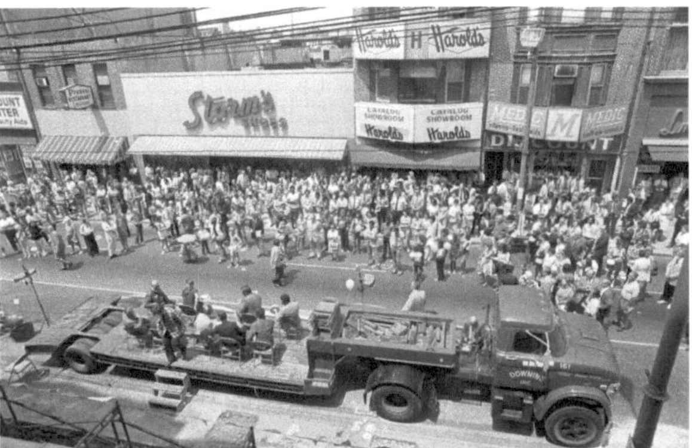

**FRED COMEGYS, *MARKET STREET MALL GROUNDBREAKING,*** JULY 16, 1974

House, Inc.—was established to receive the building title from the Masons, an architectural firm was selected, and funds were secured to undertake the massive project of restoring "the Victorian theatre in the context of a technically sound 20th-century theatre."[12] Work commenced on July 17, 1974, and continued through May 1976. The renovation project successfully restored the Grand to its 1871 glory and the inauguration-year festivities set the expectation for professional performing arts in downtown Wilmington. During that year, performers and companies included Max Morath, the Delaware Symphony Orchestra, the Philadelphia Orchestra,

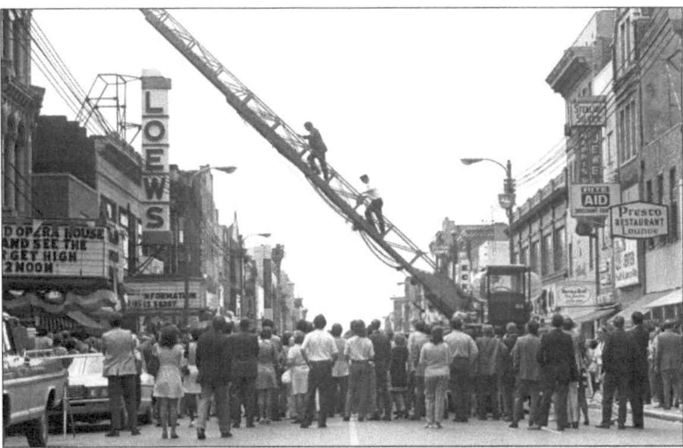

**PAT CROWE, *GRAND THEATER CEREMONIES,*** JULY 17, 1974

the Black Ensemble Theater, the Los Angeles Philharmonic, the Vienna Boys' Choir, and the Wilmington Opera Society's premiere of Alva Henderson's *Last of the Mohicans*, commissioned for the Bicentennial. The Grand restoration, and the installation of several 18th-century homes to create Willingtown Square between Fifth and Sixth Streets, bookended the Market Street Mall and provided physical spaces for centralized creativity. Spurred by the availability of commercial spaces and the reinvestment in downtown Wilmington, several artists relocated to the heart of the city.

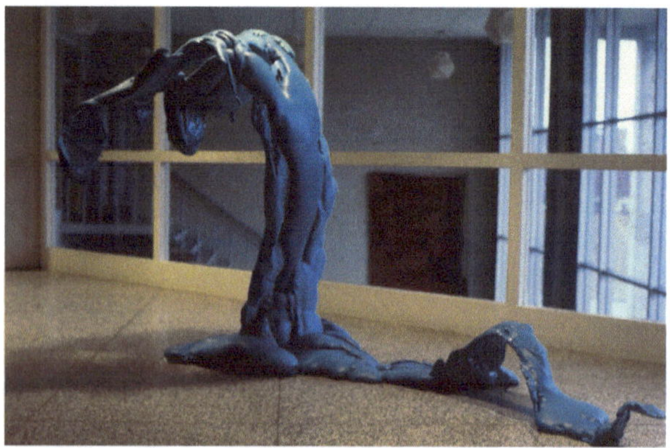

INSTALLATION VIEW OF **ROBERT JONES' *A NATURAL ENVIRONMENTAL FOAM PHENOMENON*** (MARCH 12–31, 1973)

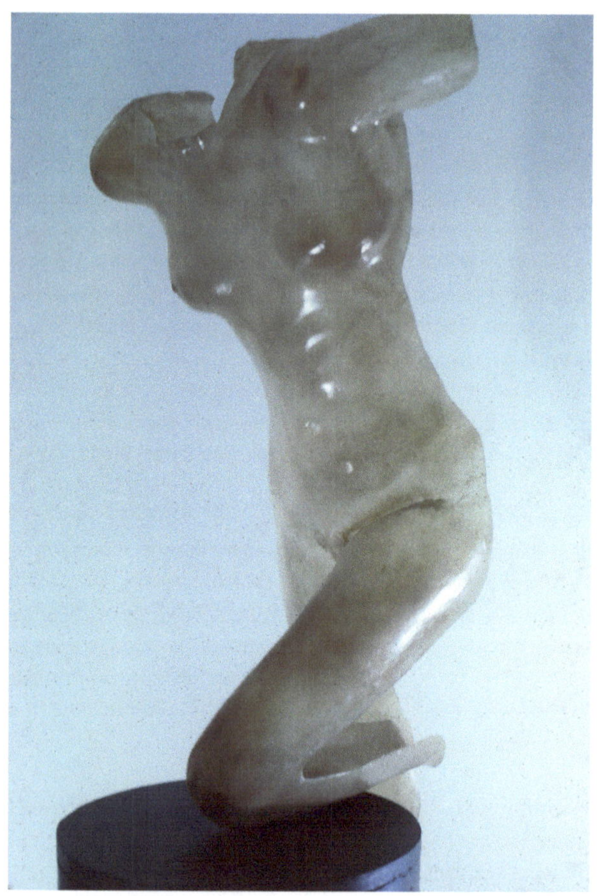

**ROBERT JONES, *FIBERGLAS NUDE*,** 1970

Robert Michael Jones, a Delaware native, attended Christiana High School before receiving his bachelor of fine arts degree in 1973 from the University of Delaware. He began exhibiting while in school, and did so more extensively after graduation, with solo presentations of his polyurethane and fiberglass sculptures in the university's Smith Hall, in the Haas Gallery at Bloomsburg State College in Pennsylvania (March 1973), and in the Delaware Art Museum's *59th Annual Delaware Show* (June 8–July 29, 1973). In a letter dated April 4, 1973, the Museum's Acting Director, Rowland Elzea, invited Jones to participate in a solo exhibition as part of the Delaware Art Museum Presents series that highlighted the work of "distinguished area artists."[13] Jones' response two months later sheds light on his opinion of Wilmington and his future intentions in regard to the establishment of Fifth Street Gallery. Jones accepted the invitation—installing his *Black Wilmington* exhibition in early 1975—and noted that instead of moving to New York, he had decided that "Wilmington seems more of a challenge. And more than anything I would love to break the Brandywine mystique."[14] His stated goal was to find a space in Wilmington and to establish a studio in the city.

The Queen Theater, a Wilmington landmark located at Market and Fifth Streets, screened its last film in 1959. While retail shops on the ground floor remained active, the upper stories were vacant for more than a decade. In his quest for a large loft space, Jones identified and rented the second floor of the Queen. The formation of Fifth Street Gallery was part of the multifaceted business of JFO Art Ltd, established by Jones and two fellow University of Delaware graduates, Jonathan R. Fox and Michael Oleksiw. The company offered a slide library, a newsletter, photography and print services, as well as art consulting, with the express desire of making "useful and strong the artistic resources of this area."[15] Fifth Street Gallery opened on April 30, 1974, with an exhibition of work by Wilmington's *News Journal* staff photographers.

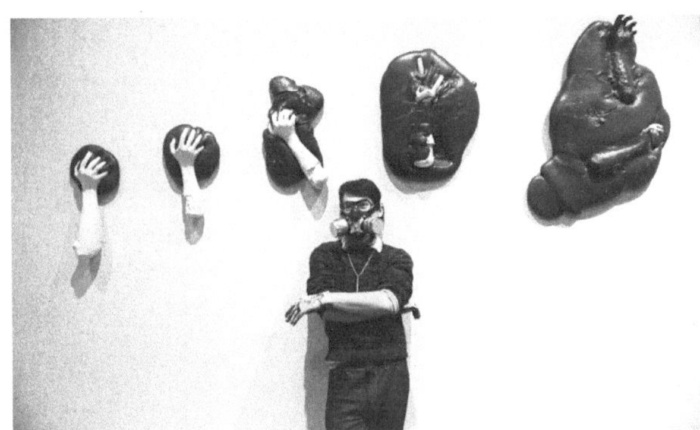

**RON DUBICK, *ROB JONES ARTIST*,** JANUARY 10, 1975

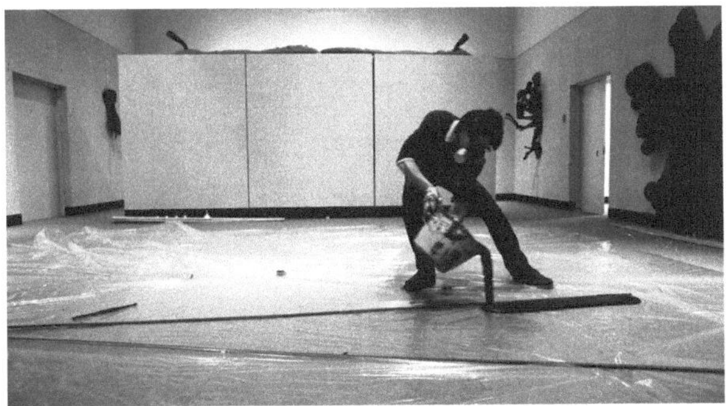

**RON DUBICK, *ROB JONES ARTIST*,** JANUARY 10, 1975

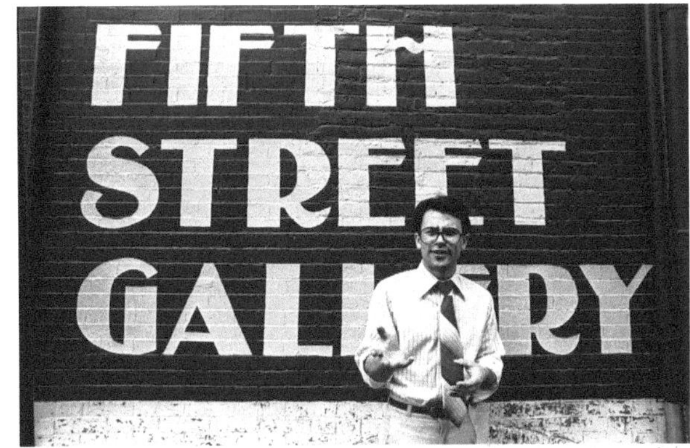


**RON DUBICK, *ROB JONES*,** APRIL 19, 1977

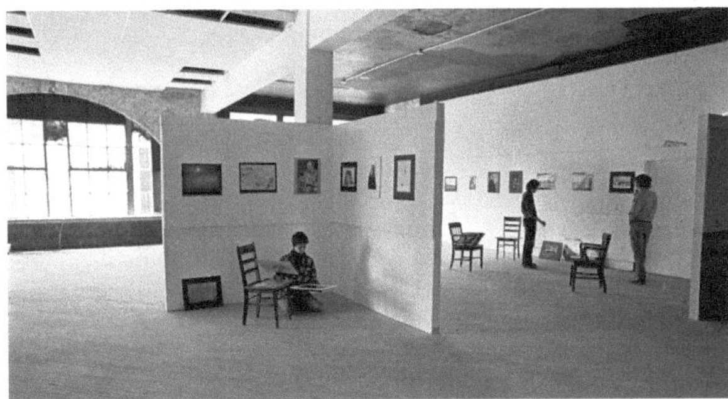

**GLENN CRAWFORD, *DOWNTOWN GALLERY*,** MAY 1, 1974

Over the next four years, Jones mounted monthly exhibitions of work by Delaware- and Philadelphia-based artists, including James A. Anderson, Julio daCunha, Traute Ishida, Vera Kaminski, Byron Shurtleff, Nick Snook, and Chun Kwang Young, among many others. Fifth Street Gallery was broadly recognized as the first commercial space to champion the work of under-recognized avant-garde painters, sculptors, and photographers. Jones' model of art advocacy extended directly into the public realm, engaging the community surrounding the gallery. On Market Street Mall, he produced—with the help of others, including Tom Watkins—the Paradise Party, the First Annual World Sleaze Convention, and *Sundial–1978*, an interactive dance performance by New York–based Battery Dance Company around

Ken Davis' sculptures. Jones also served as manager and host of the Uptown Disco that opened in the summer of 1978 on the second floor of the Grand.

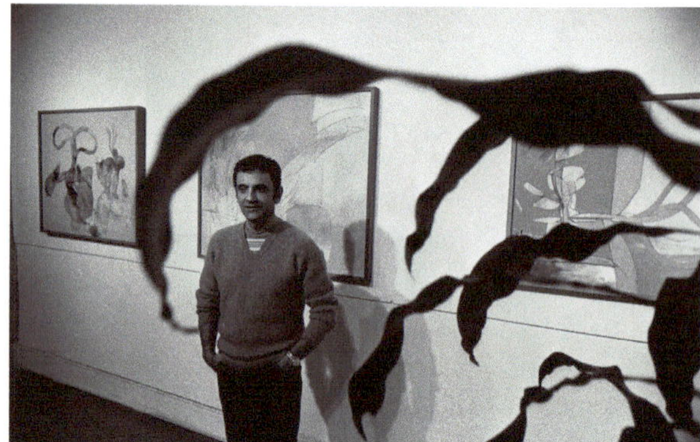

**FRED COMEGYS, *JULIO ACUNA–ARTIST,*** OCTOBER 22, 1975

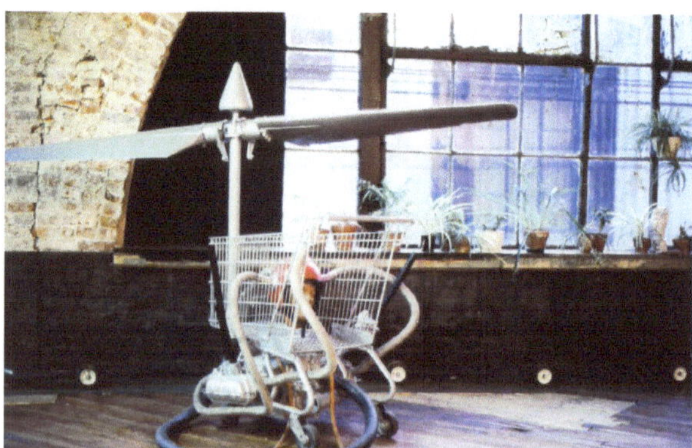

INSTALLATION VIEW OF **NICK SNOOK'S *VEHICULAR SCULPTURES*** (MAY 14–JUNE 2, 1974)

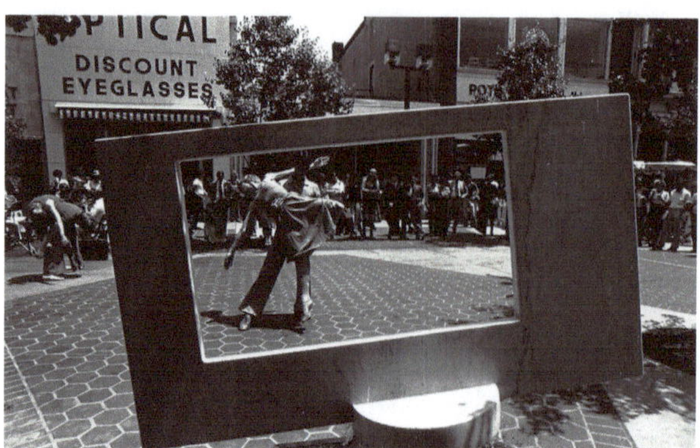


**BILL BALLENBERG, *SCULPTURE ON MALL,*** JUNE 12, 1978

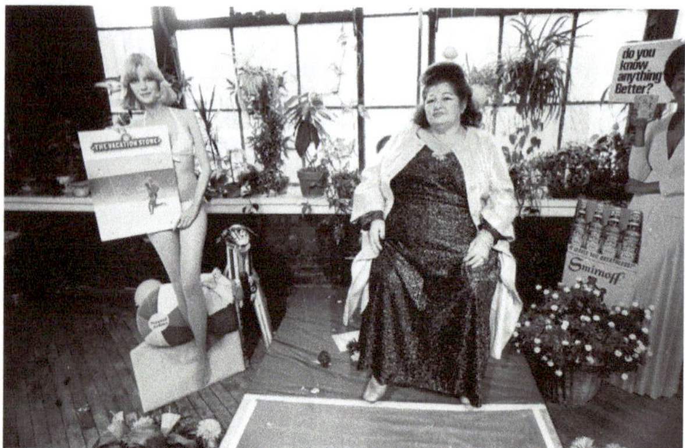


**PAT CROWE, *SLEEZE,*** SEPTEMBER 3, 1976

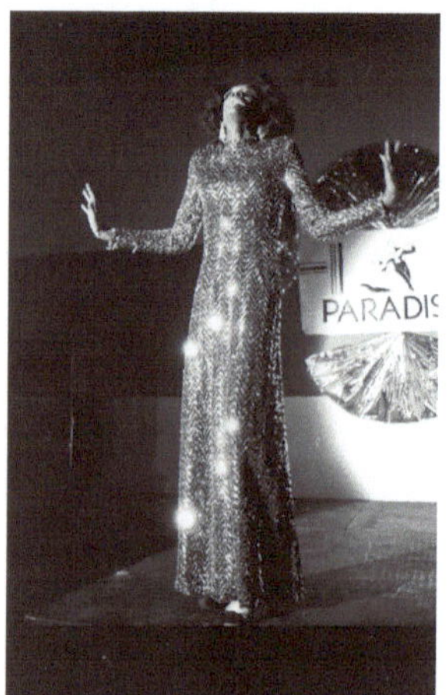

**FRED COMEGYS, *5TH ST GALLERY–PARTY,*** MAY 22, 1976

Watkins was equally responsible for infusing creative energy into Wilmington. He became a fixture in the downtown scene in the early 1970s, having lived in the city since 1967, attended H. Fletcher Brown Technical High School, and graduated with a commercial art degree in 1969. He took a sculpture course taught by Joe Moss at the University of Delaware in 1974 and, like Jones, founded an artist collective and business, Apocalyptic Productions, with Joyce Brabner and Craig Dawson that same year. While his progressive experiments in xerography would come later, in the 1980s, Watkins was engrossed in the alternative literary community from the start, serving as co-editor

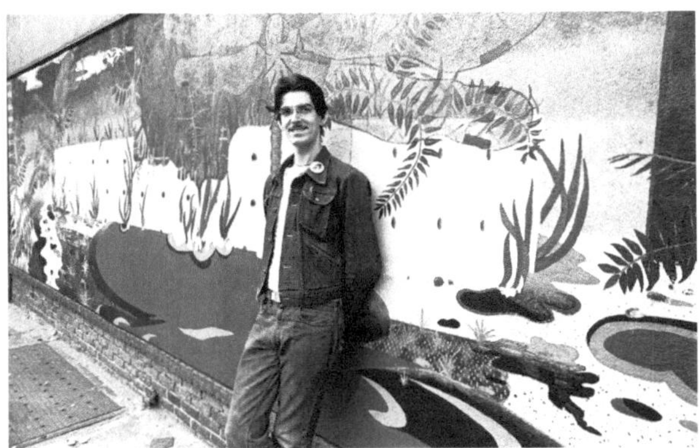
**RON DUBICK, *TOM WATKINS*,** APRIL 19, 1977

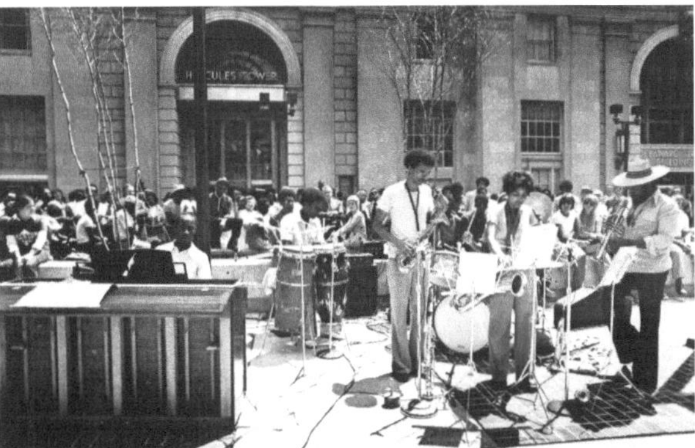
**CITYSOUNDS JAZZ MUSICIANS IN CONCERT,** WILMINGTON, 1976

and art director of *Emergency Illustrated* from 1973 to 1975 and contributing comic strips of regular characters such as Carbon Rodz, ING-7, Pat, and Sgt. Skull-Moss, a hermit crab that inhabited the skull of a dead soldier. His characters and plots offered biting criticism of both the Vietnam War and the long-term impact of nuclear energy. Watkins also covered comic art conventions in Philadelphia and social and cultural events such as that city's 1974 Gay Movement Conference. An interest in cuisine led him to contribute recipes and instructional illustrations, most often for vegetarian and macrobiotic dishes. While Fifth Street Gallery was known for displaying "modern art," Watkins's creations were "characterized as pop or ultra-modern."[16] The proximity of the two spaces to one another—on Fifth at opposite sides of Market Street—focused creative energy and encouraged visitation to the city.

Key to attracting young, working artists was not only exhibition space, but also funding for projects and living stipends. Financial support arrived in the summer of 1975 with the federal Comprehensive Employment and Training Act (CETA), via the Citysights/Citysounds (CS/CS) arts project.[17] The three-month project, which was repeated in 1976, was sponsored by the City of Wilmington under Mayor Maloney, and directed by the Wilmington Division of Manpower Development. CS/CS employed 52 "out-of-work or under-employed artists and visual artists" and was divided into two components—Citysights for the visual arts and Citysounds for music and drama.[18] Musical performers included a jazz group, an African percussion ensemble, a classical ensemble, and an eight-member theater ensemble that presented dance, dramatic readings, and skits.

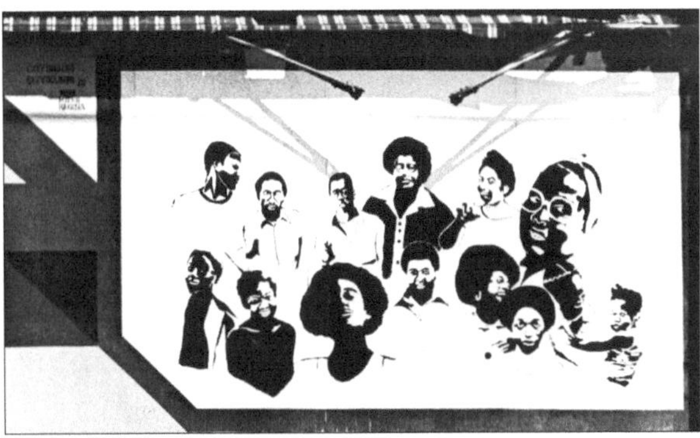
***PEOPLE ARE THE KEY* MURAL,** 1975–76

Citysights comprised two visual art programs. The first and most expansive of these produced 18 murals between the summers of 1975 and 1976. The mural movement of the early 1970s spread throughout the United States as individuals and community art workshops used large-scale public wall paintings to express sociopolitical concerns. Boston's Summerthing and New York's City Walls muralists were supported by government, corporate, and museum funding; Cincinnati's Urban Walls Project realized 10 murals between 1971 and 1973; and individuals and artist collaboratives such as St. Louis–based On the Wall Productions and the Los Angeles Fine Arts Squad realized vibrant abstract and figurative murals for businesses and communities.[19] In Wilmington, murals were located in Southbridge at Third and Harrison Streets (*People Are the Key*, under the direction of Roberto

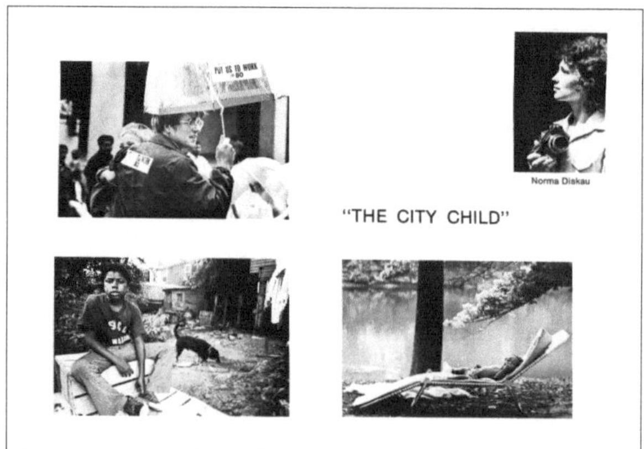


**NORMA CALABRO, *THE CITY CHILD*,** 1975

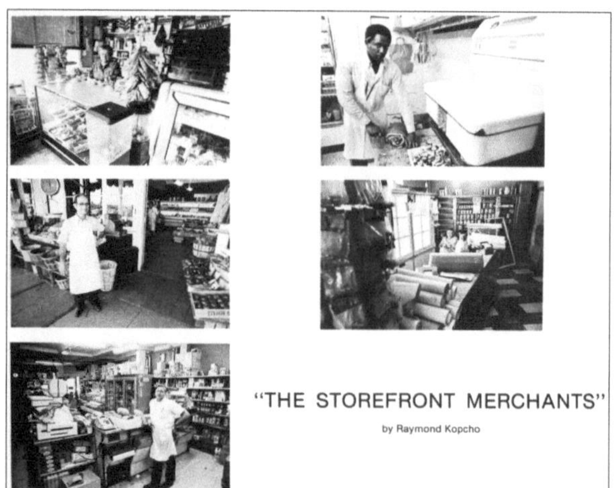


**RAYMOND KOPCHO, *THE STOREFRONT MERCHANTS*,** 1975

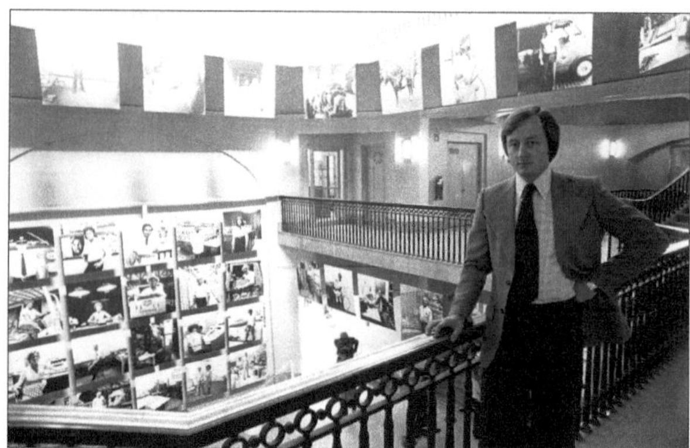

**DONAGHEY BROWN, *TOM STILTZ*,** JANUARY 25, 1976

Vega) and at the old Greyhound bus station at Second and French Streets (*In Transit* by Tom Watkins), in addition to other locations throughout the city. In September 1975, an exhibition was held in the Museum's Downtown Gallery to highlight the work of the Citysights artists.

Citysights' second visual arts project initiated what would become a series of programs supporting unemployed artists in Wilmington. In the summer of 1975, three photographers—Norma Calabro (née Diskau), Raymond Kopocho, and Thomas Stiltz—created photographic essays for Citysights. Calabro's *The City Child* was presented in a CETA exhibition in Washington, DC; Kopocho's *The Storefront Merchants* captured city vendors at work; and Stiltz's *The Urban Worker* was displayed both at AFSCME headquarters in Washington, DC and in Wilmington's Public Building. The projects funded by CS/CS led to the creation of Bicentennial Metroscope, a January 1976 through January 1977 program jointly funded by CETA and the federal American Revolution Bicentennial Administration (ARBA) dedicated to the teaching and presentation of photography throughout Delaware.[20]

While Bicentennial Metroscope received funds from these two national sources, it was "designed and operated by the City of Wilmington under the administration of Mayor

Thomas C. Maloney."[21] From the original Citysights group, only Calabro joined the program as photographer/educator. The other photographer/educators included Morris T. Brown II, Tony Calabro, Flash (née Susan) Rosenberg, Lenny Sophrin, and Floyd Van Riper. Dolores Josey joined the staff as dancer, Joseph Pinzarrone as composer, and John Mandik as historian. Added to the roster were Cynthia Burt as program administrator, Thomas Sherman as program coordinator, David Van Allen as technical administrative assistant, Jack Buxbaum as darkroom supervisor, Catherine Hatch and Kathe Morse as education coordinators, and Cheryl Wilson as secretary. The group was prolific during the bicentennial year, teaching photography in schools, community centers, and parks, and providing photographic services for nonprofit organizations and government offices. The work of the photographers was exhibited in a slideshow presentation and in the Museum's Downtown Gallery (January 7–February 20, 1977). The group published a survey of Citysights/Citysounds activities and *Wilmington Awake*, a portfolio of photographs by Tony Calabro with research and interviews by Mandik.

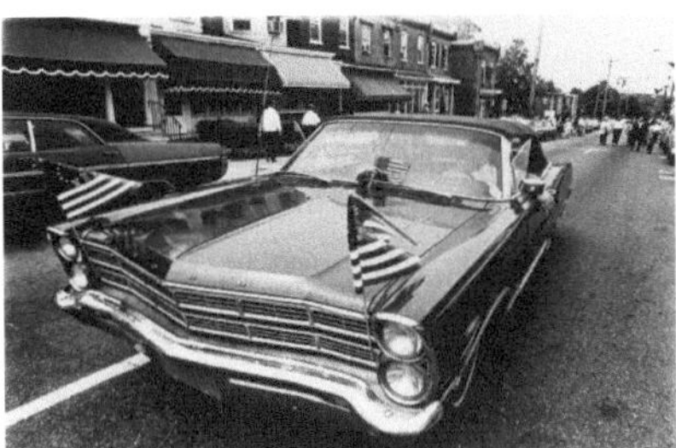

**NORMA CALABRO, *WILMINGTON PARADE*,** 1976

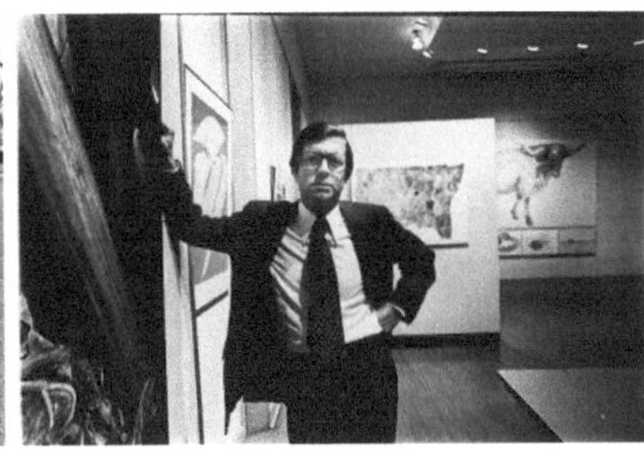

**TONY CALABRO, *CHARLES L. WYRICK, JR., DIRECTOR, DELAWARE ART MUSEUM, IN CONTEMPORARY GALLERY*,** 1976

When funding for Bicentennial Metroscope ended in February 1977, four photographers—Kopocho, Rosenberg, Van Allen, and William Pugh—joined the Delaware Art Museum staff with continued support from CETA and the NEA. That same year, CETA's available funding increased to $40 million.[22] Over the next two years, the program saw its highest level of spending, with nearly $200 million awarded by 1979 to artists and arts projects, creating a system for the creation and support of nonprofit arts organizations. Renamed Metroscope, the program was directed by Sherman and responded to photography needs within the Museum—primarily design and documentation—in addition to teaching classes on site and at the Absalom Jones Community Center.[23] CETA funding continued into 1978, and Metroscope transitioned into ArtReach, the Museum's community outreach program. ArtReach expanded previous efforts centered on photographic needs and education, and presented a curriculum focused on visual understanding in schools and community and senior centers throughout northern Delaware. Nearly 20 staff members were added to the ArtReach program, creating an influx of working artists to the Museum and supporting public art projects, including installations in the city's DART buses, a participatory exhibition in the City/County building, and continuing programs at

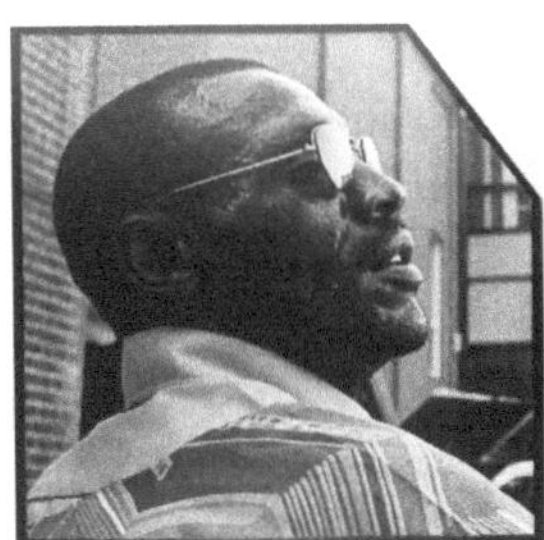

**JACK BUXBAUM, *UNTITLED*,** 1976

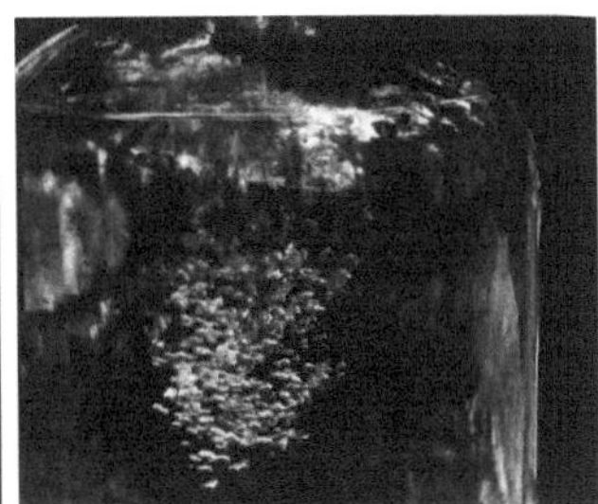

**THOMAS SHERMAN, *UNTITLED*,** 1976

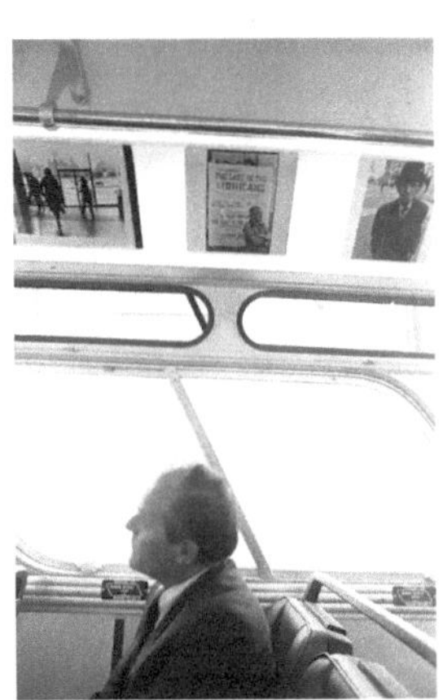

**PAT CROWE, *METROSCOPE*,**
AUGUST 13, 1976

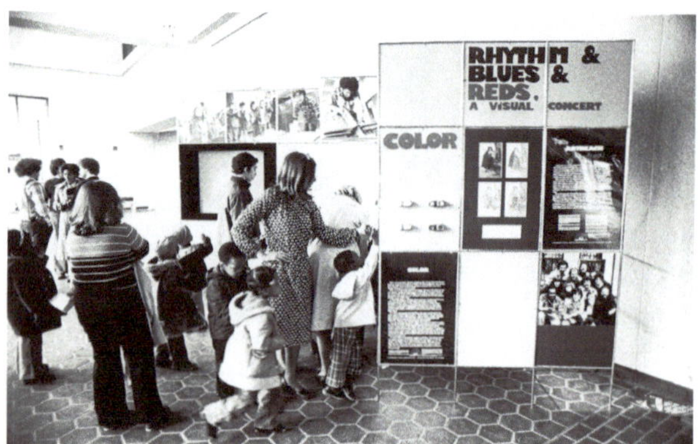


**FRED COMEGYS, *KIDS–ART REACH X-IBIT*,** APRIL 10, 1978

the Museum's Downtown Gallery.[24] ArtReach II continued in the 1979 fiscal year with similar funding, projects, and staff, although the program responsibilities were shifted to newly hired Curator of Education Diane Brandt Stillman. By 1980, decreased funding for CETA from the federal government led to the conclusion of the state-funded, community outreach programs, including ArtReach.

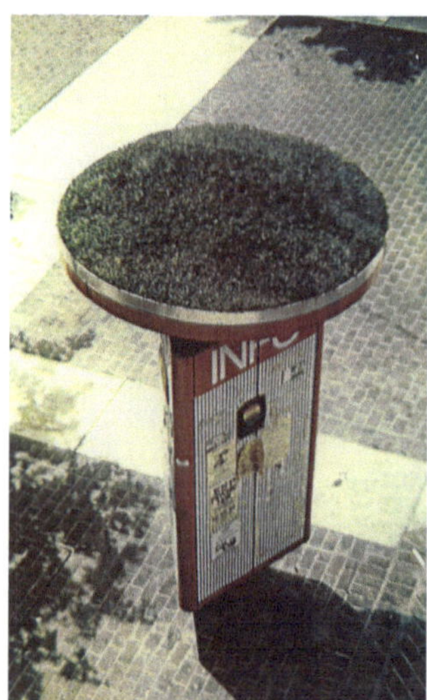

INSTALLATION VIEW OF **RICK ROTHROCK'S *WILMINGTON GREEN*,** 1978

The Museum's outreach programs supported social art practices that were gaining traction across the country in the mid- to late 1970s. Among them were Rick Rothrock's summer 1978 *Wilmington Green* and ArtSquad, the "group of artists formed to create environmental work in response to various sites in New Castle County."[25] The group was started as a county department of parks and recreation supported program of the Art Studios at the Absalom Jones Community Center, and the first episode—*The ArtSquad Goes to the Zoo*—took place at the Brandywine Zoo in early October 1978. Participants were invited to make animal masks with Stubbs Wilson, explore dance and movement with Anita Dauphin, create artwork from animal fibers, and attend a public talk by New York–based sculptor Alan Sonfist. Rothrock was a motivating force in the continuation of ArtSquad's events, which led to the March 1979 installation of an ice maze sculpture in Willingtown Square and *A Pastoral Scene*, a daylong program of site-specific installations held on the grounds of Winterthur Museum later that spring.

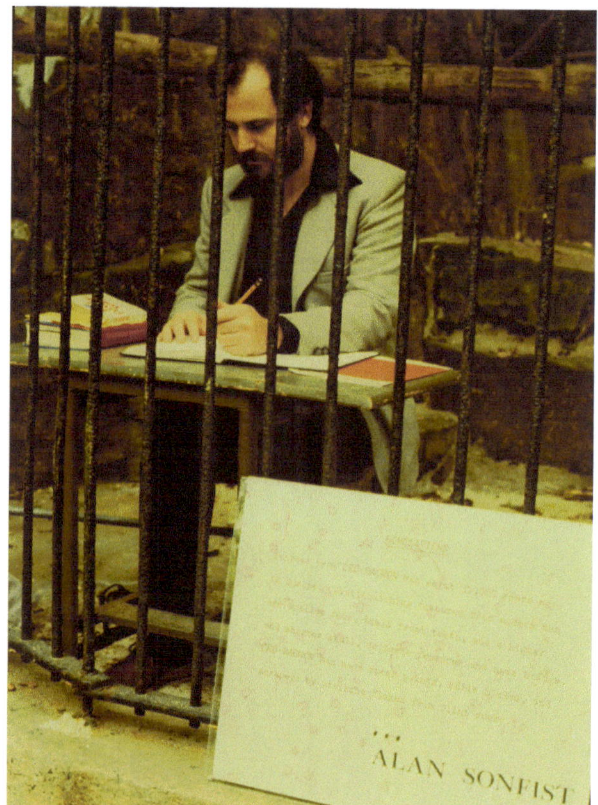


ALAN SONFIST INSTALLED IN AN ANIMAL CAGE FOR ***THE ARTSQUAD GOES TO THE ZOO***, 1978

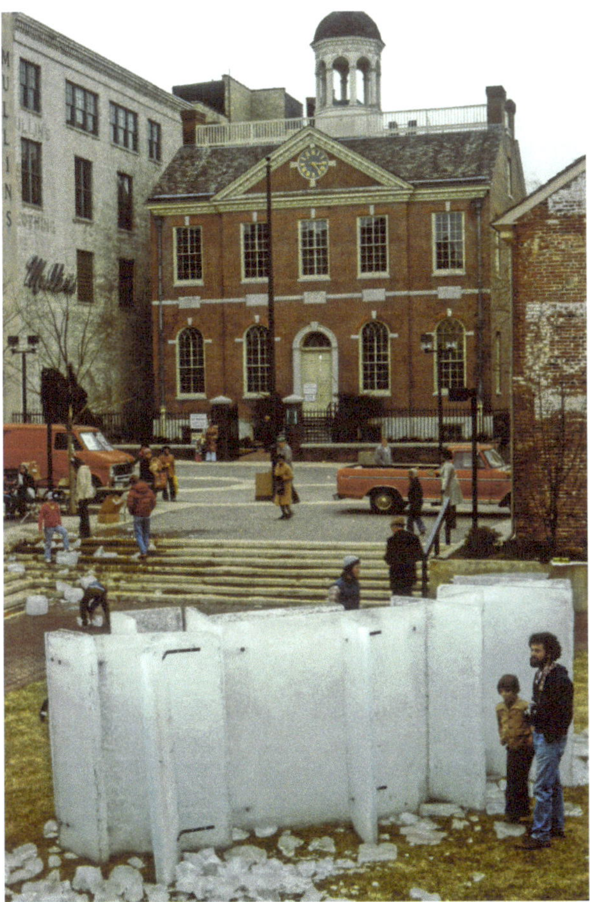

***HOMAGE TO WINTER*** ON VIEW IN WILLINGTOWN SQUARE, 1979

The convergence of federal funding; young, professional artists; and a participatory art model built on the efforts of arts advocates working in downtown Wilmington in the earlier 1970s, like Robert Jones, led to the establishment of nonprofit organizations with permanent homes within the community. Rothrock was aware of other successful models, like Hallwalls Contemporary Arts Center in Buffalo, and shortly after the start of ArtSquad, addressed the need for a space. The May 1979 issue of *The Codartist*, published by the Council of Delaware Artists (CODA), featured a report on a "yet-named" art association and center. With approximately 45 people in attendance, a permanent home from which the association would function was of primary concern. The report continues:

> It is strongly felt, and rightly so, that there is a need for artists of all persuasions to have a place to work, practice, perform, and exhibit. Such a central arts association will help by its mere concentration of members [sic] efforts in persuing [sic] answers to many of our problems and needs. Rick Rothrock, who has worked very diligently on this association idea, and who has traveled all over the country exploring similar associations has been the guiding light of the effort. [26]

It should be noted that artist associations were not absent in Delaware prior to the foundation of the Delaware Center for the Contemporary Arts (DCCA). In 1956, the first exhibition of works by CODA painters and sculptors was held in the Warehouse Gallery in the Robin Hood Theatre in Arden. The December 2 opening featured two films: Luis Buñuel and Salvador Dalí's 1929 *Un Chien Andalou* and Fernand Léger's 1924 *Ballet Mécanique*.[27] While CODA presented special workshops and lectures and exhibited regularly throughout the state, the DCCA—incorporated in May 1979—was the first, non-collecting, nonprofit contemporary art space to be established in Wilmington. The atmosphere was advantageous for other organizations and during this period the Delaware Theatre Company, Delaware Humanities Forum, and the Center for the Creative Arts in Yorklyn were also founded.

Visual and performing arts activities in and around Wilmington expanded through the 1980s as programming and funding increased. State grant funds available through the DSAC nearly doubled from the 1980 to 1981 fiscal year.[28] Additionally, a local system of commercial support expanded in Wilmington to address the needs of working artists in the form of galleries, retailers, and restaurants. In the late

1960s, only a handful of commercial galleries were operating in Wilmington and many were supported by a framing business. One of the oldest, Hardcastle Gallery, was established in 1888 by British cabinetmaker George Hardcastle on Shipley Street. In 1946, the business was purchased by Raymond Coakley and painter Bayard Taylor Berndt, and in 1979, Berndt's son, David, assumed responsibility. Hardcastle Gallery consistently represented local artists working in a traditional bent, creating a "haven for artists who follow the 'Brandywine School' of painting originated by renowned artist Howard Pyle."[29] Grace McFarren operated the Wilmington Circulating Gallery of Paintings for 25 years in the Wanamaker's store on Augustine Road following her move to the city in 1960. Her business model was based on the rental of works of art, which could be purchased at a later date if desired. In addition to displaying her own work, she showed mostly abstraction, including paintings by University of Delaware professor Dan Teis.

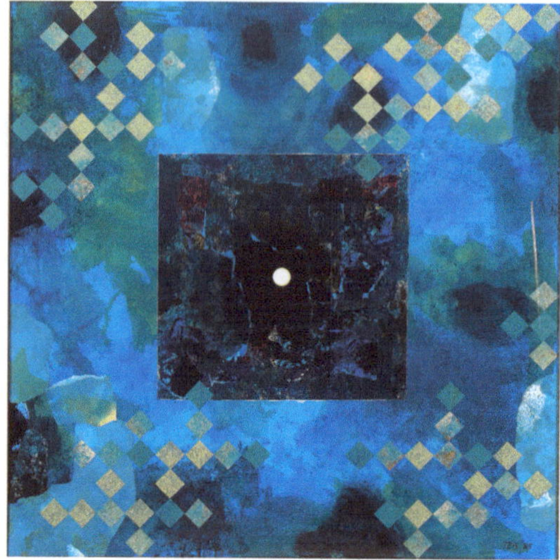

**DAN TEIS, *40 X 40 BLUE*,** 1985

While the Delaware Art Museum displayed the work of Howard Pyle and other American illustrators, few galleries were dedicated to selling this work locally until Fred Carspecken and John Schoonover—grandson of Frank Schoonover—established the Schoonover Galleries Frame Shop in the Schoonover Studies at 1616 North Rodney Street in 1969.[30] As the framing business expanded, Carspecken realized he "liked contemporary things" and opened Carspecken-Scott Gallery with Howie Scott in 1973 at 1707 North Lincoln Street.[31] From the beginning, the gallery was committed to supporting regional artists—the first show included the work of Tom Bostelle, Tania Boucher, and Mary Page Evans—and as such was the first at the start of the 1970s to do so. While Carspecken and Scott supplemented their income with the framing business, they were committed to multiple exhibitions each year, primarily of modern, representational painting, which they acknowledged as increasing in popularity locally.[32] Just two years after the opening of Carspecken-Scott, the Delaware Art Museum established an Art Sales and Rental Gallery, following the model implemented by McFarren and other national museums, including the Philadelphia Museum of Art. Alice Hupfel helped found the gallery in 1975, and ran it until it closed in early 2005. Hupfel drew from local sources while maintaining a high percentage of artists from Philadelphia and New York.

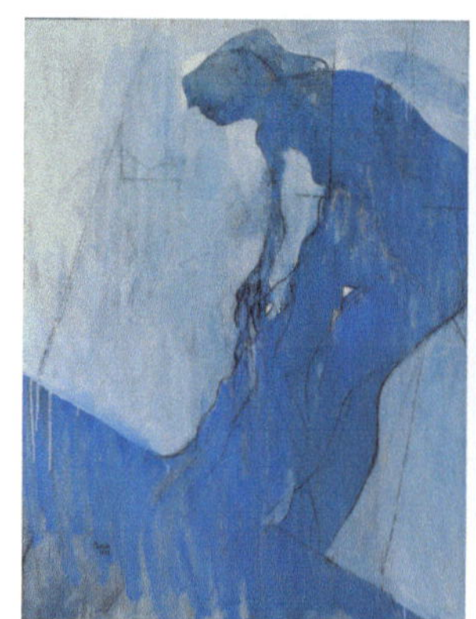

**TOM BOSTELLE, *WOMAN DRESSING*,** 1973

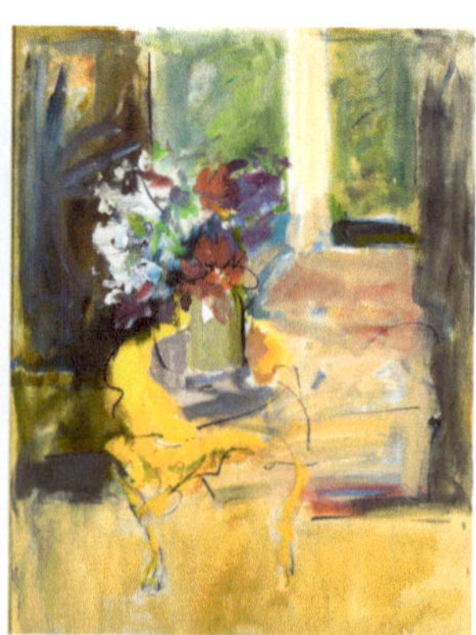

**MARY PAGE EVANS, *THE YELLOW TABLE*,** C. 1971

Concurrent with the foundation of the DCCA and Delaware Theatre Company in 1979 was the opening of the Station

Gallery in Greenville. Nancy Bercaw opened the space as a frame shop on Kennett Pike with partner Mary Shea after a brief stint at Carspecken-Scott. In 1981, Alice Crayton joined the business and, the following year, Shea sold her share of the gallery.[33] Bercaw was committed to young, emerging, Wilmington-based artists from the start: the gallery's inaugural exhibition featured the work of ceramicist and printmaker Mitch Lyons. Many of the artists the gallery represented—Lyons, James A. Anderson, and Graham Dougherty, among others—were part of the community of artists involved with the founding of the DCCA, artists documenting their surrounding city, pushing abstraction, or experimenting with

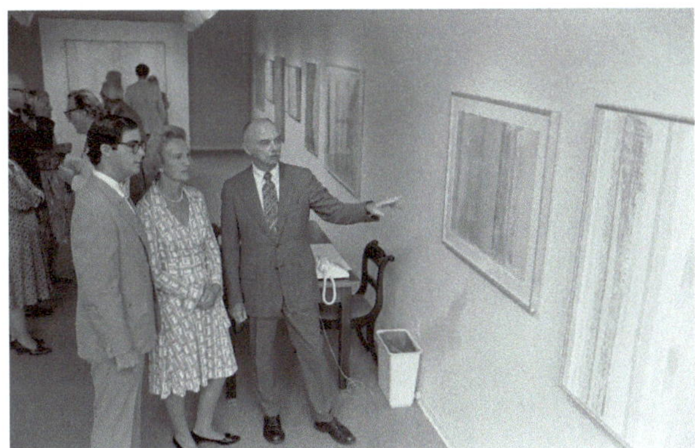

**LEO S. MATKINS, *OPENING OPERA GALLERY,*** SEPTEMBER 18, 1977

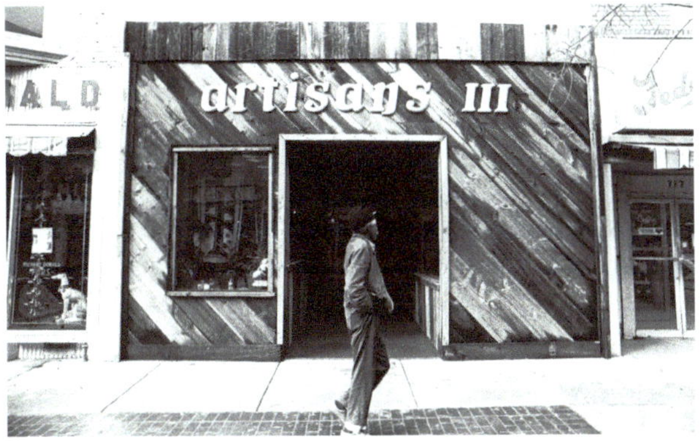


**RON DUBICK, *ARTISANS III,*** DECEMBER 6, 1977

**GRAHAM DOUGHERTY, *FLOAT,*** 1986

media. These few galleries, along with Fifth Street—which had closed by November 1978—were the key commercial supporters in the 1970s. The years that followed would usher in an expansion of the gallery scene in both downtown Wilmington and surrounding neighborhoods.

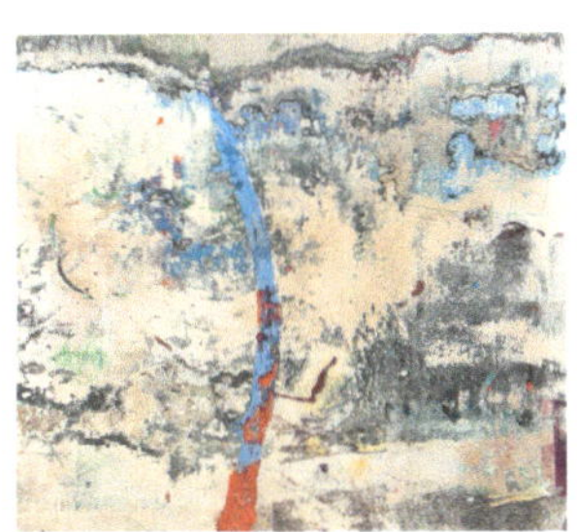

**MITCH LYONS, *UNTITLED,*** 1980

Sadie Somerville had worked first at the Brush and Palette shop in Kennett Square, Pennsylvania, before opening the Gallery at Centreville with Carol Moulton in 1981.[34] Vickie Manning, a tapestry weaver who had exhibited at Brush and Palette as well as Fifth Street Gallery, joined Gallery at Centreville shortly after and quickly became Somerville's partner, renaming the gallery Somerville Manning. They maintained the same Centreville location until the gallery's move to Breck's Mill in 1993. Somerville Manning Gallery focused on "full-time artists" with national reputations and local ties, such as John McCoy, Peter Sculthorpe, and the Wyeths—N.C., Andrew, Jamie, and others in the family.[35] The Blue Streak Gallery was incorporated in 1982 by Avery Draper and opened at 1723 Delaware Avenue in 1983, providing for the first time a gallery solely dedicated to the growing American craft movement.[36] The range of media—ceramics, fiber, glass, jewelry, pottery—represented the variant approaches seen nationally and locally. After Draper's sudden death in 1987, her sister, Reeve, assumed responsibility for the gallery with Ellen Bartholomaus, whom she had met in a weaving class taught by Sigrid Meier at the Delaware Art Museum.

In 1986, Susan Isaacs and Linda Brennan-Jones opened the L. B. Jones Gallery at 709 North Tatnall Street after working together in a private psychiatric hospital.[37] Isaacs assumed much of the responsibility for setting the exhibition program, in addition to offering framing services, and in 1988, she undertook full control of the three-story gallery, changing the name to the Susan Isaacs Gallery. Committed to promoting contemporary art she described as "figurative to abstract—landscape to non-objective—funky to refined," Isaacs was the first gallery owner with advanced degrees in both painting and art history to establish a commercial space in downtown Wilmington.[38] Her dedication to supporting the most avant-garde art practices was reminiscent of Robert Jones' agenda and strengthened by her expertise in the field and supplemented through framing work. The closing of the Isaacs Gallery in 1992—following an advantageous move into a larger space at 222 Delaware Avenue in 1991—was bemoaned by many and represented the "latest blow" to contemporary art at the start of the 1990s.[39] Prior to those financial crises was the opening Rue Lam's Tatnall Street Gallery in 1987 with a program of a few local artists—John Gatti and Roberta Tucci included—along with under-recognized artists from around the nation. The next year, Wilmington's Art on the Town was launched as a Wilmington Arts Commission and DSAC supported endeavor to connect participating art galleries and "to accelerate interest in the Wilmington art scene."[40] The Art Loop linked exhibitions in the Redding City/County and Carvel State buildings as well as galleries in Trolley Square and downtown with local restaurants—Oscar's, Scotty's, and Crumbs Upstairs—that supported art programs.

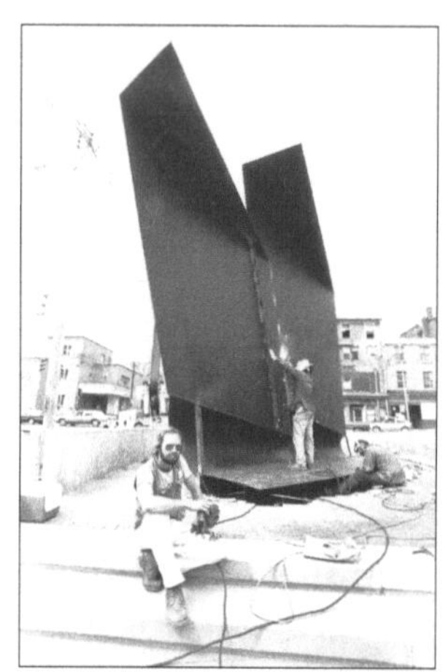

**FRED COMEGYS, *SNEAD SCULPTURE*,**
JUNE 3–8, 1985

Wilmington reestablished its commitment to public art in 1981 with a permanent sculpture program made possible in large part by the city's Percent for Arts fund. A city code was initiated requiring that all public construction projects dedicate five percent of building costs to ornamentation. In the event that not all the sum is used, the remaining monies are placed in a reserved city fund, which can be used for public art projects.[41] (Philadelphia was the first to establish such a program, in 1959; many other cities and states adopted the requirement in the late 1970s and early 1980s.[42]) Wilmington's first commission was Ric Snead's *PROA*, installed at the corner of Fourth and Shipley Streets. The competition for this public sculpture was administered by the Wilmington Arts Commission and the final selection was made by a committee of individuals from the Commission, the City administration, Delaware Technical Community College, and the Delaware Art Museum.[43] Later acquisitions and commissions in the 1980s included Richard Stankiewicz's *Untitled 1979-8*, unveiled following the completion of the Louis L. Redding City/County Building at 800 North French Street, Ken Davis' *Kinetic Sculptures* at 1313 North Market Street, Manuel Neri's *Passage* at 201 North Walnut Street, Ned Smyth's *Landfall* at French Street and Martin Luther King Boulevard, and Xavier Corbero's *Christina Sunrise* at 301 North Walnut Street.

The financial crises of the late 1980s and nationwide criticism of government funding for the arts led to a decrease in the creative fervor of the preceding two decades. The more than 20 percent drop in the Dow Jones Inductrial Average stock market index on October 19, 1987 ("Black Monday"), the Iraqi invasion of Kuwait in August 1990, and subsequent corporate reorganizations that led to the elimination of 9,000 DuPont positions in 1991 impacted financial stability worldwide and locally.[44] As Susan Isaacs explained, the crash "literally closed my business."[45] The impact of these economic crises on the arts community was exacerbated by the 1989 attacks by conservative politicians—Senators Jesse Helms and Alfonse D'Amato, among others—on NEA funding of the contemporary work of Karen Finley, Robert Mapplethorpe, and Andres Serrano. Designated today as the "culture wars," the fight over federal funding of what some Republicans referred to as "obscene and indecent" art predicted the tone of cultural support of the 1990s.[46] In Wilmington, the heyday of government funding had come to an end, but in its wake were two of the most artistically vibrant decades of the 20th century.

1. "Arts Council Forms Subcommittees," *Evening Journal*, September 17, 1969.
2. Jonathan D. Lippincott, *Large Scale: Fabricating Sculpture in the 1960s and 1970s* (New York: Princeton Architectural Press, 2010). Lippincott provides a thorough overview of the company's history, and Patterson Sims' introduction to the text traces public art and large-scale sculpture exhibitions in the 1960s and 1970s.
3. Bill Frank, "Sculpture Gets to You after a While," *Morning News*, June 18, 1970.
4. "Artmobile," *Delaware State Arts Council 15 Year Report 1969–1984* (Wilmington: Delaware State Arts Council, 1984), 22.
5. Fine Art Gallery postcard, Delaware Historical Society, Fine Arts Ephemera.
6. Exhibitions were held in two additional off-site locations—the Goodstay Center and the Branmar Plaza Gallery—during the 1970–71 exhibition season due to the expansion project.
7. Dorothy Grafly, "New Art Look in Delaware," *Art in Focus* 22, no. 8 (May 1971): 1.
8. Eric D. Robinson served as Downtown Gallery Assistant through federal funding in 1978 and 1979. The gallery closed in 2005, following the exhibition *Cross Country Run: Recent Work by Ken Mabrey* (October 21, 2004–September 30, 2005).
9. Ruth Jilla Kaplan, "Exhibit Looks at City's Future," *Evening Journal*, February 10, 1972.
10. Carol E. Hoffecker, *Corporate Capital: Wilmington in the Twentieth Century* (Philadelphia: Temple University Press, 1983), 234. Hoffecker's text surveys the developments within the city from the late 19th century through the late 1970s. Leah Virginia Kacanda's 2011 thesis, *"A Street of Hopes and Dreams": Rehabilitation, Revitalization, and Gentrification Along Market Street in Wilmington, Delaware* addresses the Market Street Mall initiative specifically.
11. Toni Young's *The Grand Experience: A History of the Grand Opera House* (Watkins Glen, New York: American Life Foundation for the Grand Opera House, 1976) is a thoroughly researched and well-presented text on the history of the Grand Opera House. It includes extensive details on the restoration project from the late 1960s through the reopening in 1976.
12. Young, *The Grand Experience*, 152.
13. Rowland Elzea, letter to Robert Jones, April 4, 1973. *Black Wilmington* exhibition files, Delaware Art Museum, Institutional Archives.
14. Robert Jones, letter to Rowland Elzea, June 4, 1973. *Black Wilmington* exhibition files, Delaware Art Museum, Institutional Archives.
15. Philip F. Crosland, "A New Art Gallery—and New Art Services," *Evening Journal*, May 2, 1974.
16. Steve Leech, "Wilmington's New Art Movement," *Greater Wilmington Sunday Advertiser*, September 19, 1976.
17. Mirasol Riojas, "The Accidental Arts Supporter: An Assessment of the Comprehensive Employment and Training Act (CETA)," *UCLA Chicano Studies Research Center Research Report 8* (May 2006): 2. CETA had its basis in President John F. Kennedy's Manpower Development and Training Act of 1962 and other manpower programs of the 1960s and was enacted in December 1973 as funding for unemployed and typically disadvantaged communities. While the program started as a manpower project, it soon addressed the employment needs of unemployed artists and funds were distributed to local and state governments that then distributed monies to organizations and projects at the local level. CETA funded staff positions at the Delaware Art Museum including a registrar and docent training supervisor, among others.
18. "The Urban Worker," *The Partnership of CETA and the Arts: Six Reprints from Worklife Magazine* (Washington, DC: Employment and Training Administration, 1978): 21.
19. Eva Cockcroft, James Cockcroft, and John Weber, *Toward a People's Art: The Contemporary Mural Movement* (New York: E. P. Dutton & Co., Inc., 1977). Several publications from the mid-1970s trace the history of the mural movement and provide instructions for realizing projects within one's own city.
20. "Delaware Bicentennial Body Created," *Morning News*, July 2, 1971. Delaware's commitment to bicentennial programming began in 1971 when Governor Russell W. Peterson signed into law Senate Bill 340, which created a Delaware American Revolution Bicentennial Commission.
21. Bicentennial Metroscope brochure, c. 1977. *Metroscope Photographers* exhibition file, Delaware Art Museum, Institutional Archives.
22. Riojas, "The Accidental Arts Supporter: An Assessment of the Comprehensive Employment and Training Act (CETA)," 3
23. Thomas L. Sherman, "Report of the Photography Program," *Delaware Art Museum Annual Report 1977* (Wilmington: Delaware Art Museum, 1977), 9. Delaware Art Museum, Institutional Archives.
24. Sherman, "Report of the ArtReach Program," *Delaware Art Museum Annual Report 1978* (Wilmington: Delaware Art Museum, 1978), 8. Delaware Art Museum, Institutional Archives.
25. *The ArtSquad Goes to the Zoo* poster, 1978. Collection of Rick Rothrock.
26. "Art Association and Center Proposed," *The Codartist 1*, no. 8 (May 1979): 3. Council of Delaware Artists Records, 1966–2000, deposit 2000.89, box 2, folder 1. Delaware Historical Society
27. Council of Delaware Artists Records, 1966–2000, deposit 2000.89, box 2, folder 21. Delaware Historical Society.
28. *Delaware State Arts Council 15 Year Report: 1969–1984* (Wilmington: Delaware State Arts Council, 1984), 7. The Governor's Awards for the Arts were also established in 1981, bringing statewide recognition to artists and arts organizations.
29. "About the Gallery," *Hardcastle Galleries*, accessed November 25, 2014, http://www.hardcastlegallery.com/Pages/About.php.
30. Fred Carspecken, interview by Margaret Winslow, August 17, 2013. Delaware Art Museum, Institutional Archives. Carspecken and Schoonover were fraternity brothers at the University of Virginia, and Schoonover's invitation brought Carspecken to Wilmington from St. Louis following graduation.
31. Fred Carspecken, interview by Margaret Winslow.
32. Judy Pennebaker, "Gallery Hopping: Art to Art," *Delaware Today* (November 1988): 121.
33. Nancy Bercaw and Alice Crayton, interview by Margaret Winslow, August 19, 2013. Delaware Art Museum, Institutional Archives.
34. Sadie Somerville and Vickie Manning, interview by Margaret Winslow, August 21, 2013. Delaware Art Museum, Institutional Archives.
35. Sadie Somerville and Vickie Manning, interview by Margaret Winslow.
36. Ellen Bartholomaus, interview by Margaret Winslow, June 3, 2013. Delaware Art Museum, Institutional Archives.
37. Linda Brennan-Jones, interview by Caitlin Davis, April 3, 2012. Delaware Art Museum, Institutional Archives.
38. Pennebaker, 95.
39. Gary Mullinax, "Avant-Garde Artist Goes Mainstream," *The News Journal*, April 16, 1992.
40. Pennebaker, 94.
41. "New Riverfront Sculpture Honors Underground Railroad Champions Harriet Tubman and Thomas Garrett," *The City of Wilmington Delaware*, accessed October 3, 2012, http://www.wilmingtonde.gov/residents/news.php?newsID=546.
42. *Philadelphia Redevelopment Authority (PRA)*, accessed January 20, 2014, http://www.phila.gov/pra/percentForArt.html. According to the PRA, Philadelphia pioneered the Percent for Art Program, becoming the first city to require developers to commission public art during the planning process.
43. Robert T. Silver, *Outdoor Sculpture in Wilmington* (Wilmington: Wilmington Arts Commission, 1987), 61.
44. Mark Carlson, *A Brief History of the 1987 Stock Market Crash with a Discussion of the Federal Reserve Response* (Washington, DC: Board of Governors of the Federal Reserve, November 2006), 2, http://www.federalreserve.gov/pubs/feds/2007/200713/200713pap.pdf. Donna Shaw, "DuPont Plans Up to 4,500 More Layoffs in U.S.," *Philadelphia Inquirer*, September 14, 1993, http://articles.philly.com/1993-09-14/business/25985593_1_dupont-plans-dupont-stock-dupont-officials.
45. J. Susan Isaacs, interview by Margaret Winslow, October 28, 2013. Delaware Art Museum, Institutional Archives.
46. Maureen Dowd, "Unruffled Helms Basks in Eye of Arts Storm," *New York Times*, July 28, 1989, http://www.nytimes.com/1989/07/28/arts/unruffled-helms-basks-in-eye-of-arts-storm.html.

# PERCY EUGENE RICKS AND AESTHETIC DYNAMICS, INC.

**Dr. James E. Newton**
*Artist and Professor Emeritus, Black American Studies, University of Delaware*

"The main purpose of Aesthetic Dynamics, Inc. is to increase awareness and understanding of the need to place the cultural contributions of *all* groups in proper perspective."[1]
—Percy Eugene Ricks, February 1973

An artist, humanist, educator, arts advocate, and visionary, Percy Eugene Ricks (1923–2008) was born in Washington, DC. He attended public schools and received a bachelor's degree in art and liberal arts from Howard University. After serving as an artist and combat soldier during World War II, he continued his studies, obtaining a master's in art education from Columbia University and a master's in fine art from Temple University's Tyler School of Art. In 1947, Ricks began working as an art teacher at the Absalom Jones School in Wilmington. The following year, he was hired as the first full-time black instructor of art in the city's all-black segregated school district. Since space and resources were lacking, he often conducted his classes in church basements and other venues. These experiences boded well for Ricks in later years.

Ricks was keenly aware of the difficult road that African Americans had to travel to achieve parity in the mainstream art world. Earlier generations of black artists had sought greener pastures—and recognition—in Europe. But Ricks was among a handful of artists who were determined to forge a career in Delaware. He conceived of Aesthetic Dynamics, Inc. in the late 1960s, though the organization was not officially incorporated until March 10, 1971. In his "Profile of Aesthetic Dynamics," he clearly stated the purpose of his new, community-based nonprofit:

> Aesthetic Dynamics is designed to have impact as a multiracial, grassroots organization with the purpose of creating a catalyst for cross-cultural communication within the Delaware community. It was conceived with the intention to utilize to the maximum the creative contributions of all people who desired to participate in our projects. Our primary goal is to promote and broaden the role of the arts and those who produce it. Our vision is to contribute to the cultural growth of the City and State.[2]

The organization's first major project was an ambitious presentation of African American art in February 1971. Sponsored by the Delaware State Arts Council, *Afro-American Images 1971* took place at the National Guard Armory in Wilmington. Consultants for the exhibition were Romare Bearden, Lois Mailou Jones, and Hale Woodruff. This major exhibition might easily serve as a roadmap for the agency's future plans and project developments. Although it was the group's first major effort, from a historical viewpoint, it may be a pivotal moment in the history of African American art. For Aesthetic Dynamics it serves as the foundation of its mission and its legacy.

Exhibiting artists in the "Armory Show" read like a Who's Who of African American artists: Romare Bearden, Lois Jones, Norman Lewis, Ernest Crichlow, Sam Gilliam, Humbert Howard, Jacob Lawrence, Samella Lewis, Delilah W. Pierce, James Porter, Raymond Saunders, Alma Thomas, James L. Wells, Charles White, Walter Williams, and Hale Woodruff, among others. Delaware Valley artists included Walter Edmonds, Barkley Hendricks, Simmie Knox, Robert Moore, Ed Loper Jr., Percy Eugene Ricks, Charles Searles, John Simpson, John Wade, and Theodore Wells II.

The exhibition was the first of its kind in Delaware, with 140 works by 66 nationally and regionally known contem-

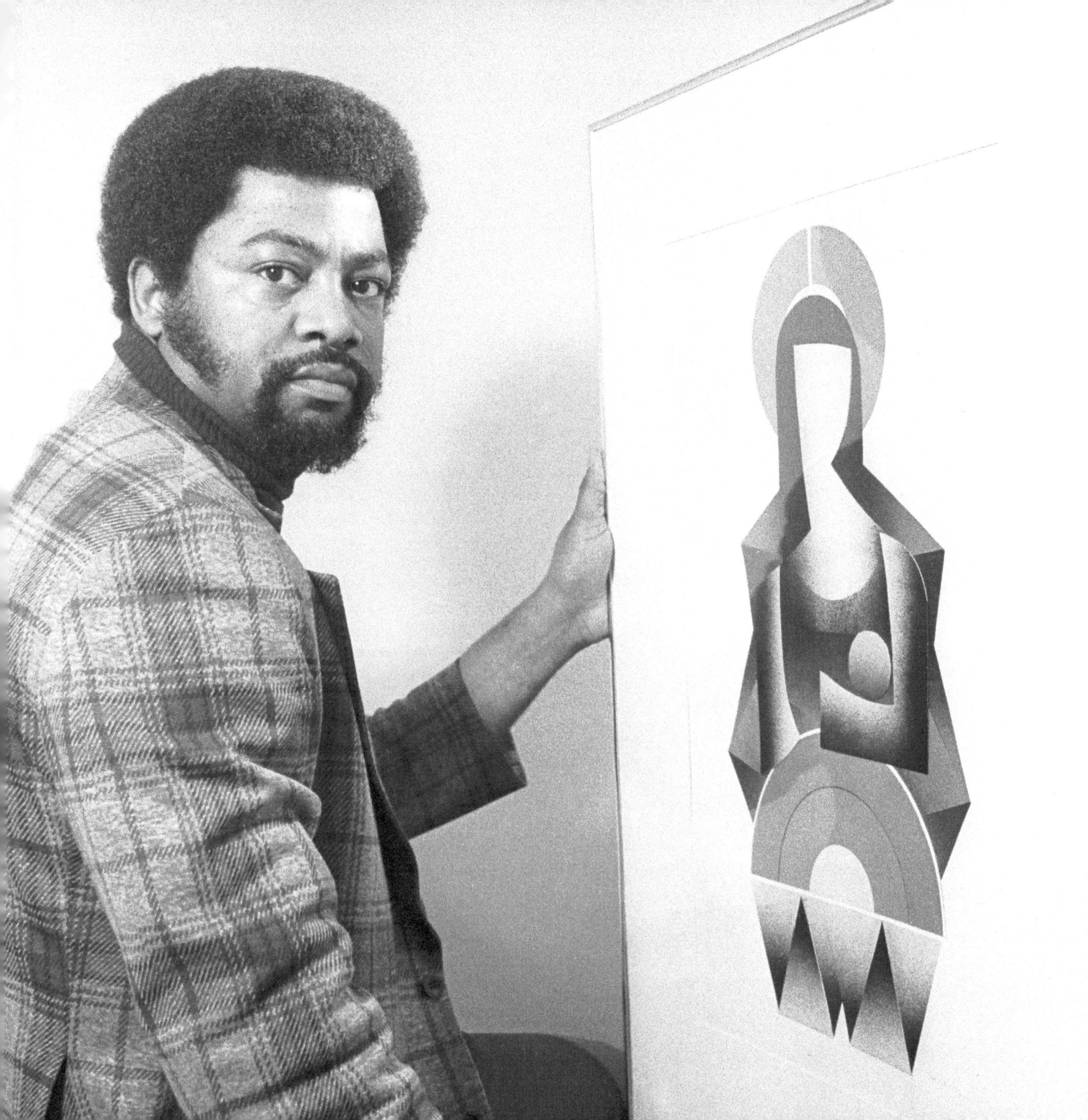

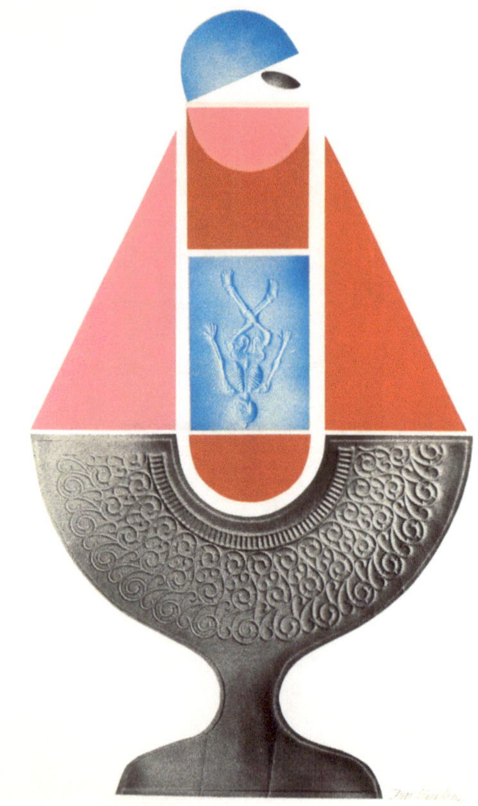

**JAMES E. NEWTON, *THE PILL*,** 1972

porary black artists. More than 7,000 people visited the show, including students from 49 schools in Delaware and Pennsylvania. One critic praised it as "very exciting"; another declared, "We need more displays of this caliber."[3] The exhibition was considered the most significant of its time on the Northeast corridor.

In 1976, Aesthetic Dynamics organized Blackaleidoscope, which combined African American music—classical, Negro spirituals, gospel, rock, and jazz—and art. In his proposal to the Delaware American Revolution Bicentennial Commission, which provided financial backing for the project, Ricks wrote, "The focus of our effort is to bring to the general public the awareness of the cultural contributions made by our minority citizens which are of far-reaching and lasting value."[4] Musical performers included Four Souls Plus One, the Al Cato Jazz Ensemble, Dr. Charles Moore, and Lonnie Thomas. The visual component consisted of work by such prominent artists as Edward Loper, Sr. and William Lee Howell. Listed among those involved with the production of Blackaleidoscope were Marcia Charleston, Rene Evans, Cookie Diaz, Al Cato, Margaret Owens, Eric D. Robinson, Bernard Brooks, Percy Eugene Ricks, and James E. Newton.

The organization's 1980 *Delaware African American Art Exhibition*, sponsored by the Delaware Historical Society and the Delaware Division of the Arts, was hung in the Dingee House Gallery in Willingtown Square during Black History Month. The presentation included 56 works by artists who lived in Delaware. While paintings dominated the show, sculpture, mixed media, collages, drawings, mosaics, carvings, and photography were also featured. As explained in the introduction, "The works presented in this exhibition affirm the vitality of art in the ethnic community. It especially attests to the fact that the African American artist is no stranger to the American art scene."[5] The exhibition was one of the few devoted exclusively to Delaware-based black artists at the time.

The reputation of Wilmington jazz phenomenon Clifford Brown did not escape the culturally conscious Aesthetic Dynamics leadership. In 1982, the group put forward a proposal to give the public a taste of the big band sound, using the jazz-conscious city as a background. Robert "Boysie" Lowery, the longtime musical teacher of Brown and other Wilmington jazzmen, and Gerald Chavis spearheaded the production. The three-and-a-half-hour event was held at the Forum II on Governor Printz Boulevard and drew a standing-room-only crowd, who heard renditions of works by Charlie Parker, Miles Davis, Duke Ellington, and Horace Silver. The 50 musicians on the roster were familiar names to the hometown crowd: Lydia Anderson, Dean Jenkins, Al Cato, Wilby Fletcher,

Sr., Wilby Fletcher, Jr., Millie Cannon, Gerald Price, Sr., Gerald Price, Jr., Tommy Ryan, Tony Smith, Stan Williams, and Kenny Brown. In some ways, mid-August 1982 was a flashback to the earlier days in Wilmington—the days when jazz was a welcomed sound in the birthplace of Clifford Brown. Ethnomusicologist Dr. George Ricks wrote in the event brochure, "Jazz is an authentic and original Afro-American art form. It is the spiritual and musical gift of creative black musicians to America and to the world."[6]

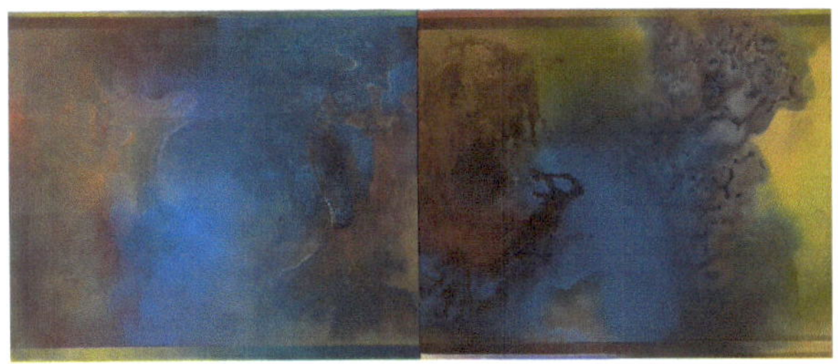

**SIMMIE KNOX, *A PLACE: SUSPENDED*,** 1970

Over more than three decades, Percy Eugene Ricks and Aesthetic Dynamics brought exhibitions, musical extravaganzas, lectures, seminars, and cultural forums to the citizens of Delaware as a way of cultivating, perpetuating, and advocating for the arts. Ricks almost single-handedly changed Delaware's perspectives on multicultural education in the visual arts. His vision was best reflected in his lemming-like drive, his persistence, and his monk-like discipline in implementing cultural arts programs through Aesthetic Dynamics. The arts community, public school students, and particularly Delaware's cadre of African American artists can all tip their hats to Ricks and the members of his visionary organization for their vanguard leadership in raising artistic consciousness for generations to come. For those of us who knew Ricks personally, it is difficult to conceive of anyone taking the reins following his passing. In short, Percy Ricks was Aesthetic Dynamics and Aesthetic Dynamics was Percy Eugene Ricks.

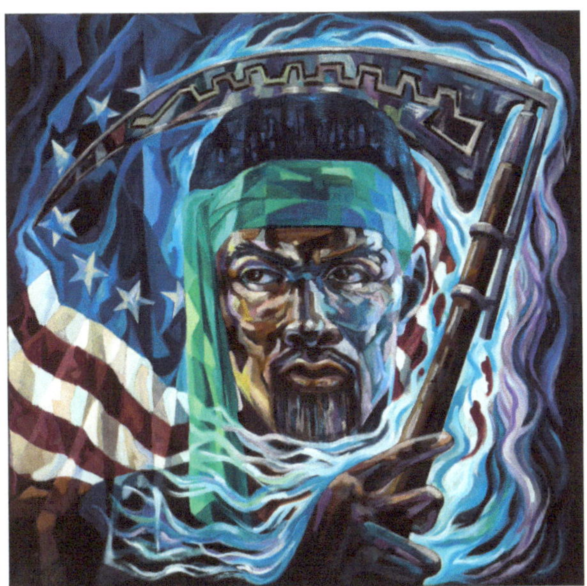

**PERCY EUGENE RICKS, *BLACK SAMSON OF BRANDYWINE*,** C. 1989

1. Interview with Percy Eugene Ricks, 7 February 1973. Wilmington Institute Library.
2. Percy Ricks, charter papers of Aesthetic Dynamics, Inc., March 1971.
3. *Art Exhibition of Contemporary Paintings and Sculpture by African American Artists (African American Images, 1971)*, An Evaluation submitted to the Delaware State Arts Council (Wilmington, Delaware: Aesthetics Dynamics, Inc., May 1971), 4.
4. Percy Ricks, "Proposal to the Delaware American Revolution Bicentennial Commission" (Wilmington, Delaware: Aesthetics Dynamics Inc., February 1976).
5. James E. Newton, "Introduction," *The 1980 Delaware African American Art Exhibition* (Wilmington, Delaware: Aesthetic Dynamics, Inc. and Delaware Historical Society, February 1980).
6. Dr. George Ricks, "The Phoenix," *Apollo Rising: The Big Band Sound* (Wilmington, Delaware: Aesthetic Dynamics, Inc., May 1982).

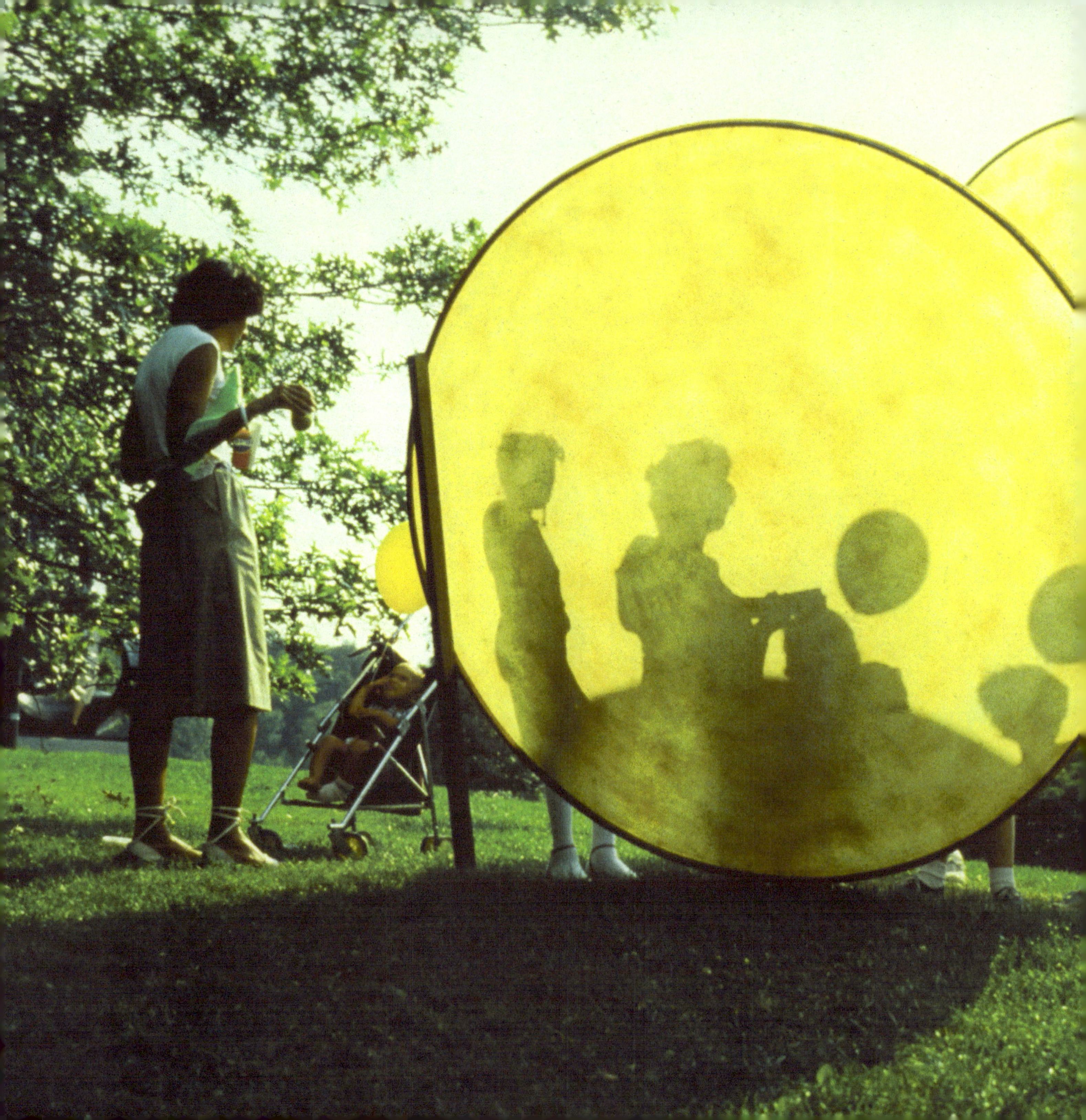

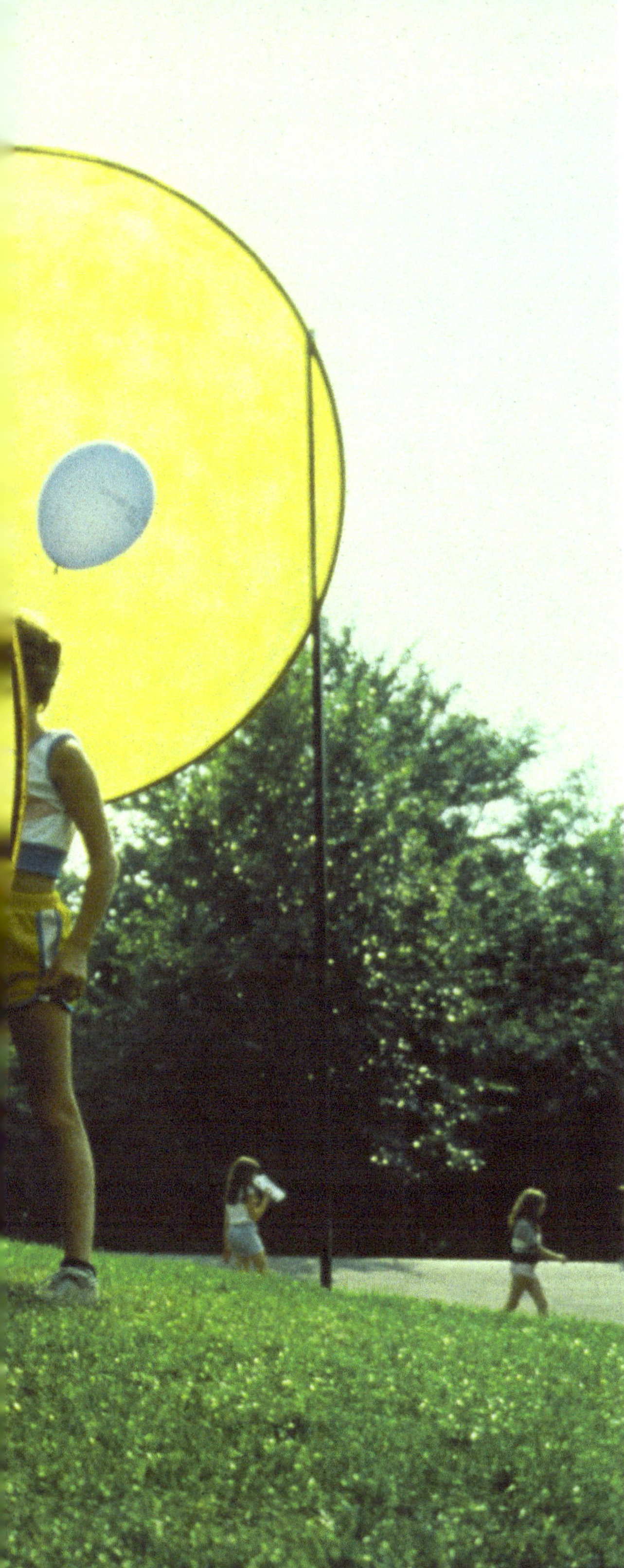

# UNIVERSITY OF DELAWARE DEPARTMENT OF ART IN THE 1970S AND '80S

**Stephen Tanis**
*Artist and University of Delaware Professor Emeritus*

I began teaching in the University of Delaware's Department of Art in 1972. At that time, I found a medium-size department reflecting the model of a small college art program. Art education and graphic design were the major degree programs; fine arts was offered only as a bachelor's degree. When Dan Teis, a painter with extensive experience in arts administration and a doctorate in art education, succeeded George Nocito as department chair in 1974, he developed a more in-depth Bachelor of Fine Arts curriculum and established the Master of Fine Arts. Later, in 1982, when painting professor Larry Holmes took over as chair, he focused on securing more funding for graduate assistantships and scholarships, and collaborated with professor Charles Rowe to start a new concentration in illustration. Beginning in the early 1980s, professors Ray Nichols and Vera Kaminski spearheaded the introduction and subsequent expansion of the personal computer into the department's curriculum. Nichols recognized early on that design would be a digital medium; his leadership contributed enormously to the success of the department's visual communication program.

The fine arts faculty embraced the concept that the artist/teacher should participate in art making in the highest professional sphere. As such, a remarkable number of faculty exhibited their work in New York City galleries during the 1970s and '80s: sculptor Joe Moss at Max Hutchinson's 142 Greene Street Sculpture Now gallery and Madison Square Park, ceramicist Victor Spinski at Theo Portnoy Gallery, photographer Wallace Wilson at OK Harris, and painter Robert Straight at Barbara Toll Fine Arts. Larry Holmes, the department chair, showed at Littlejohn-Smith Gallery, painter Dan Teis with Hansen Gallery, and printmaker Rosie Bernardi

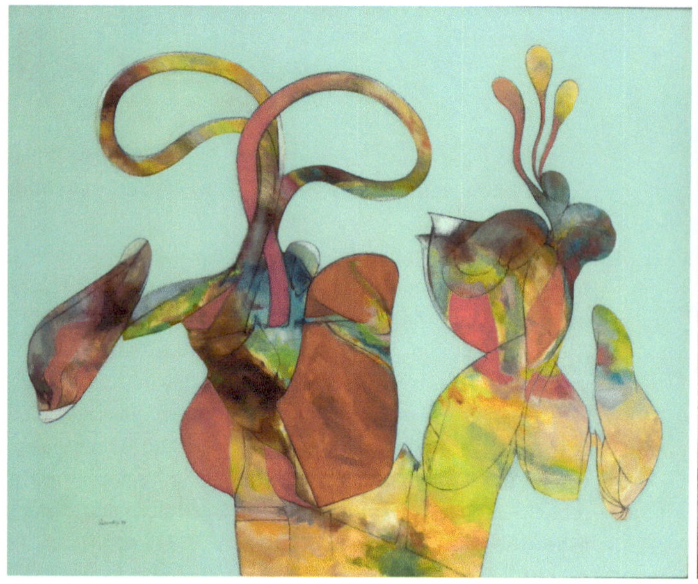

**JULIO DACUNHA, *ENTANGLEMENTS II*,** 1975

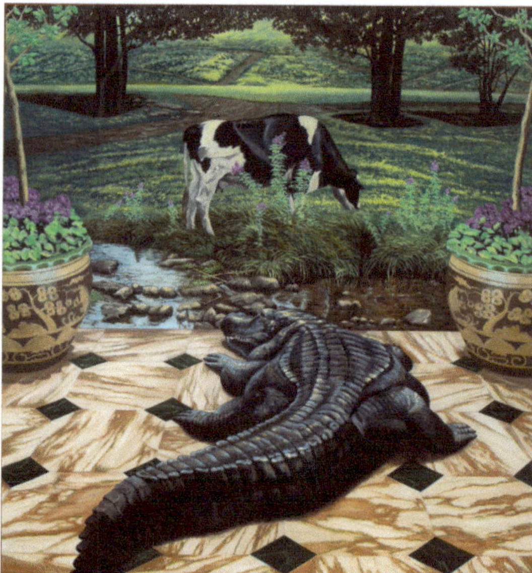

**LARRY HOLMES, *ALLIGATOR PAINTING #6*,** 1984

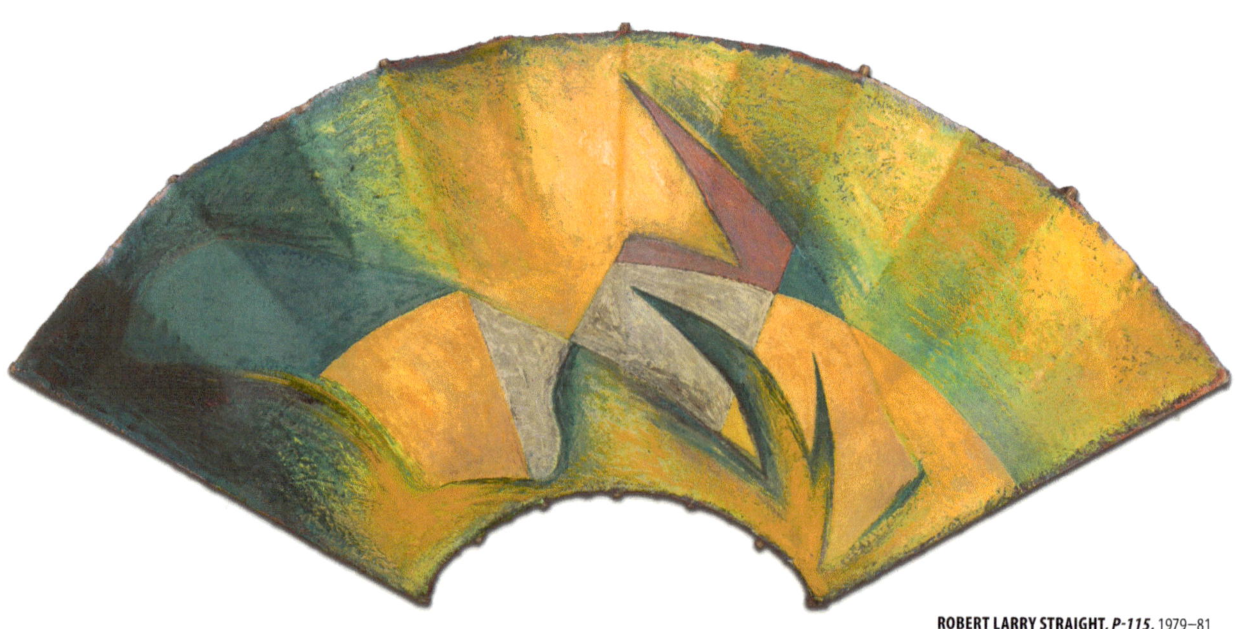

**ROBERT LARRY STRAIGHT, *P-115*,** 1979–81

at A.I.R. Gallery. Finally, both illustrator Charles Rowe and painter Julio daCunha of the honors program had shows at the Pleiades/Cloud Gallery. I, too, exhibited in New York, at FAR Gallery and then, beginning in 1986, at Sherry French Gallery. With so many faculty showing their work at this level, the department was an exciting place to be.

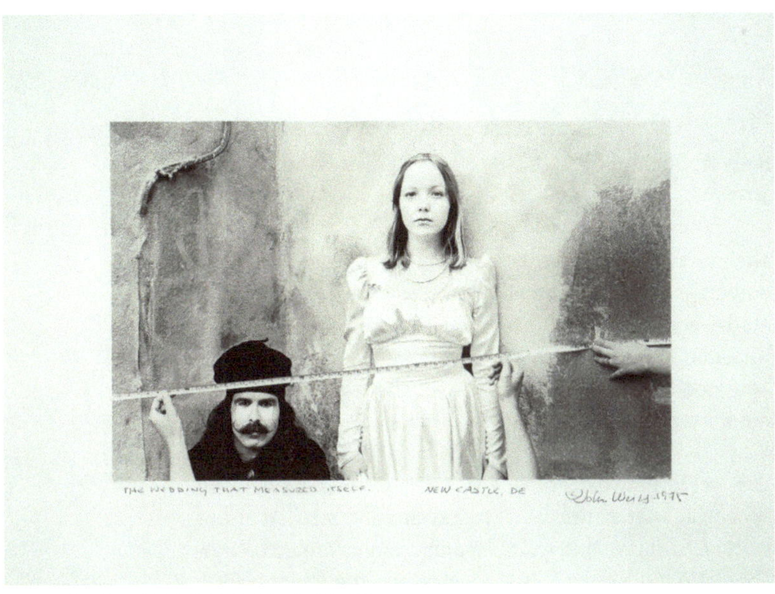


**JOHN WEISS, *THE WEDDING THAT MEASURED ITSELF*,** 1974

A major component of the MFA program was to bring nationally recognized artists to meet with students, providing them insight and fresh criticism. The students were energized as they became more ambitious and their work advanced. Among the long list of outstanding visiting artists and critics were Elizabeth Murray, Gary Stefan, and James Turrell. In 1980, photography professor John Weiss, along with several graduate students, produced a major exhibition and catalogue at the Delaware Art Museum of the photographs of Frederick Sommer. As part of a concerted push for greater diversification during those years, we recruited outstanding minority graduate students and were privileged to have two distinguished African American artists, Jerry Pinkney and Joyce Scott, join the faculty as adjunct professors.

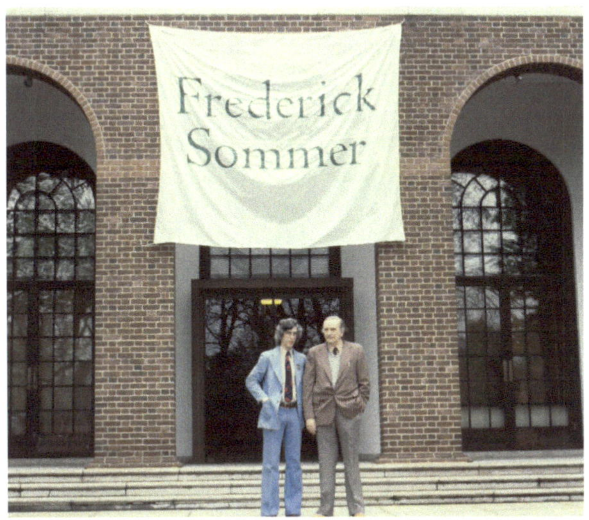


FREDERICK SOMMER AND JOHN WEISS AT THE OPENING OF ***VENUS, JUPITER, AND MARS: FREDERICK SOMMER PHOTOGRAPHS*** (APRIL 27–JUNE 8, 1980)

Today, leading members of Delaware's visual arts community have ties to the department: art historian and curator J. Susan Isaacs; painters Lisa Bartolozzi, Jon Redmond, and Robert and Daniel Jackson; printmakers Laura Hickman and Deborah Stelling; photographers Connie Imboden, Chris Wells, and Nancy Brokaw; and sculptors Matt Geller, Dennis Beach, and Rick Rothrock, to name a few. I think I can speak for the entire department from the '70s and '80s in saying it has been an honor to have witnessed the evolution of so many successful art careers.

# AMERICAN CRAFT: THE CONFLUENCE OF ART AND THE HANDMADE OBJECT

**Sally W. Donatello**
*Scholar*

The capacity to invent handmade objects is deeply embedded in human civilization. Early handwork permeated everyday life: our dexterity gave us skills to redefine raw materials into household items and tools. Clay, fibers, metal, and wood became entry points for the transformation of natural resources and agrarian byproducts.

The years between 1970 and 1990 were a time when American craft artists looked backward and forward at our cultural heritage. Bold experimentation transformed boundaries of self-expression. Individuality was the impetus for a new aesthetic and cutting-edge work. As interest in the field grew, craft became an economic engine. Private and public participation in the arts increased, and vibrant art communities and collections blossomed. The success of American craft infused our culture, permanently influencing the art world.

The craft scenes in Newark and Wilmington were closely tied, with artists in these cities flowing back and forth to curate, exhibit, sell, and teach. The University of Delaware studio arts program became a center of fresh talent. Faculty like Anne Krohn Graham, Vera E. Kaminski, and Victor Spinski, along with students such as Betty Helen Longhi and Helen Mason, gained prominence as proponents and practitioners of craft.

The Financial Center Development Act (1981) liberalized laws governing Delaware banks, which brought a steady flow of new money to the state. The marketplace expanded with craft shops and small galleries. Wilmington boasted Blue Streak Gallery, L. B. Jones Gallery, Susan Isaacs Gallery, and Artisans III, while Newark was home to Gallery 20, on the University of Delaware campus, and Grassroots. As quality

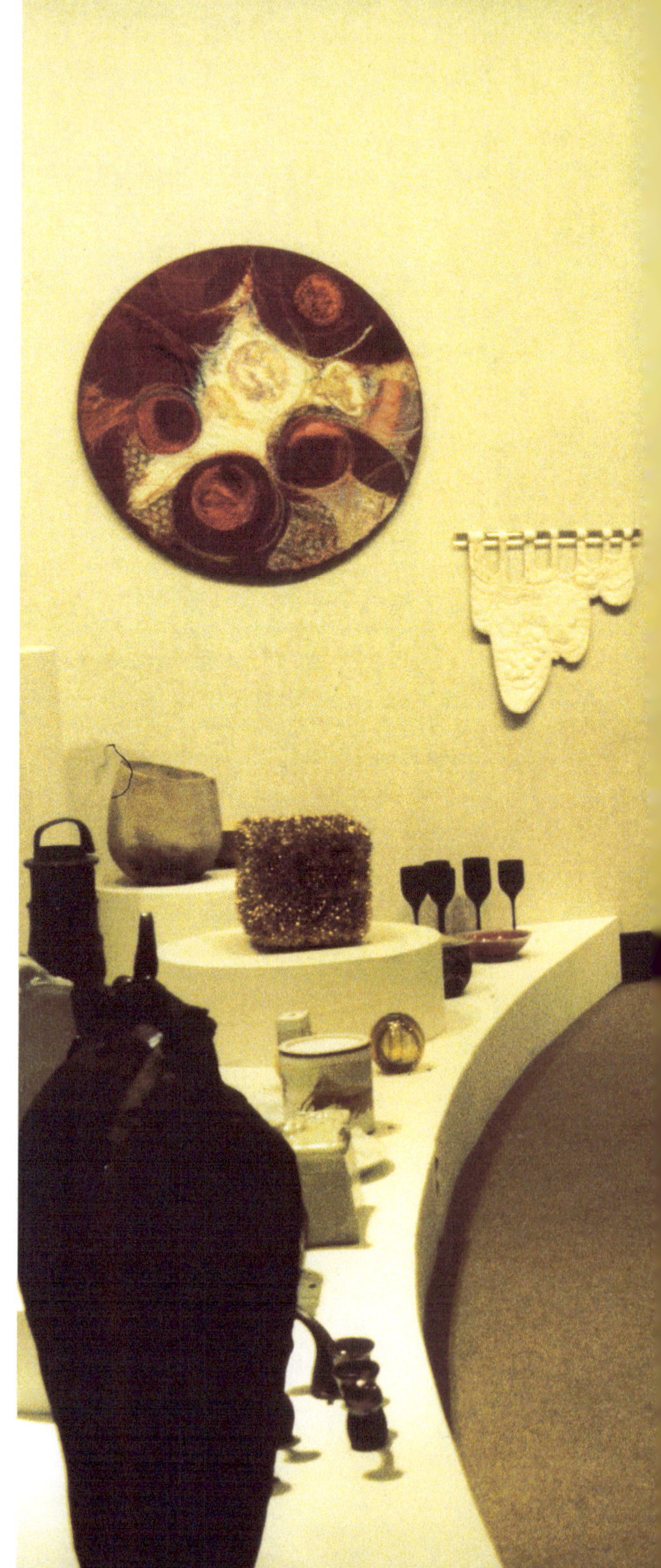

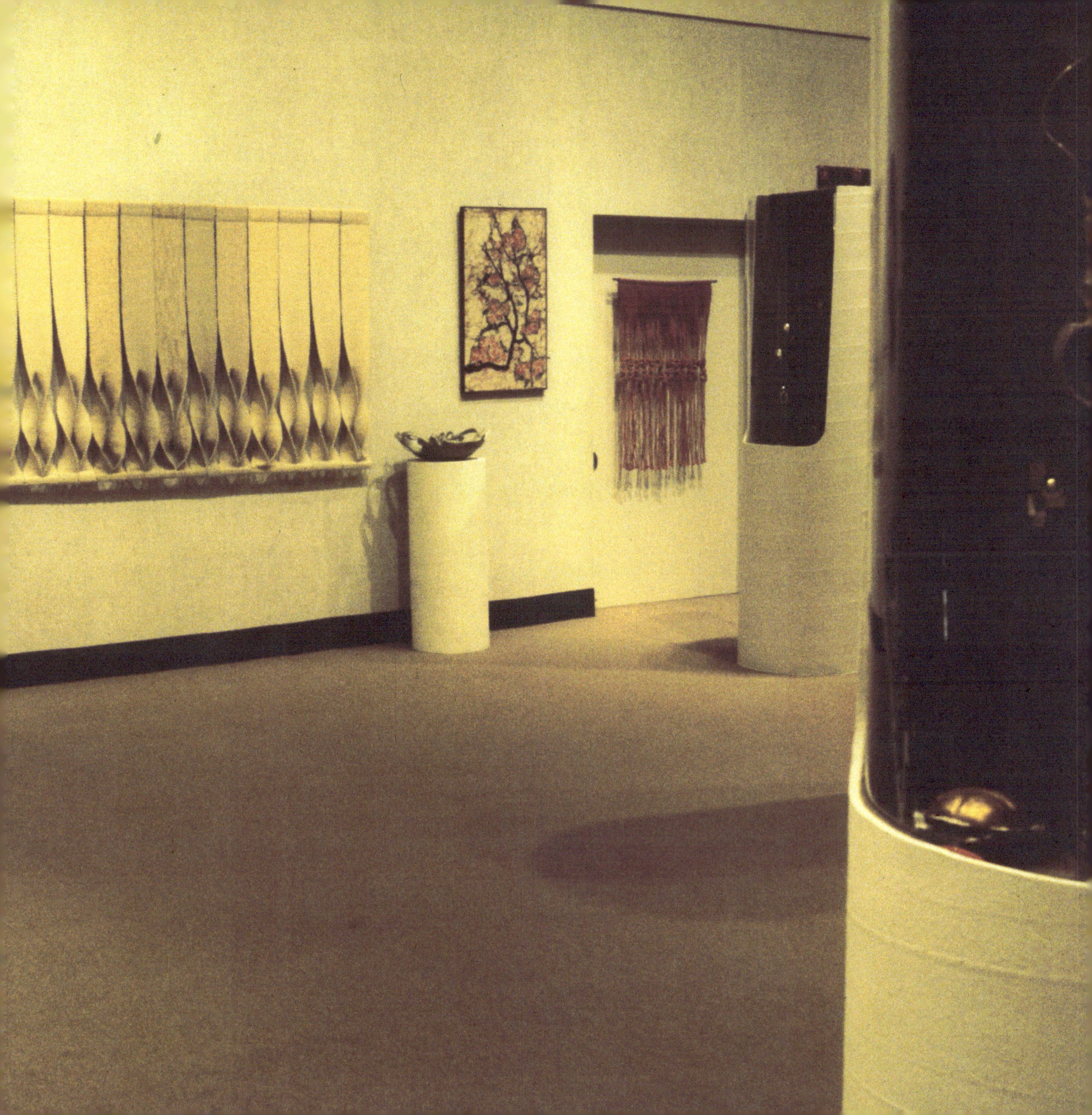

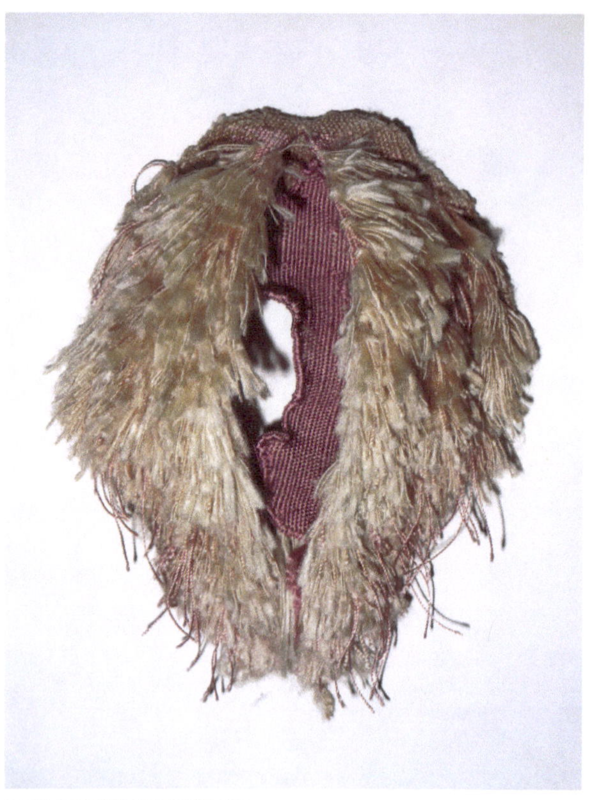

**VERA E. KAMINSKI, *ANDROGYNE*,** 1976

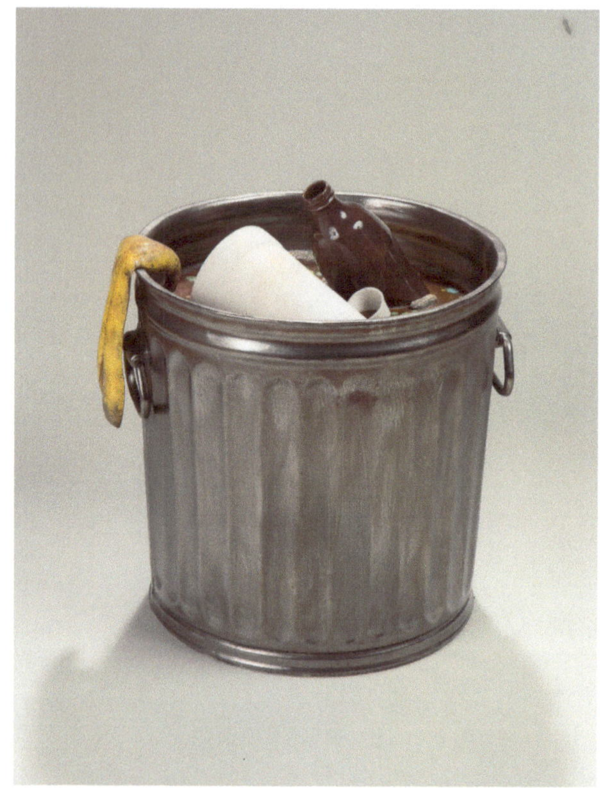

**VICTOR SPINSKI, *SLUDGE TRASHCAN*,** 1986

and refinement met imagination, barriers between so-called high and low culture were leveled. The confluence of fine art and the handmade was sealed.

The Delaware Art Museum held over 30 exhibitions that featured work by nationally recognized clay, glass, metal, wood, textile, and mixed media artists, among them Wendell Castle, Judith Ingram, and Jack Lenor Larsen. The Museum sponsored its *Annual Contemporary Crafts Exhibition* and crafts fair, whose reputation drew local and regional artists and enthusiastic audiences.

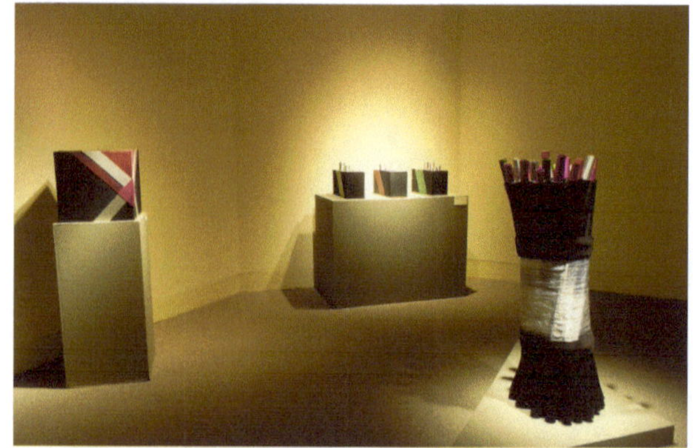

INSTALLATION VIEW OF ***HELEN MASON: FORM AND SPIRIT*** (MAY 20–JUNE 19, 1988)

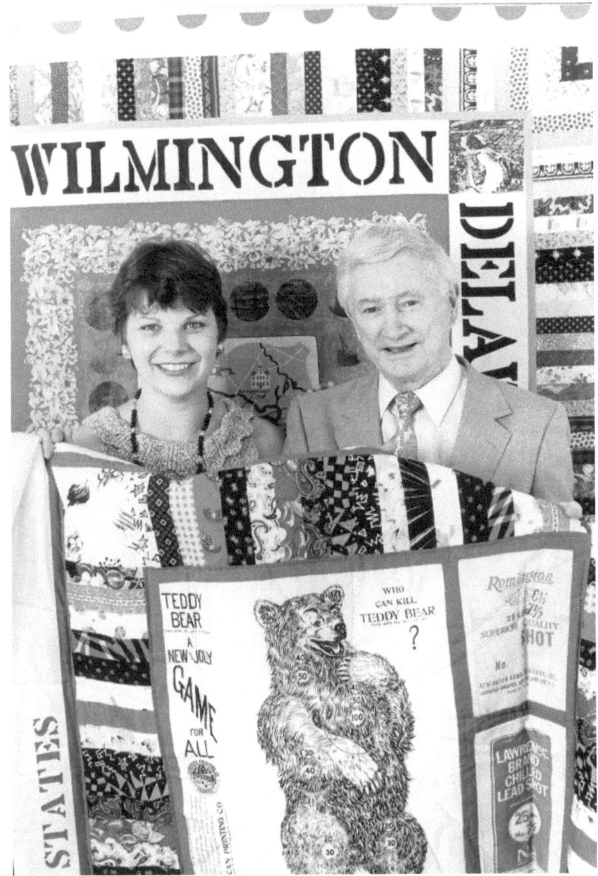


**TERENCE ROBERTS, *TERESA BARKLEY AND FORMER WILMINGTON MAYOR WILLIAM T. MCLAUGHLIN,*** 1987

The American Craft movement brought capital to small businesses such as advertising agencies and print shops. Gallery guides steered consumers to events. *The Craft Guide, Delaware* (1981–82) sponsored a juried submission for each publication and a 1982 exhibition. Artists included Kaminski, Longhi, Mason, and Spinski, as well as Sheila Ashby and Teresa Barkley. Additionally, local artists' works were reviewed in national publications such as *The New Art Examiner.*

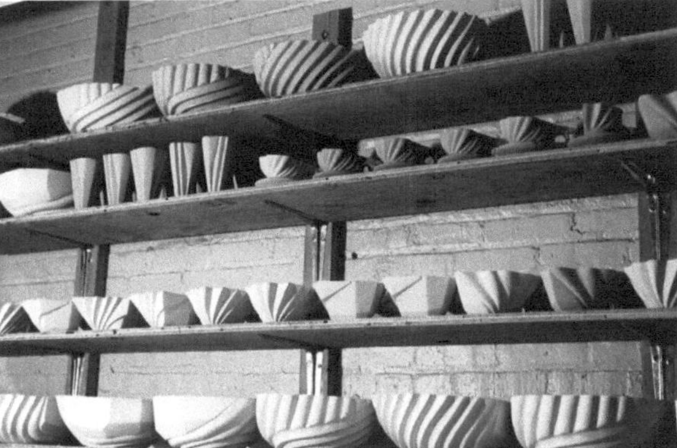

**CHARLES NALLE STUDIO AND WAREHOUSE IN DOWNTOWN WILMINGTON**

Corporations, government agencies, and public and private venues became ardent supporters of craft organizations. Even a White House collection of American craft was built from the Carter administration to the Clinton administration. Each object was chiseled from the artist's vision that reflected the human narrative. Acceptance of craft as fine art was a historic milestone, and this recognition of the handmade reflects its timeless quality.

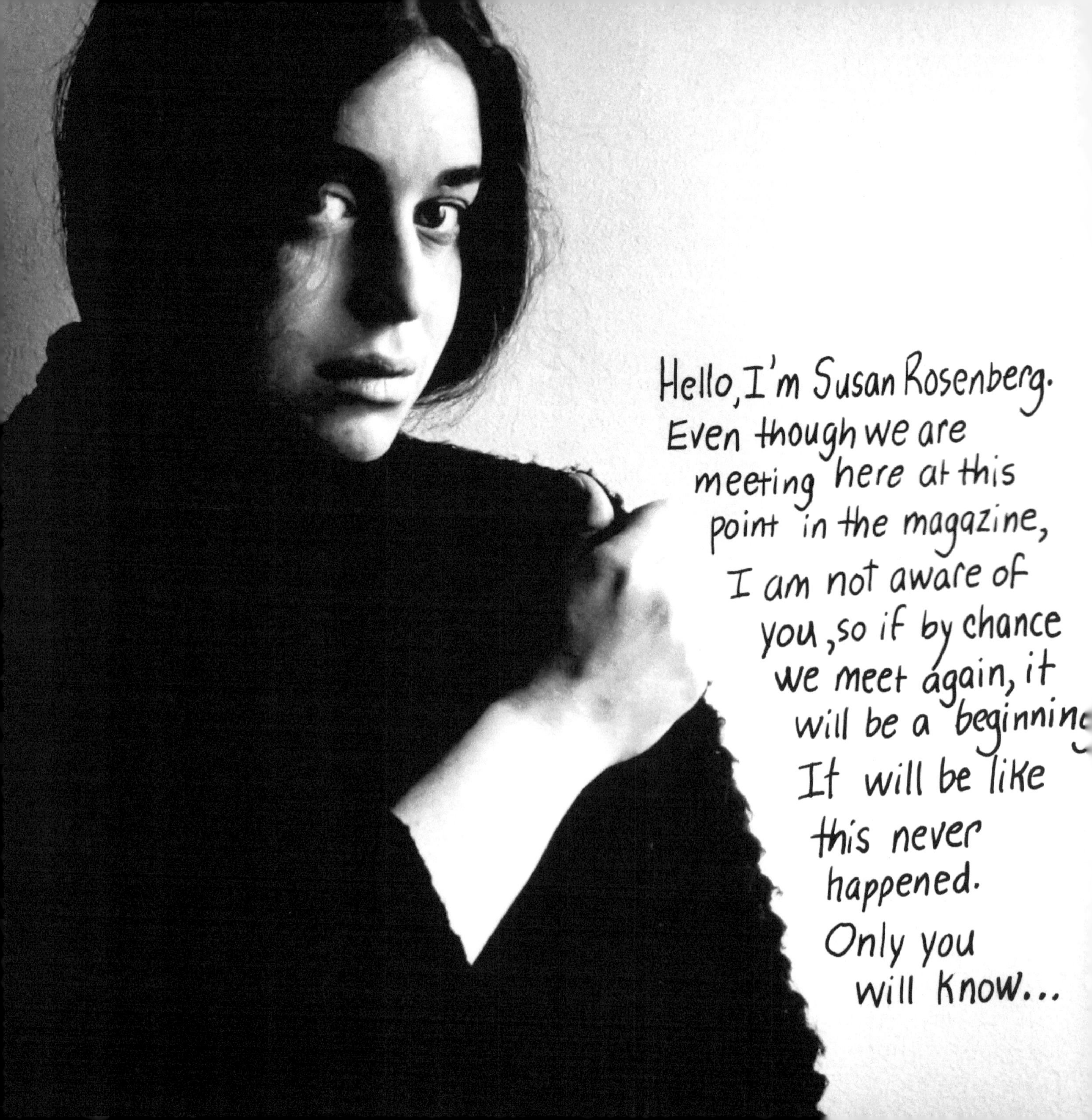
Hello, I'm Susan Rosenberg.
Even though we are
meeting here at this
point in the magazine,
I am not aware of
you, so if by chance
we meet again, it
will be a beginning
It will be like
this never
happened.
Only you
will know...

# THE SENSATION OF PHOTOGRAPHY IN DELAWARE 1970S AND '80S: "THE PHOTOS SEEN"

**Flash Rosenberg**
*Photographer, Filmmaker, and Cartoonist*

What does photography reveal? Most pictures show us how we used to *look*. I have always been determined to create images to capture how we used to think. I was first drawn to photography by the perceptual sensibilities it offers, rather than by its dazzling (and often laborious) technology. Ever since I began using a camera, I have been fascinated by the discovery that how we make pictures is connected to how we think in words.

But how does that relate to what we want to remember? Can we re-experience the texture of being alive at any given time by looking at a photo of it? Revisiting the work I made in the 1970s and '80s—when I was in my 20s and 30s—has brought me back to a very fraught, passionate, and playful time. Decades later, I have come to realize that wherever you are in life right now, you are still inseparably connected with your own moment in history. It was a heady time of upheaval. Photographers felt an exhilarating responsibility to document injustice, as well as create images to express the counterculture. For me to recall those days as a time of great energy and artistic possibility is to cuddle nostalgically with the idealistic hopes of my youth.

One thing I do know for sure is that the photos I made as *art*, now probably have more value as historic documents. Since I enlisted my artist friends to pose in photo scenarios, I now have a vast, meaningful record of who lived here, how we played, and what everything we loved and loathed used to look like.

Back then I worked primarily in black and white. My fascination with summarizing experience into images was shaped by the way black and white naturally abstracts the complexity of color and visual information into a simpler form. Only black and white was archival (color print chemistry was not yet stable), so that's why it was deliberately used to make art. I was also shaped by how negative film made time linear. Shooting film, like handwriting, was done in a flow, without stopping to review or edit in the midst of paying attention. How we see ourselves in time is now intrinsically more jagged and eye-popping due to digital technology.

So what about "The Delaware Photo Scene: 1970–90?" *Wait. There was a photo scene?* As humble artists in a small state, we were pretty sure that capital A-Art was happening in New York City, or maybe Philadelphia, but not in our backyard. Of course we photographers knew of one another. But our energy was for photos seen, without much awareness of any "photo scene." Who knew we needed to join a group to decide when to press the shutter? The art scene seemed to reside within each of us, which I view as one of the great perks of evolving as a Delaware artist. With little expectation for being noticed, I was formed by the notion that what I got to know was far more important than who got to know me.

At that time, there were few galleries for contemporary artists. This was not wholly a bad thing, because it meant I could merrily show anywhere and everywhere. Art was territorially unlimited and not precious. I installed vending machines in restaurants filled with *Sue-venirs*—tiny photo frames cut from contact sheets, mounted and displayed in plastic globes. Insert two quarters, turn the handle, and out popped art.

I collaborated with dancer Dolores Josey to take pictures of her frolicking dramatically in public spaces to create *Dance Around the Town*, displayed gallery-style on a public bus

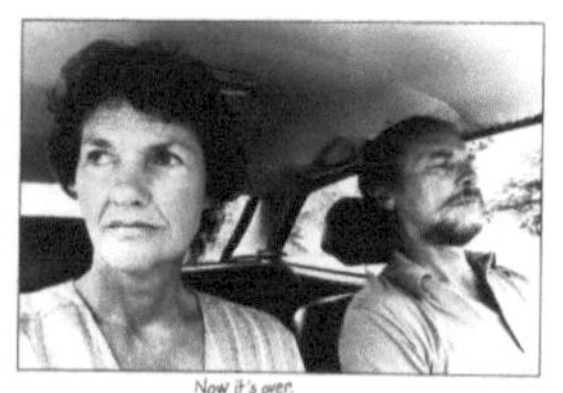

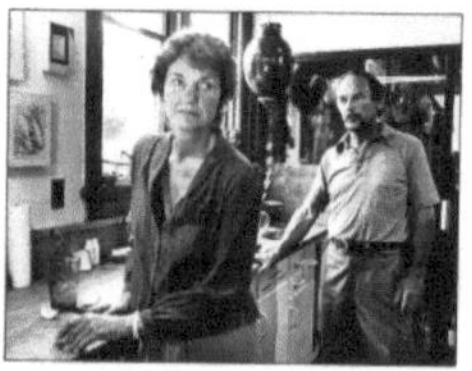
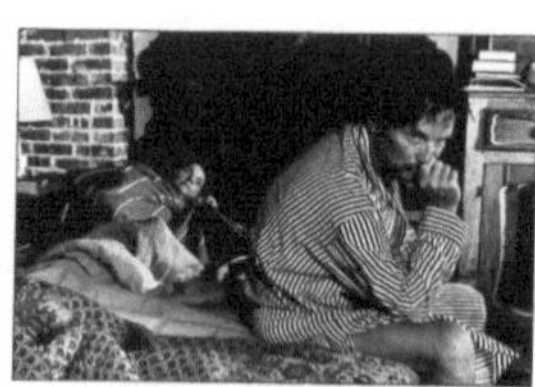
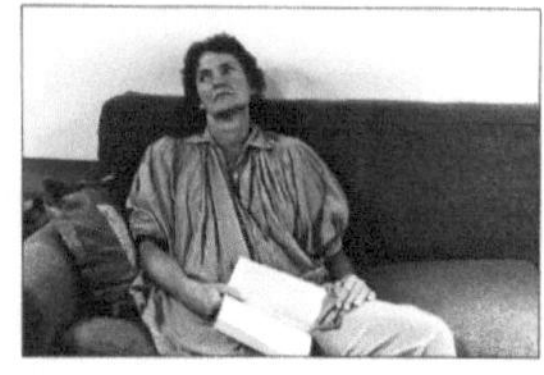
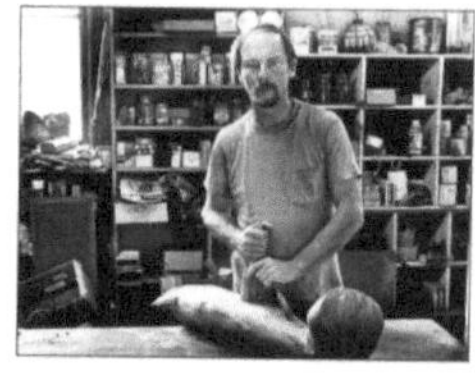
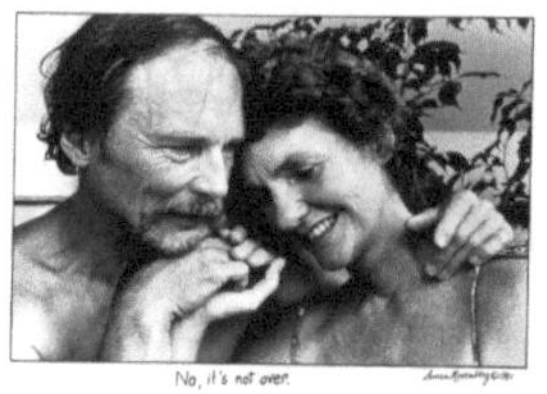


**FLASH ROSENBERG, *NOW IT'S OVER. NO, IT'S NOT OVER.*,** 1981

renamed *L'Autobus* D'ART—a Frenchification for Delaware Area Rapid Transit—that ran on a new route each day so all commuters could enjoy the show in rotation. Passengers were greeted with cider and cookies for the opening.

*Listening Photos* featured folks I photographed and interviewed while strolling around town. Their portraits were captioned with handwritten notes expressing how they felt about living in Delaware, and displayed in libraries, office buildings, town halls, and theater lobbies.

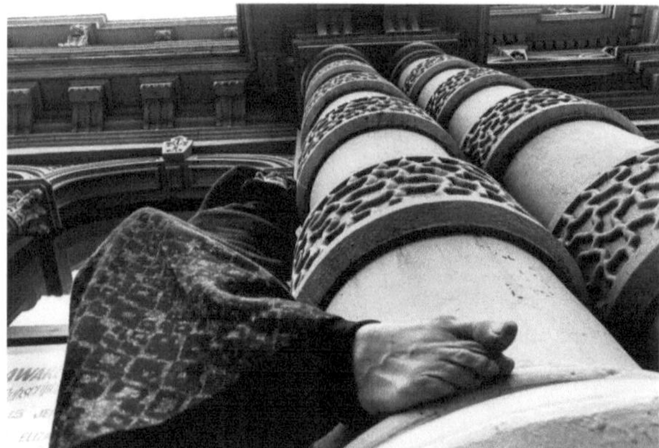

**FLASH ROSENBERG, *DANCE AROUND THE TOWN*,** 1976–77

As a Delaware Artist-in-the-Schools, I posed high school students in scenes they storyboarded to illustrate their English class compositions based on real dreams, to create *Dream Visions*, exhibited in schools and educational administrative bureaus throughout the state.

At art festivals and heritage fairs I invited folks who happened onto a designated spot to reveal to me how they felt at that moment, in one word, to create a giant, instant-photo *Mood Quilt*.

And as much fun as all those antics were, it was momentous when Robbie Jones, director of the Fifth Street Gallery in Wilmington, invited David Tonnesen, David Pugh, Shawna Reilley, Mimi Greenberg, John Gatti, and me to be in the major exhibition *Six Shooters*. To show our work in a gallery was validating, because photography was not fully respected or accepted in those days. Pugh, Reilley, Greenberg, and I were members of a loose lark of approximately 25 artists in Phark (Photographers of Newark), who gathered monthly (from 1977 to 1980) to *socialize* and sometimes critique work.

The most influential person committed to championing photography during this time was my teacher, mentor, and dear friend Byron Shurtleff. In 1966, he was hired to start a photography program at the University of Delaware. He led a national movement to aesthetically insinuate photography into university art departments. He had a degree in painting, because when he was in college, photography was still considered a mere technical skill to be taught in vocational schools.

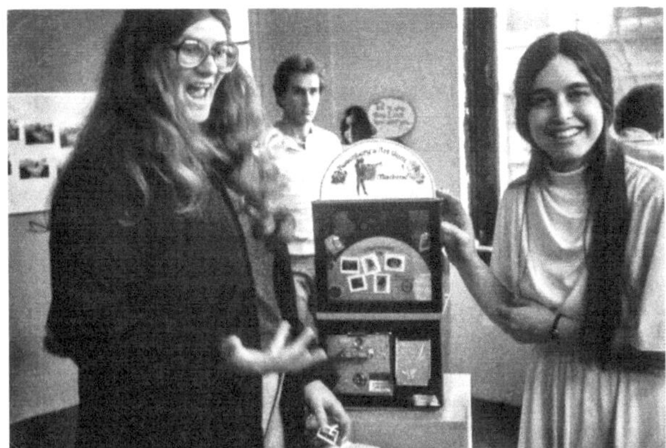

INSTALLATION VIEW OF ***SIX SHOOTERS*** (MARCH 12–APRIL 1, 1978)

In 1972, while serving as vice-chair for the National Society for Photographic Education, he told Wilmington's *Evening Journal* that "photography exerts a powerful influence on the whole fabric of society today. Although the concept of photography in universities is a new discipline, students should be taught the subject right along with 'the three R's.'"[1]

Shurtleff was a brilliant instructor. Unlike Minor White or other charismatic photo superstars of the time, he did not urge imitation, but demanded that we discover our own unique visions. He pushed us to understand the inner sensation of sight, to experience how depth of feeling could be most vivid during the solitude of looking. He taught photography as a language. He'd joke, "Sit down, I want to talk your picture." He taught us to be tuned-in to when our expectations collide with what's really there. I've blissfully carried his teachings with me for years.

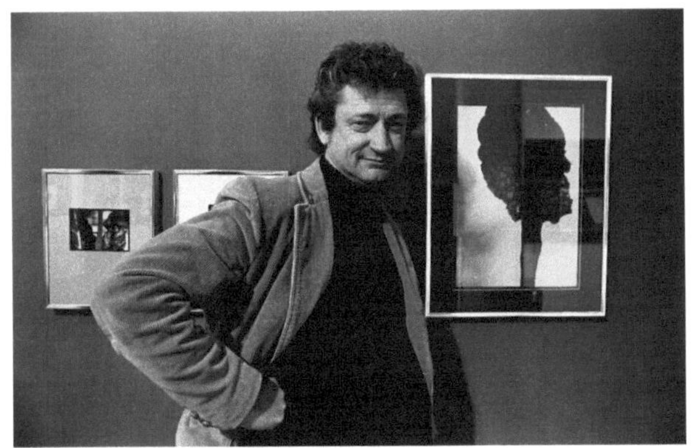

**RON DUBICK, *BYRON SHURTLEFF*,** MARCH 19, 1976

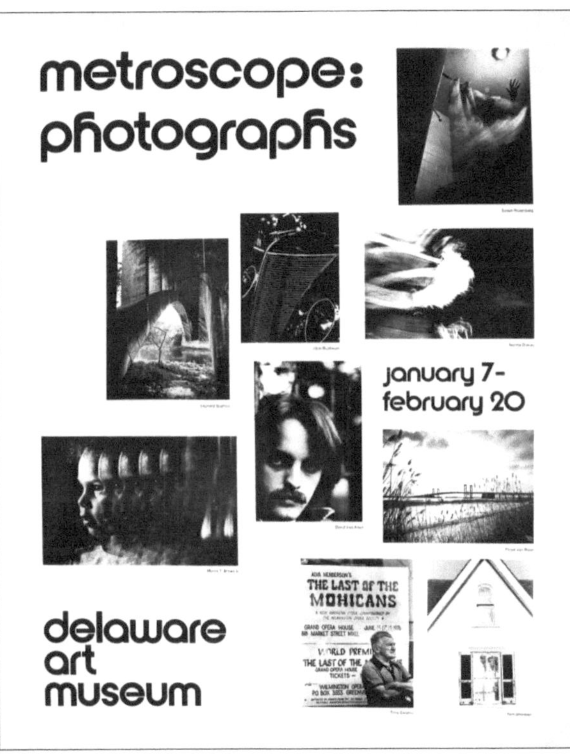


EXHIBITION POSTER FOR ***METROSCOPE: PHOTOGRAPHS*** (JANUARY 7–FEBRUARY 20, 1977)

That said, these recollections should serve as profound comfort for artists currently hard at work in sleepy towns, who might be wondering, "Where is the art scene?" Just wait 40 years and—surprise—you might discover you were it!

1. "Delaware Teacher Reorganizing Photo Society" *Evening Journal*, January 13, 1972, 40.

# ARTSQUAD AND THE DELAWARE CENTER FOR THE CONTEMPORARY ARTS

**Rick Rothrock**
*Artist and Founder of the Delaware Center for the Contemporary Arts*

In the summer of 1978 I was hired as the Community Arts Coordinator for the New Castle County Art Studio at the Absalom Jones Community Center. A recent graduate of the University of Delaware's master of fine arts program, I had undertaken a number of large-scale public art projects where public or group participation was encouraged. People

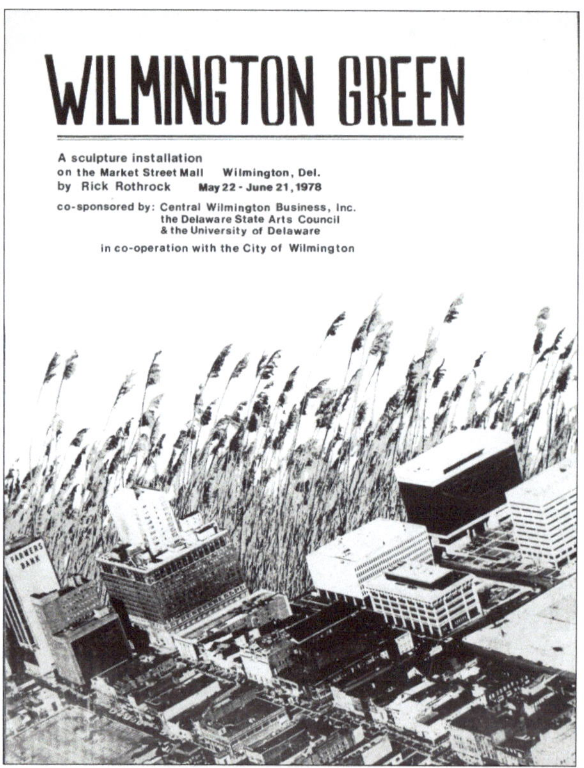


**RICK ROTHROCK, *WILMINGTON GREEN* POSTER,** 1978

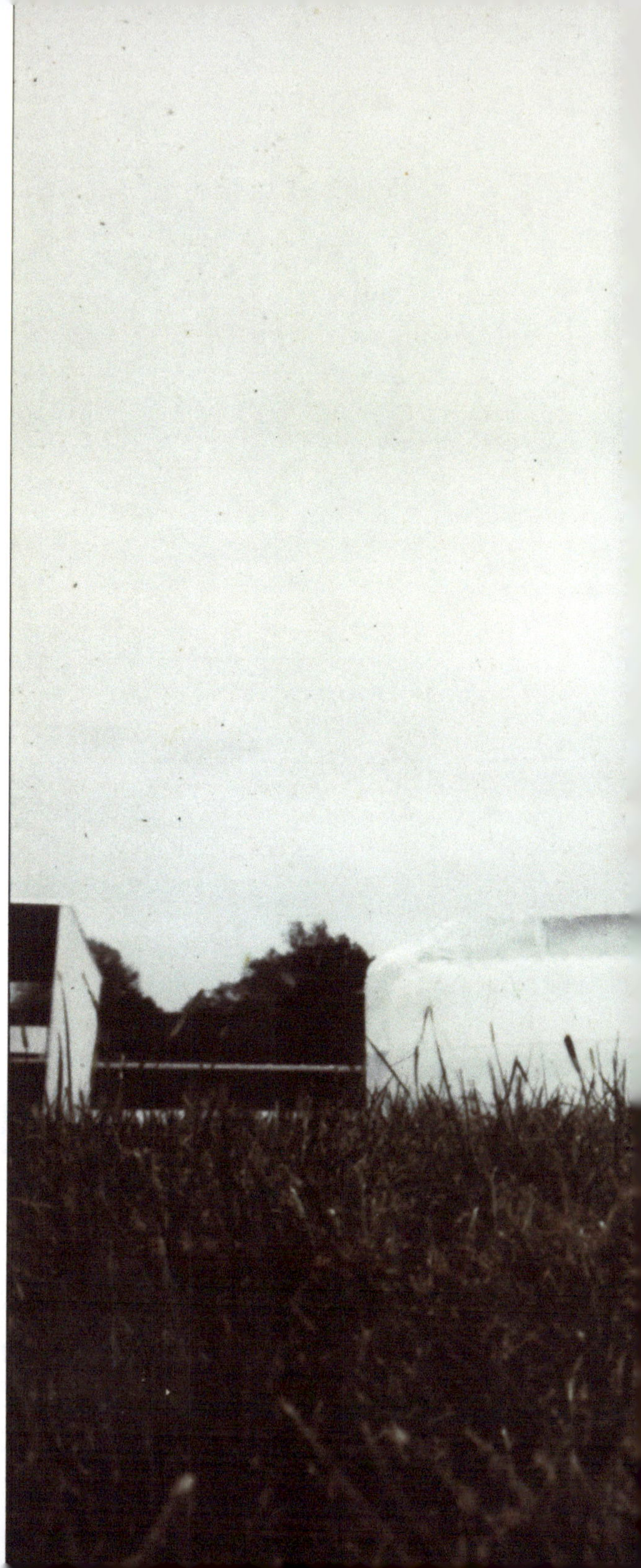

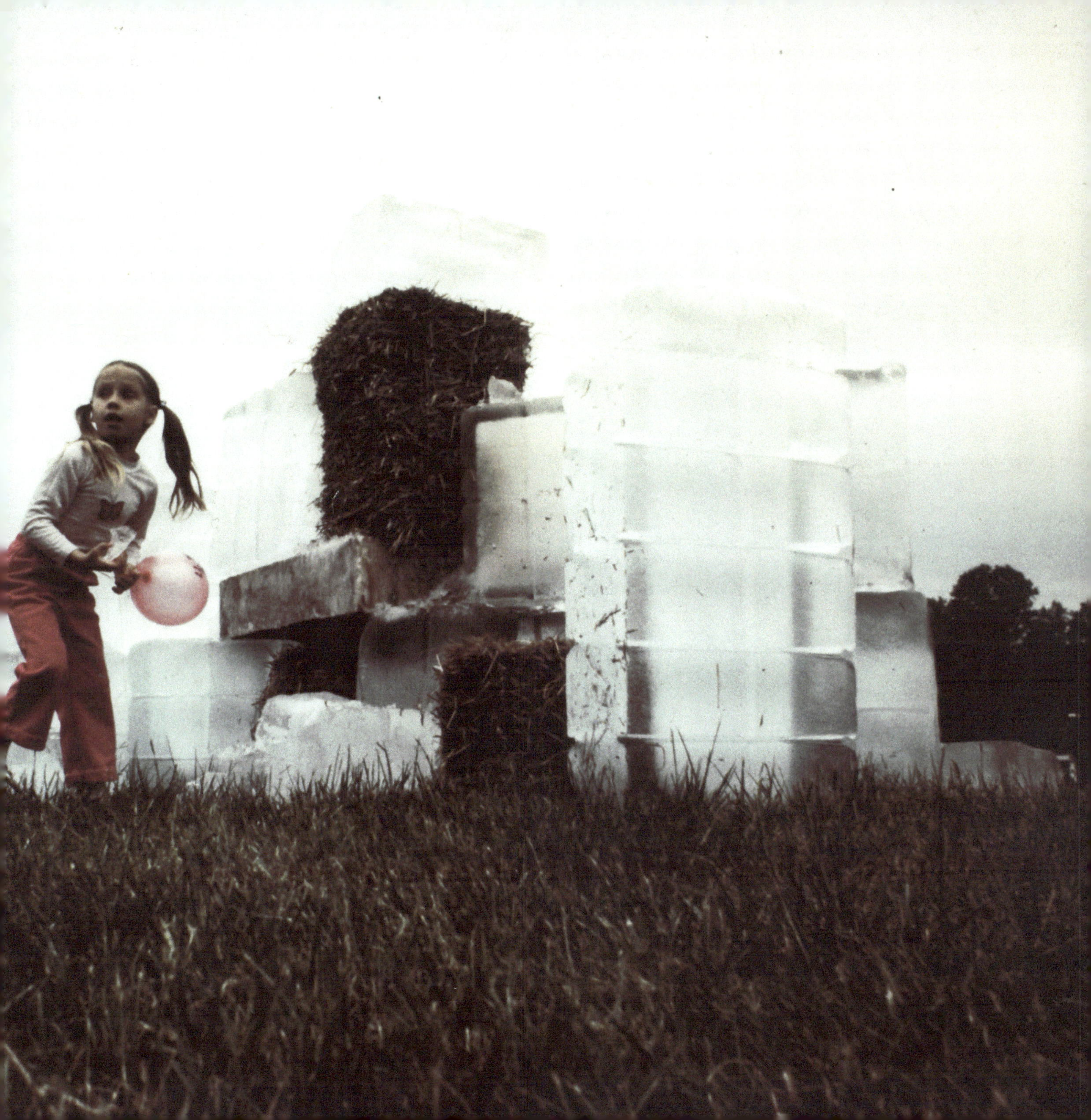

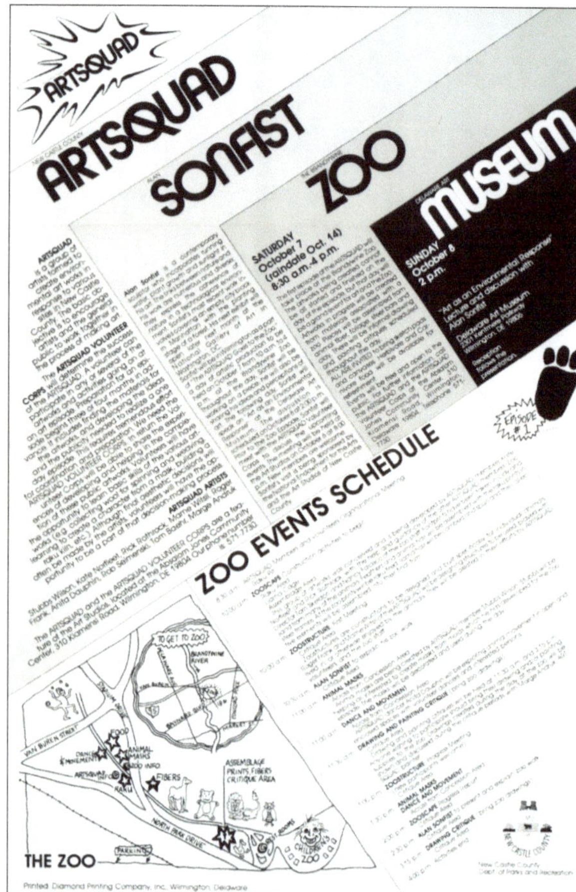

ARTSQUAD ARTISTS, *THE ARTSQUAD GOES TO THE ZOO* POSTER, 1978

well as ideas about authorship, originality, and individuality.

in Delaware were challenged and excited by this "new" kind of artwork.

As Community Arts Coordinator, I invited professional local and guest artists and volunteers to create different "episodes" focused on a variety of art activities. The group met for the first time on September 11, 1978, and the ArtSquad was born. We believed in the importance of the creative process and were willing to share it. We discussed artistic principles as well as ideas about authorship, originality, and individuality.

The ArtSquad's first episode took place at the Brandywine Zoo in Wilmington on October 7, 1978 with guest artist Alan Sonfist. We organized several more episodes at other venues in the city, including Willingtown Square, Banning Park, and Winterthur Museum, as well as Lums Pond State Park in Bear. We reveled in our freedom and shared our youthful passion and joy until the grant that fueled our fire was exhausted.

The energy and enthusiasm generated by the ArtSquad convinced me of the need for a permanent art center where Delaware-area artists could create, exhibit, and learn from one

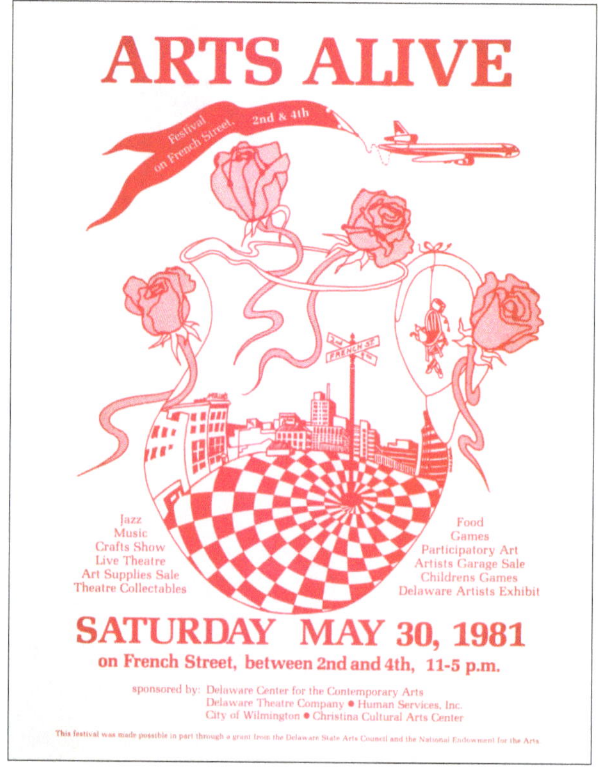

VARIOUS ARTISTS, *ARTS ALIVE* POSTER, 1981

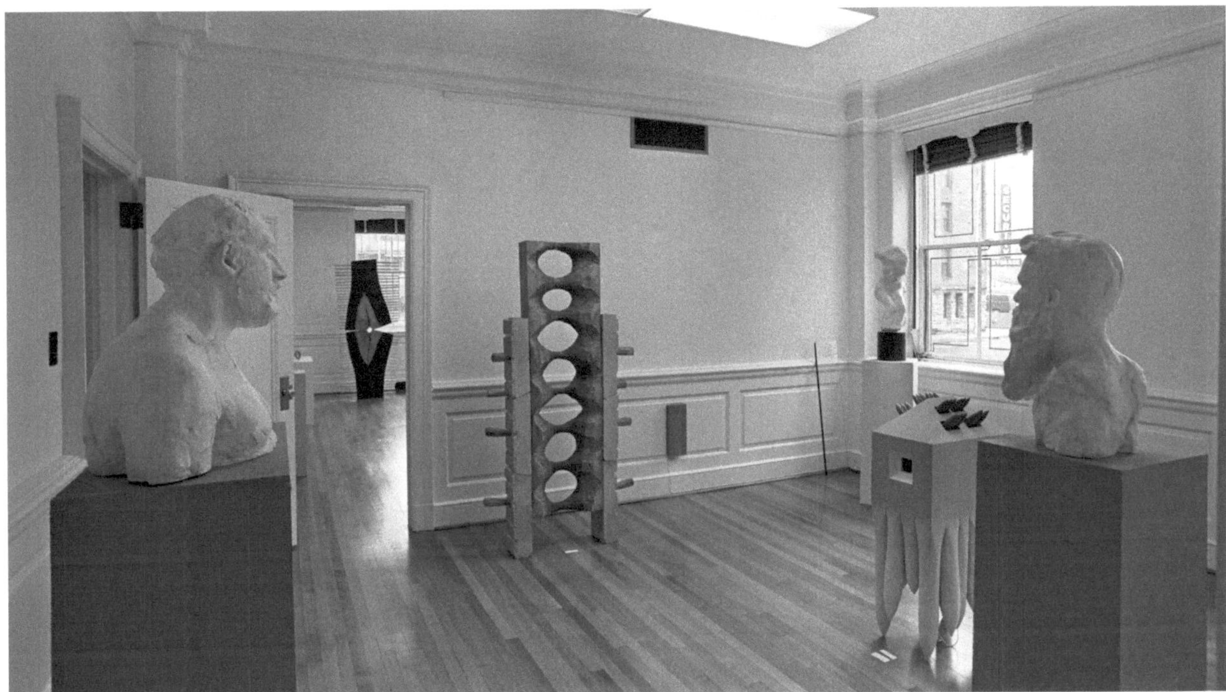

**LEO S. MATKINS, *DCCA NEW MUSEUM*,** MAY 13, 1984

another. Over the next several months, I gathered information by meeting with directors at several art centers throughout the eastern United States as Gina Bosworth gathered information in the Northeast. Fresh with new ideas, I organized meetings with artists and community members in private homes, galleries, and schools, where we shared our ideas and concepts for a contemporary art space in Wilmington.

In early 1979 the Delaware Center for the Contemporary Arts (DCCA) was incorporated and a board of directors was formed. I became the first acting director and Gina became the first president. We leased a former sheet metal factory at 224 French Street in Wilmington from the State and, in 1981, began renovations to create artist studios and gallery space. The first juried show, curated by J. Susan Isaacs, consisted of sculpture and works on canvas and paper. Along with the Delaware Theatre Company and the Christina Cultural Arts Center, the DCCA held Arts Alive festivals to promote the arts and funds were raised for the DCCA and its roster of more than 120 affiliated artists. In 1983 the organization moved to the Waterworks Building at 103 East 16th Street, then, in 2000, to its present location at 200 South Madison Street, under the guidance of its first full-time director, Steve Lanier. Today the space features seven galleries, a 100-seat auditorium, and 26 studios for resident artists.

The Delaware Center for the Contemporary Arts is a non-collecting museum that presents annual exhibitions of regionally, nationally, and internationally recognized artists. The DCCA commits to educational and community outreach through various programs and fosters a greater appreciation and understanding of contemporary art.

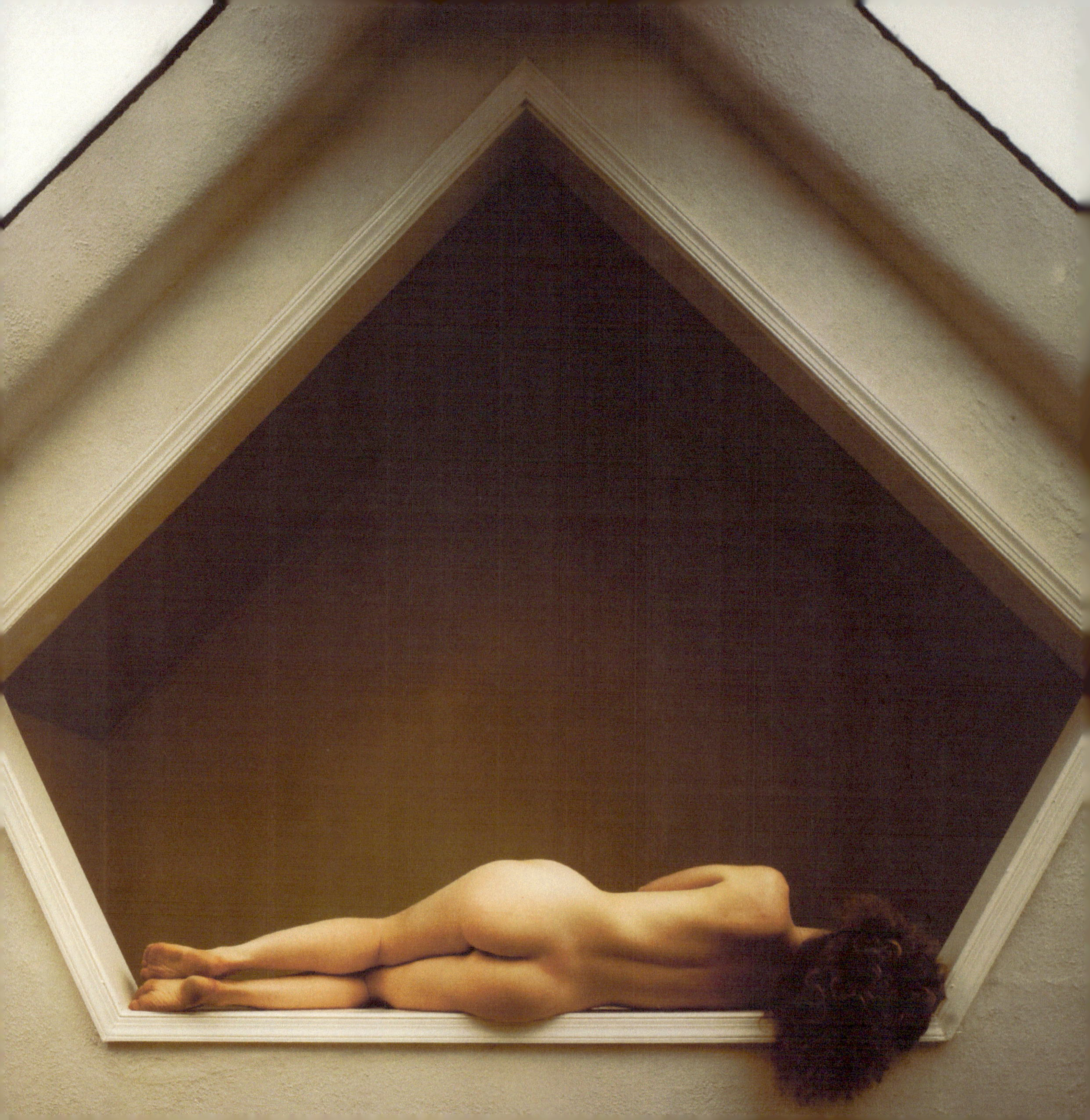

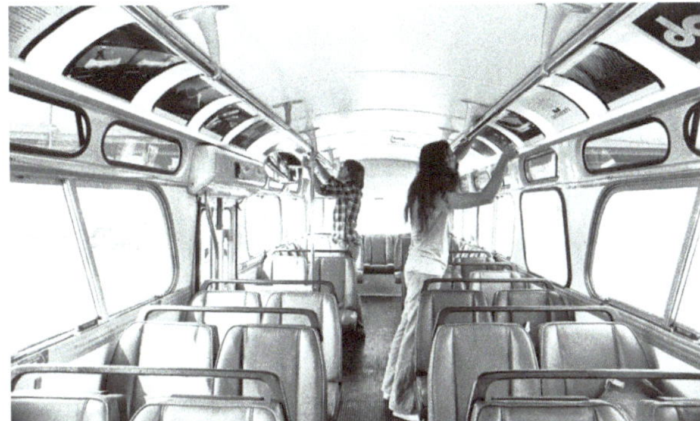

**FRED COMEGYS, *DART ART*,** SEPTEMBER 20, 1977

I was fortunate to have participated in the blossoming of Delaware's arts community in the late 1970s and early '80s. No single event sparked this surge in creativity—there were many: Rob Jones opened his Fifth Street Gallery; ArtSquad was established; Xanadu Comics and Collectables began staging performances; the Delaware Center for the Contemporary Arts (DCCA) and the Delaware Theatre Company were founded; and the Delaware Art Museum embarked on an expansion, just to name a few. Perhaps the time was fertile, as the woes of the day gave us something to respond to: the end of the Vietnam War, recession, gas shortages, and sky-high interest rates. Many of us channeled our artistic energy and talent into making our community a more livable and vibrant place to be.

In 1978, with a grant from the federal Comprehensive Employment and Training Act, the Delaware Art Museum launched ArtReach, a community-based art education program. I was hired, along with others, to develop arts programming for the public schools. We would spend an entire month in a school, working every day to transform students' lives through multiple art projects, with a final exhibit that parents were invited to. The culture of the Museum changed radically with the infusion of so much young talent. Even after federal funding ended, the Museum remained committed to more ambitious curatorial

**Carson Zullinger**
*Photographer*

and education projects, including a seminal series of exhibitions examining art and culture from 1890 to 1940.

In 1978, I also became involved with ArtSquad, a group of artists that Rick Rothrock organized to produce interactive public art installations. The ArtSquad evolved into the DCCA as Rick and others put together a series of community meetings to assess what we wanted for our creative lives. I joined the organization's board of directors, and later served as president. We moved temporarily into a state-owned building at 224 French Street, then, after losing that lease, successfully negotiated with the City of Wilmington to procure a new space in the Waterworks Building at 103 East 16th Street. At that time, as an organization, we felt strongly that we needed to establish a separate visual arts voice that was not connected to the Brandywine tradition. From the beginning, we envisioned a space to exhibit and promote contemporary art—both local and national in scope—as well as to develop affordable artist rental studios and education programming for the community. Once we had a permanent home, a place for new ideas and new art, the DCCA grew quickly. It was an exciting time.

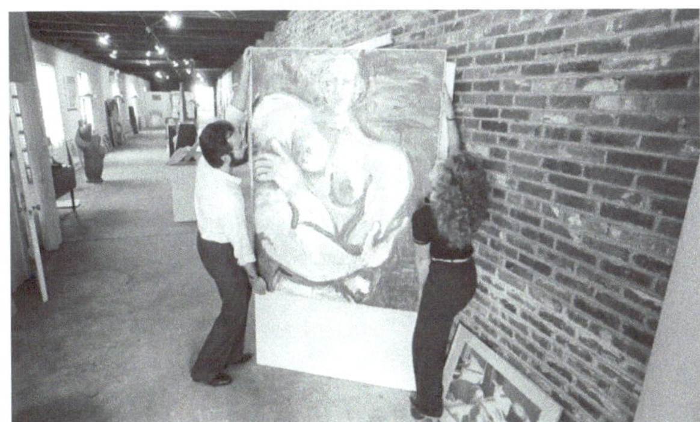

**LEO S. MATKINS, *GALLERY SHOW*,** SEPTEMBER 26, 1982

**Caitlin Davis**
*Curatorial Intern*

Not typically considered a major player in the art world, Wilmington is perhaps best recognized as the home of the DuPont family and the headquarters of major financial institutions. Less well known is the thriving community of artists who, in the 1970s and 1980s, generated work rivaling that produced in New York and Los Angeles. Taking full advantage of the advent of the color photocopier and joining the burgeoning "xerographic art" movement, Wilmington natives Anne Eder and Tom Watkins pushed their city away from the landscapes and farm scenes that then dominated its gallery walls and toward more cutting edge, provocative work.[1]

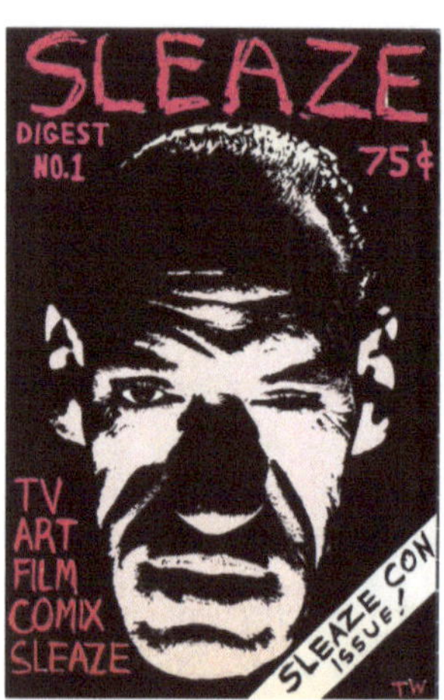


**TOM WATKINS, *SLEAZE DIGEST*,** NO. 1, 1976

The original black-and-white copier was invented by Chester Carlson in 1938.[2] A law student at the time, Carlson could not afford the expensive textbooks required for his classes. He spent his days at the New York Public Library, using a mimeograph to copy the pages of the text he needed to review. He grew tired of the time-consuming procedure, and set about trying to develop a machine that could make copies more quickly. Through a series of experiments conducted in his own living room, he invented an electrostatic process that could reproduce words on pages in just minutes. Carlson patented his work and sold his machine to the Xerox Company, but it was not until 1959 that it came onto the marketplace. For the next 20 years, the "Xerox machine" was a fixture in commercial offices around the world.

By the early 1980s, copying technology had advanced significantly and the first color copiers were introduced. Artists quickly adopted the new machines as part of their practice. As Dave Hamill wrote in *Big Shout Magazine,* they were able "to produce professional-quality four-color separations without the use of more expensive printing techniques. This process allows an artist to produce limited editions of prints, posters or other visual formats without incurring prohibitive production costs; it also allows for the creation of transfers that can then be applied to articles of clothing, such as T-shirts."[3] Artists were able to manipulate their images in ways they had never before considered. They could change the color composition of the piece, introduce layering of colors, and experiment with a variety of supports. No longer used solely to duplicate pages of text, the copier had become the catalyst for a new art form.

*Electroworks*, the first exhibition featuring this type of work, was organized in 1979 by the George Eastman House. The show included over two hundred prints, books, and three-dimensional objects; the related Copy Art Symposium provided artists and critics with a forum to discuss the new movement and its impact on contemporary art.[4] Soon after this landmark exhibition, a number of galleries devoted to xerography were established, among them Ginny Lloyd's Electro Arts Gallery in San Francisco. Louise Neaderland founded the nonprofit International Society of Copier Artists in New York City, and, in April 1982, began publishing a quarterly magazine that would showcase xerographic work by international artists for the next two decades.[5]

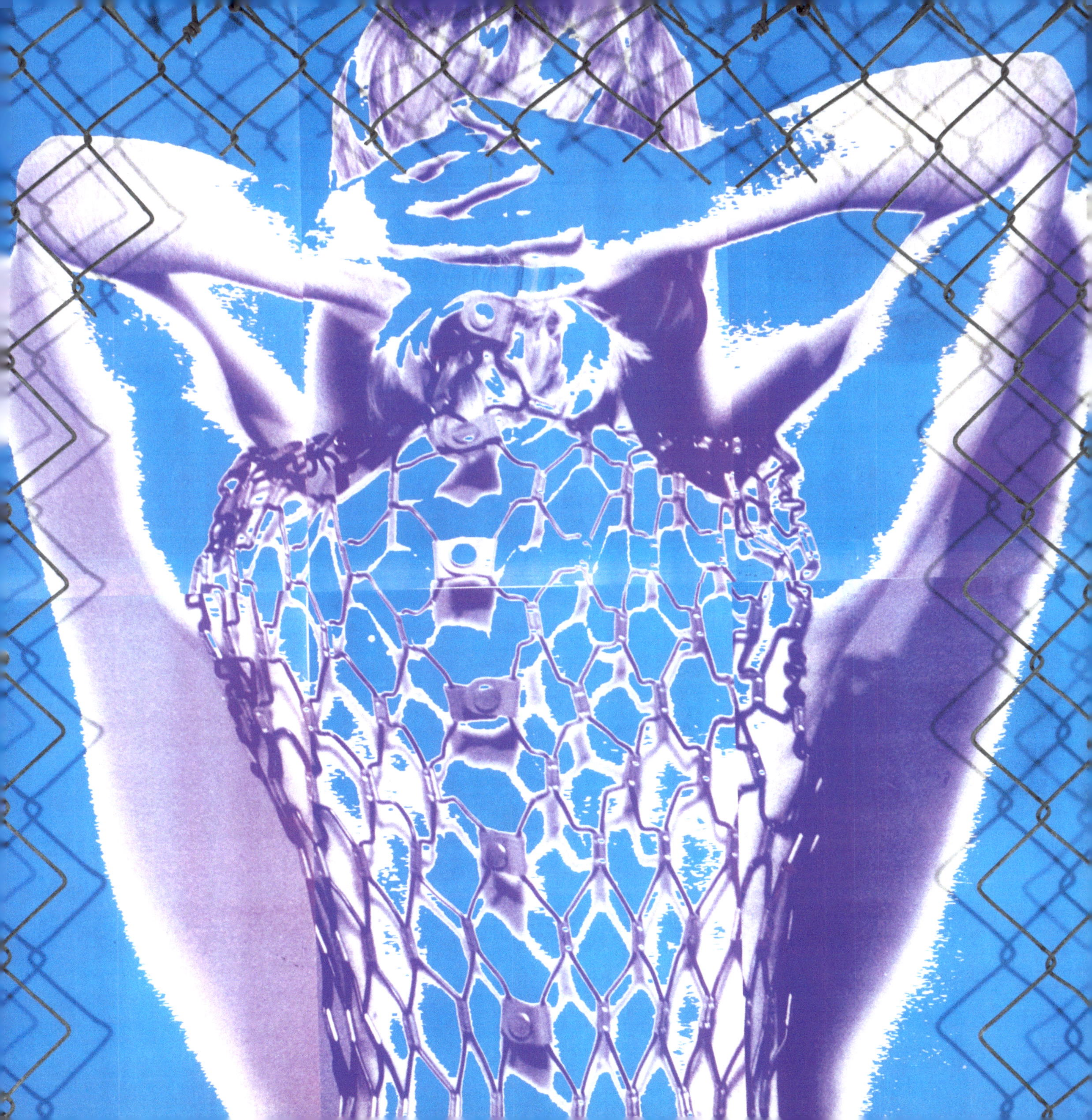

Anne Eder, a graduate of Saint Mark's High School, was eight years old when she received her first camera. In her early 20s, after a short stint in which she studied acting at New York University and toured the United States with a band, she returned to Wilmington as an apprentice to local photographers Jon Schladen and Peter DeLaurier. Following her apprenticeship, she worked at Karl Richeson's 25th Street Studio at 217 West 25th Street, developing, printing, and retouching photographs and assisting on commercial shoots. It was during this time that she wandered into two of Tom Watkins' businesses, Xanadu Comics and the Wilmington Costume Shop, both located just off the Market Street Mall at 2 West Fifth Street. She recalls the Alice in Wonderland effect that these places had on her: "Tom was six-and-a-half feet tall, so everything in the shop was built to his size."[6] And she notes that Watkins "had the power to hound people into believing what he had to say. He had the power to inspire other artists and would always pull people together."[7] She was captivated by this magnetism, and, having developed an interest in Watkins' xerographic work, she began collaborating with him.

Watkins was a graduate of Brown Technical High School. After a debilitating accident sustained while working as a longshoreman, he enrolled in a sculpture class being taught by Joe Moss at the University of Delaware. There he befriended Robert Jones, a graduate of the university and a sculptor who worked with industrially produced materials such as polyurethane and fiberglass. Jones also owned the Fifth Street Gallery, Wilmington's only avant-garde commercial art space at the time, which gave Watkins entrée into the city's art scene.

A self-described Renaissance man, Watkins got involved with many different projects. He helped organize a Sleaze Convention, a weekend event that featured "sleazy" movies such as *I Was a Teenage Frankenstein* and *Pink Flamingos* along with a tour of Wilmington's Sleaze District. The events were attended by celebrities Edith Massey—Edie the Egg Lady in John Waters' films—and Blondie band members Debbie Harry and Chris Stein, along with Anya Phillips and Marty Thou.[8] Watkins' artwork was often featured in the "Off Center" section of *Fine Times* magazine, where he wrote about pop culture with a dose of humor. With the help of Hank Goldstein, Bill Lynch, and Ed Wesolowski, he designed a 1960s counterculture-inspired zine called *Emergency Illustrated*, which featured comics, unique stories, and editorial reviews. According to Watkins, the magazine was primarily considered a student publication and, as such, it struggled

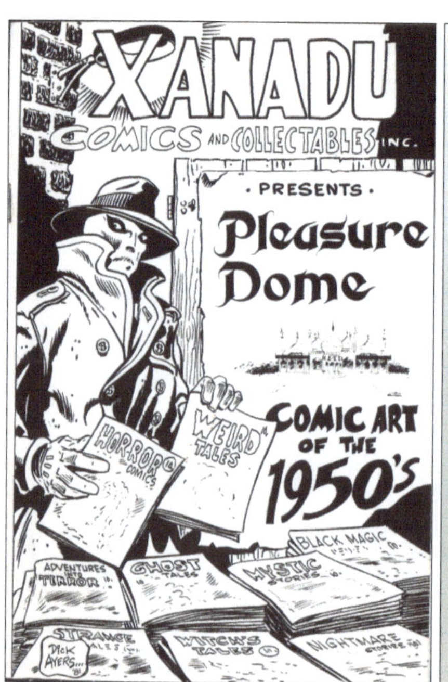


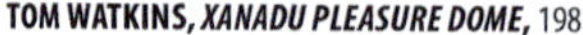
**TOM WATKINS, *XANADU PLEASURE DOME*,** 1981

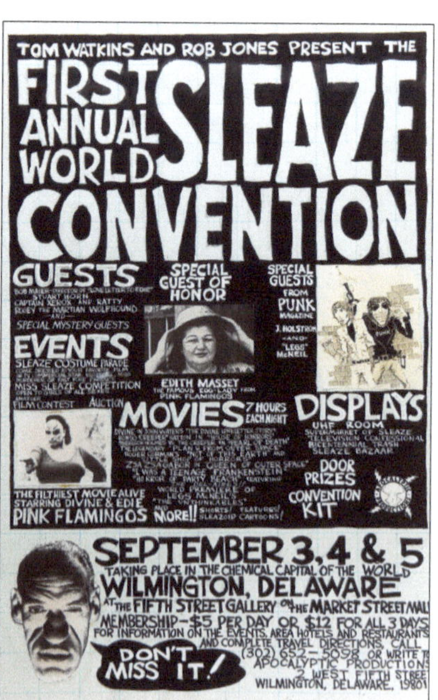


**BILL LYNCH AND TOM WATKINS, *SLEAZE CONVENTION POSTER*,** 1976

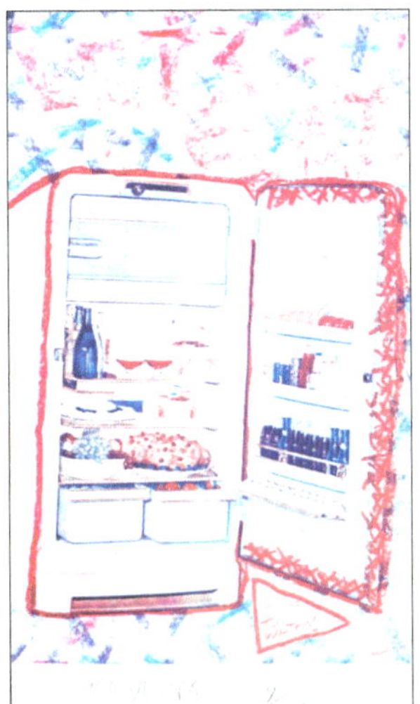

**TOM WATKINS, *UNTITLED*,** 1983

to gain respect among the literary community. But while its existence was relatively brief—only five issues were published—*Emergency Illustrated* united many local artists and sparked the formation of an underground community.

In 1974, Watkins, Craig Dawson, and Joyce Brabner—wife of the late Harvey Pekar, creator of the *American Splendor* comic series—opened Apocalyptic Productions, a commercial art studio where Watkins sold his unique artwork. Shortly afterward, Watkins formed the Wilmington Costume Company, hoping to turn his passion for creating characters into something profitable. Through the publication *Famous Monsters of Filmland*, he learned about film, directing, acting, and script-writing. He taught himself how to apply stage make-up, produce special effects, and design and create custom masks and costumes that he made available for rent.[9]

Watkins says he "came into xerography through the back door," explaining that he "used it as a low-cost way of beating the cost of photostats and other processes used in magazine and commercial art production."[10] Discouraged by a lack of government funding, he began using the Xerox 6500 to create inexpensive works. He first sold his xerographic T-shirts at the Brandywine Arts Festival. The positive response encouraged him to delve further into the medium.

Before the invention of color copying, illustrations for commercial pieces were done "twice-up," the term used to describe the process by which an illustration is created. For example, a standard color magazine cover of 8 1/2 inches by 11 inches had to be painted as a larger original piece with dimensions of approximately 17 inches by 23 inches. The painting was then photoengraved using four plates—one each for magenta, cyan, yellow, and black—to create the desired image. This resulted in the print becoming reduced to 9 inches by 12 inches. It was then trimmed down to the precise size of the cover, which gave it a clean edge called a "bleed." Black-and-white illustrations that incorporated shading required additional steps. To create a 25 percent gray, the artist had to prepare the work with a 50 percent tone that was then reduced at 50 percent to a density of 25 percent. Watkins notes that these processes were tedious and rather expensive, so it is little wonder that he and Eder jumped at the chance to use the color copier. This did not mean, however, that producing color illustrations would be effortless. There were still several challenges in utilizing this new technology and an infinite number of discoveries to be made along the way.[11]

Due to the threat of reproducing this coveted technology, manufacturers did not produce black toners for their early color copiers. Instead, artists had to mix color inks to get the desired effect. Eder remembers, "Since early copiers had no black toner, we had to manipulate the color balances and the amount of toner deposited to achieve blacks. It meant taking that into consideration when laying out the original artwork as well, since prints with high percentages of black areas tended to blister and crack." She also recalls having to make her own text: "It is crazy to think how difficult it was to even add text to an image at that point. I usually would type my text, have a photostat made, reverse the stat in the darkroom and then double expose the image in order to photographically print the text onto the photo itself."[12] Despite the challenges, Eder and Watkins were committed to advancing xerography as an artistic process.

According to Eder, she and Watkins "were always trying to push what was possible—heavier papers, fibers, and so on—and sometimes the accidents were as interesting as the projects that went smoothly." [13] This was the part of copy art that made it revolutionary. One could rapidly work through an idea, seeing immediately if it was a success or a failure. Eder and Watkins often traveled to the Philadelphia print shop, Copy Center, where the staff allowed them to experiment with machines to understand how they would perform under different conditions. The staff was just as curious about the ability of the new technology to bridge the gap between the art and business worlds.

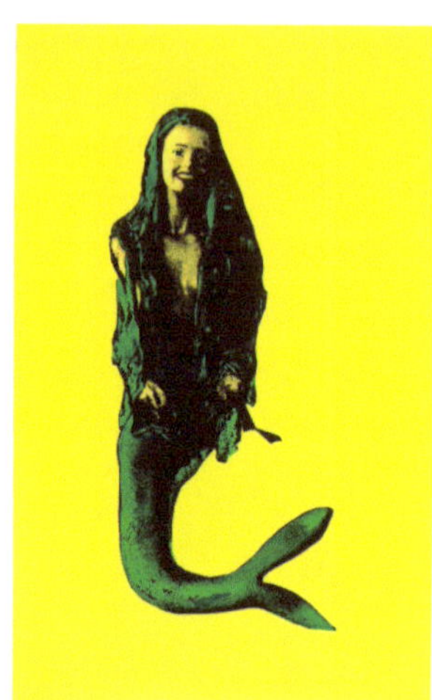

**ANNE EDER, *MERMAIDS*,** 1984

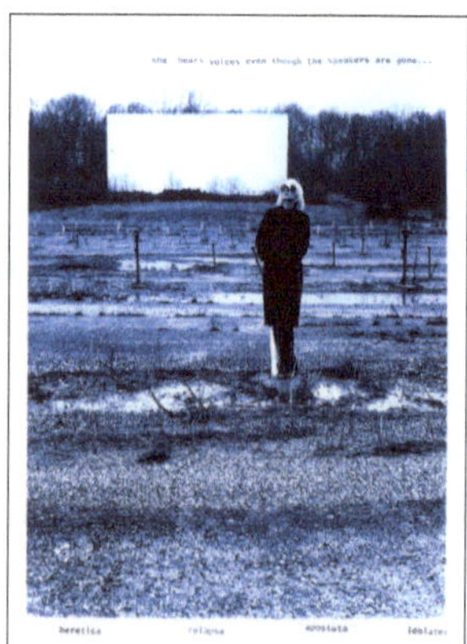

**ANNE EDER, *SHE HEARS VOICES (EVEN THOUGH THE SPEAKERS ARE GONE)*,** 1987

For Eder, an artist coming from a background in black-and-white photography, the color copier significantly changed her artistic practice. "Having color to work with was new and inspiring, and I often gave in to the temptation to print an image in a series of monotones or go Andy Warhol on it, as in the *Mermaids* prints," she recalls.[14] Her work consisted of 50 percent mixed media and 50 percent fabric with heat transfer. As Eder describes it, her xerographic technique "almost always started with black-and-white photography, and then used layering, hand-coloring, collages, assemblages, or machine-generated color."[15] Even though she felt that Xerox was an innovative company, she preferred working on Canon copiers, which produced high saturation and softening, for her portraits, so she would go to Wilmington Blueprint and Metrocolor to create her pieces.

Watkins' comic work, which the artist had previously drawn by hand, could now reach a much larger audience. According to Watkins, his biggest discovery was that he could copy his images onto vellum paper. "This had a big result. I could now make art in any size, make corrections of the black-and-white art...I could then add tones with no concern about 'losing' the art because of a mistake on tone work."[16] He used dye pens as toner to create different textures, as there was no commitment to an original, making it easier to dispose of a drawing if he was dissatisfied. He remembers purchasing self-filling marker sets. "They had variable nibs and allowed a huge range of line weights, so I could now do 'pure tone' modeled effects. I could also do 'camera ready' toned art in varying sizes and final looks, and create complicated color by hand."[17] Watkins could now layer color effects in sequence, similar to the manual process he had used before the advent of the color copier. He also had the freedom to mix technical approaches, such as pen and ink, brush and ink, pastel and crayon, duo shade, photo collage, or even original color photographs.[18] Eder and Watkins were both creating artwork in the 1980s that would not be replicated by modern computer software until the mid-1990s.

While the two artists worked together over the years, their subject matter was extremely varied. One of Eder's consistent themes was the strong, fearless woman. During this period, Eder was a single mother raising two young children, and she gathered inspiration from female leaders and made them the subjects of her prints. She incorporated photographs of herself, creating self-portraits in the guise of the historical characters she admired. Joan of Arc was a recurrent figure in her work. The artist notes, "My fascination with St. Joan of Arc is obvious, and I have included her in the trilogy work as well as in *She Hears Voices (even though the speakers are gone)*. The latter piece was an intentional double entendre—it was as much about my own history and childhood trauma as it was about Joan of Arc, and visually about what I imagined she might look like in a 1960s Italian movie."[19] *She Hears Voices* features a solitary image of Eder in an abandoned drive-in movie theater lot. She poses against a pole that is fixed to the ground and stares upward into the sky. The light coloring of the blank film screen and of Eder's blonde hair contrasts with her black attire and dark sunglasses. In one self-portrait from the Joan of Arc trilogy, Eder is surrounded by crosses made of twigs and twine. Another shows Eder wrapped in rope around a cluster of trees with a cutout of fire at her feet, a reference to Joan of Arc's martyrdom.

The primary themes in Watkins' xerographic work were inspired by his lifelong love of comics. As a child, he learned to read from the *Alley Oop* and *Batman* comics of the 1950s, and was captivated by the illustrations of *Avengers* creator Jack Kirby as well as the science fiction and monster stories of Steve Ditko, who created *Spider-Man* and *Doctor Strange*. When Stan Lee's *Fantastic Four* series was published in 1961, Watkins realized that he wanted to become a comic illustrator. He spent hours emulating his idols' hands and attempting to master the skill of inking, a technique he jokes that he is still learning 50 years later.

For Watkins, no subject was off-limits: he sketched everything from men in electric chairs to Easter Island statues and underwater maidens. In 1984, he created the *Waitresses from Outer Space* series, which featured caricatures of cigarette-smoking female servers in brightly colored uniforms with over-the-top hairstyles. The artist notes that the series was initially intended to "parody the awful 'glamour' art so popular in the late 1970s to mid-1980s."[20] He got the idea to incorporate science fiction from hearing his friends refer to waitresses as "waitrons." He also took inspiration from Japanese manga; Veronica from the Archie comics of the 1940s to mid-1950s; bondage art from the 1950s, including the work of Irving Klaw and Eric Stanton; and *Heavy Metal*, an adult science fiction/fantasy magazine first published in 1977. Watkins explains that the final concept behind *Waitresses from Outer Space* "was to catch 'real' situations with this science fiction/sex overlay."[21] He was friends with many waitresses who worked midnight shifts, and he tried to capture their monotonous late-night world. He then incorporated the planets—Venus, Saturn, and Uranus, among others—and referenced each in the imagery. For example, works in the Saturn series feature the waitresses' breasts as the rings of the planet. The sense of robotic shifting is no doubt a reference to the science fiction influences of his childhood.

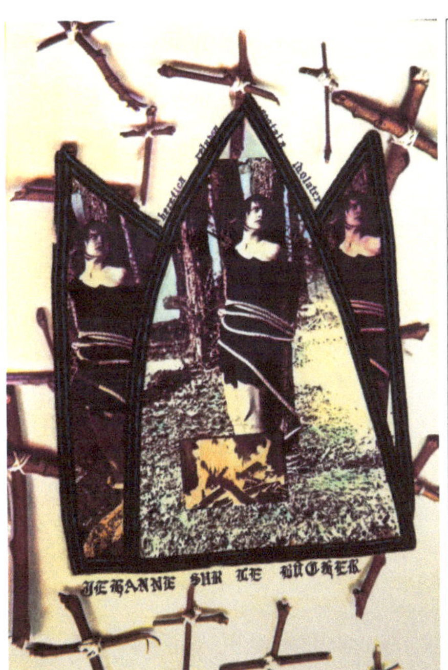


**ANNE EDER, *JEHANNE SUR LE BUCHER* FROM *JOAN OF ARC TRILOGY*,** 1985–86

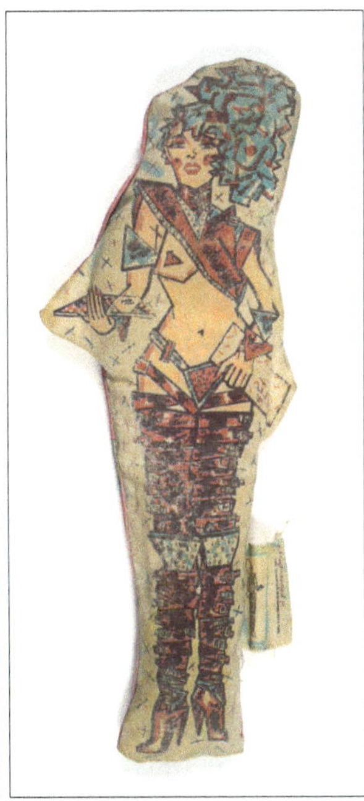

**TOM WATKINS, *WAITRESSES FROM OUTER SPACE DOLL*,** 1984

In addition to science fiction and fantasy, Watkins was fascinated by serial killers and death. His 1985 booklet called *Suicide Notes* included a razorblade, poems about death (featuring lines such as "Rub a dub dub, bleeding in the tub"), single-panel cartoons, photography, and xerographic manipulations of skulls. "It was an effort to treat a very serious subject with humor. Very black humor, but humor," says Watkins.[22] The work helped him cope with the loss of several friends who committed suicide.

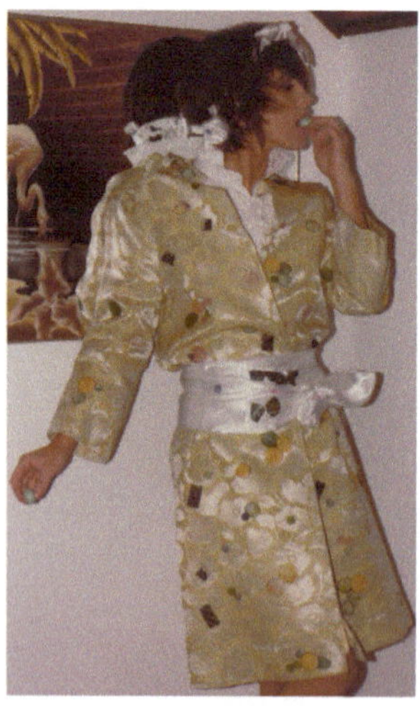
ANNE EDER MODELING ***XEROGRAPHIC CLOTHING LINE***, 1985–86

As color copier technology advanced, Watkins and Eder began creating their own wearable art using heat transfers to print images on fabric. Watkins focused on shirts featuring his quirky prints, while Eder created her own clothing lines. She purchased garments in antique stores, then added her unique designs. Her process "involved a lot of cutting out of tiny detailed images placed on either found or handmade clothing items and applied with a tipping iron."[23] At the peak of her xerographic work, she was producing "cocktail party wear, a cloaks and daggers and miscellaneous line, which includes a line called 'tarot,' and a new theme called 'genetic dress' based on government-funded DNA experiments".[24]

In 1984, Watkins and Eder organized a show at the Neither/Nor Gallery in New York City's East Village. (Watkins had previously exhibited there in 1980, in a show called *Love Letters and Suicide Notes.*) Eder showed limited-edition prints as well as creatures that she called Dendis—demons in various household situations. She remembers, "They were sort of these terrifying little finger puppets made from glove finger ends with big teeth and crazy hair, very primitive. But there was also something very happy about them, like they were SO happy being terrifying. I made outfits for them and dioramas using xerographic transfers and prints."[25] Watkins showed various examples of his comic art as well as image transfer shirts. The exhibition was well received by critics and the public.

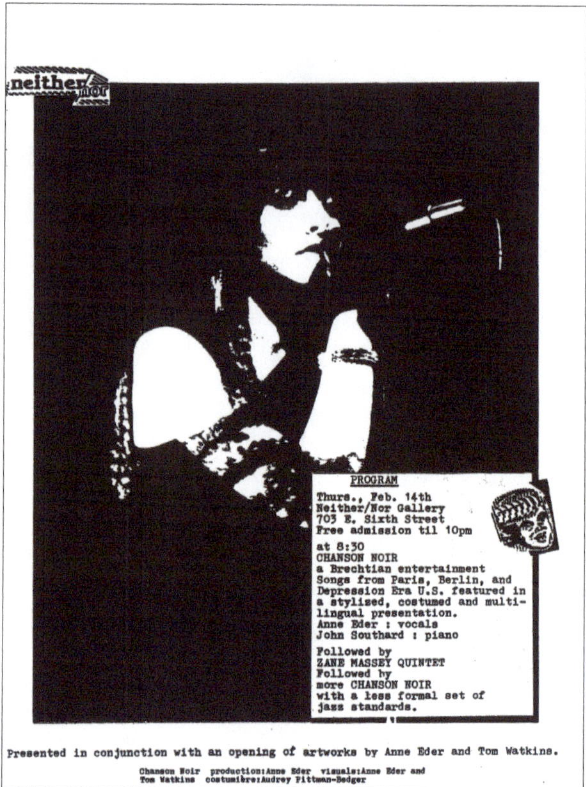

POSTCARD FOR SHOW AT **NEITHER/NOR GALLERY, NEW YORK EXHIBITION**, 1985

Both artists also showed at galleries in and around Wilmington. Eder exhibited her xerographic photography at the Delaware State Arts Council Gallery, the State Theatre, and various festivals throughout the area. Watkins showed his black-and-white manipulated prints at L. B. Jones Gallery, and his work was frequently on view at Crumbs and Oscar's restaurants. He also organized several experimental presentations within the city and hosted at his own Gallery X on Seventh Street. Eder participated in the events, making it a priority to feature a variety of artwork, including decorative arts and jewelry. Both artists disliked what they considered to be the pretentious nature of the art world and purposefully created a welcoming space with affordable art. At one exhibition opening, Eder remembers offering Twinkies and cartons of milk. They often displayed free artwork outside Gallery X, making it available to passersby, to encourage engagement with the gallery space and the artists' alternative art practices.

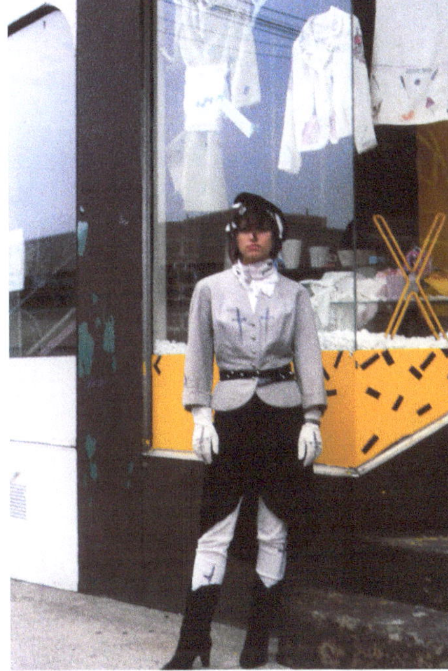

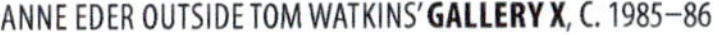

ANNE EDER OUTSIDE TOM WATKINS' **GALLERY X**, C. 1985–86

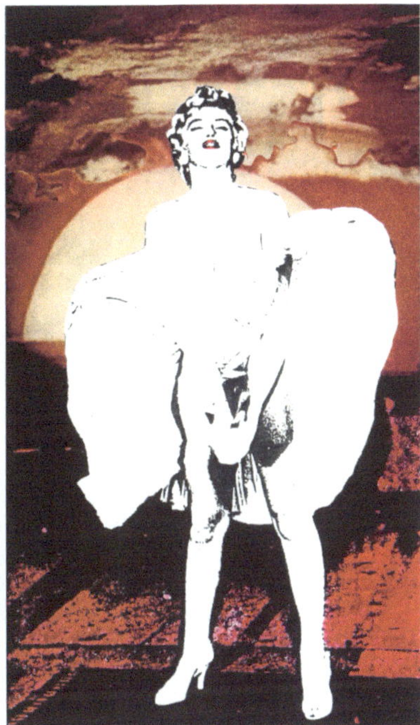

**TOM WATKINS, *HOT BLONDE*,** 1990

Watkins and Eder reluctantly witnessed the collapse of xerography in the early 1990s. With the prevalence of computers and the invention of the Internet, fewer artists practiced this unique art form—the cutting of bits of fabric to create heat transfers or the hand application of toners. These effects were now easily and more economically produced with computer software. As Watkins explained in a 1988 article in *X-Ray Magazine,* "Like so many of the finer things in life, xerography represents the triumph over the mundane, the creative over the commercial. The varied and exciting manifestations of copy art share that same impulse that elevates the results of a silkscreen into a seriograph, an acid-etched plate into a lithograph. Xerography is simply the creative deliberate use of this decades-old tool to create art."[26]

1. Dave Hamill, "Copy Cats: Delaware Artists Make Fashion Statement with Xerography," *Big Shout Magazine*, July 1989, 15, 19.
2. "Celebrating 75 Years of Xerography: Still Simplifying How the World Works," *Xerox*, accessed March 1, 2014, http://www.xerox.com/about-xerox/75th-anniversary/enus.html.
3. Hamill, "Copy Cats," 15.
4. Judith Hoffberg, "Copy Art Symposium," *Umbrella 2*, no. 6 (1979): 131–132.
5. John A. Walker, "Copy This! A Historical Perspective on the Use of the Photocopier in Art," *Plagiary: Cross-Disciplinary Studies in Plagiarism, Fabrication, and Falsification* 1, no. 3 (2006): 1–3.
6. Anne Eder, interview by Caitlin Davis, November 28, 2011.
7. Anne Eder, interview by Caitlin Davis.
8. Steven Leech, "The Sleaze District: An interesting and authentic subculture is developing in a section of Wilmington, affectionately named the 'Sleaze,'" *Wilmington Sunday Advertiser*, September 5, 1976
9. Tom Watkins, interview by Caitlin Davis, August 2013.
10. Hamill, "Copy Cats," 15.
11. Tom Watkins, interview by Caitlin Davis.
12. Anne Eder, interview by Caitlin Davis.
13. Anne Eder, interview by Caitlin Davis.
14. Anne Eder, interview by Caitlin Davis.
15. Anne Eder, interview by Caitlin Davis.
16. Tom Watkins, interview by Caitlin Davis
17. Tom Watkins, interview by Caitlin Davis
18. Tom Watkins, interview by Caitlin Davis
19. Anne Eder, interview by Caitlin Davis.
20. Tom Watkins, interview by Caitlin Davis.
21. Tom Watkins, interview by Caitlin Davis.
22. Tom Watkins, interview by Caitlin Davis.
23. Anne Eder, interview by Caitlin Davis.
24. Hamill, "Copy Cats," 15.
25. Anne Eder, interview by Caitlin Davis.
26. *Tom Watkins' X-Ray*, January 1988, 32.

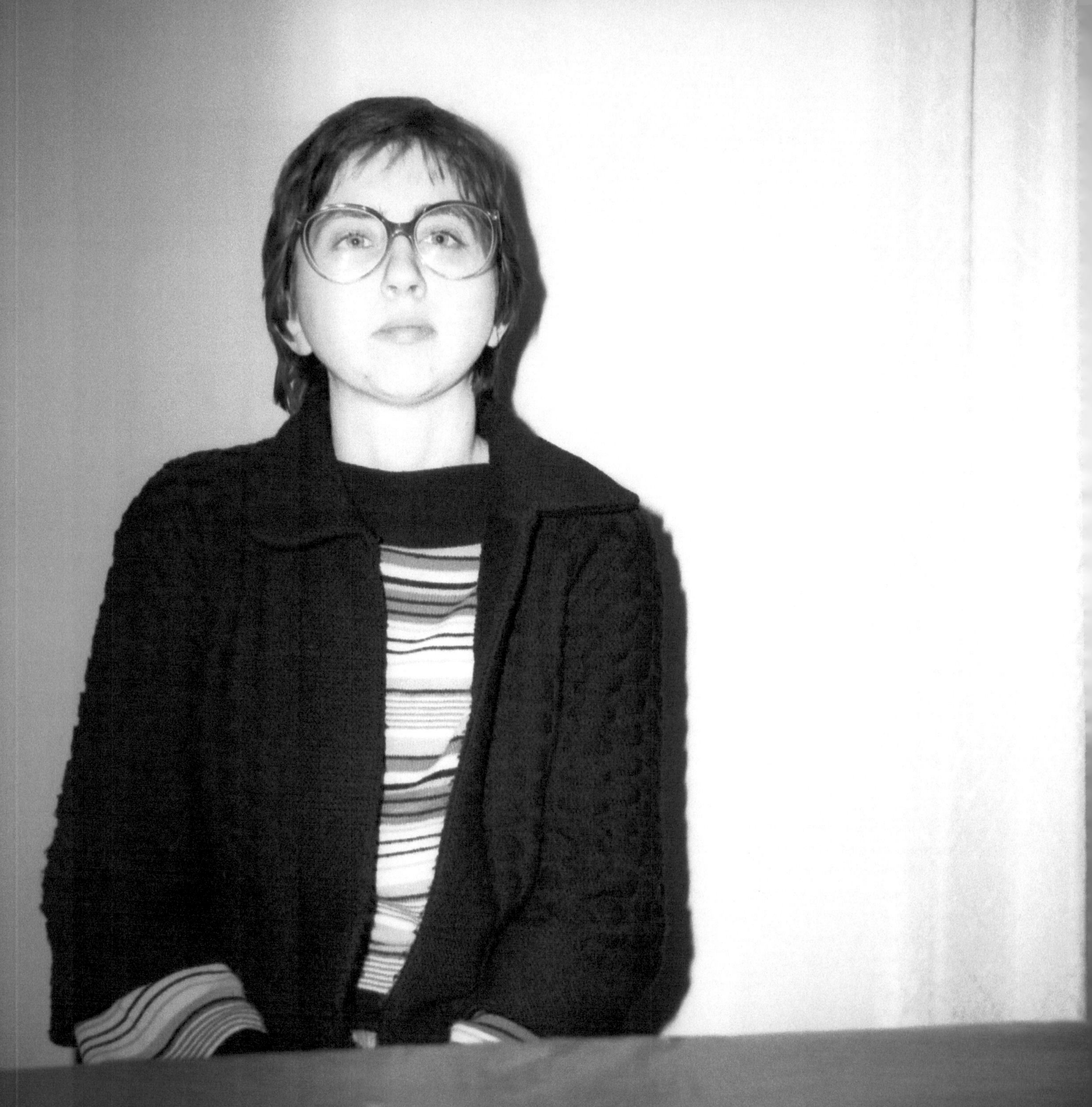

**Joyce Brabner**
*Writer*

In November 1982 I wrote letters to Cleveland comic book writer and critic Harvey Pekar (1939–2010). We married the following year. Our life together was chronicled in various books we wrote in tandem and individually, four stage plays, one feature film (*American Splendor*), several documentaries, an opera, and some other projects I am probably wisely forgetting.[1] Here's the way I explained myself then, when my epistolary suitor asked:

What do you do, Ms. Brabner?

*Costumes, comics and convicts…*

Tom [Watkins], Craig [Dawson], and I were co-owners of several rickety floors of a warehouse located at 2 West Fifth Street.[2] Once a month, in our long upstairs that was previously an indoor driving range, we held a sort of movable feast and cinematheque that we called the Rondo Hatton Center for the Deforming Arts.[3] We stripped down the art studio, set up chairs and a screen, served a Japanese-style vegetarian dinner, and showed cult/classic films or our own work. This was funded for several years by the Delaware State Arts Council until they finally objected—*not* to us showing the work of quirky filmmaker John Waters, but to the tofu. We weren't supposed to feed our audience.

On the ground floor was Xanadu Comics and Collectables, Inc. We sold comic books, science fiction and movie memorabilia, robots, gum cards, and buttons. The street kids who had no money but wanted the overpriced collectible comics often ran errands and did cleanup in exchange for issues of *Superman* and *Spider-Man*. Adult collectors built shelves, balanced our books, hauled trash, and patched the roof. We'd usually try to beat the crap out of shoplifters. One booster escaped with his skin, but left his wallet; Craig divvied up the cash among the witnesses before turning the wallet—including the thief's driver's license—over to the cops.

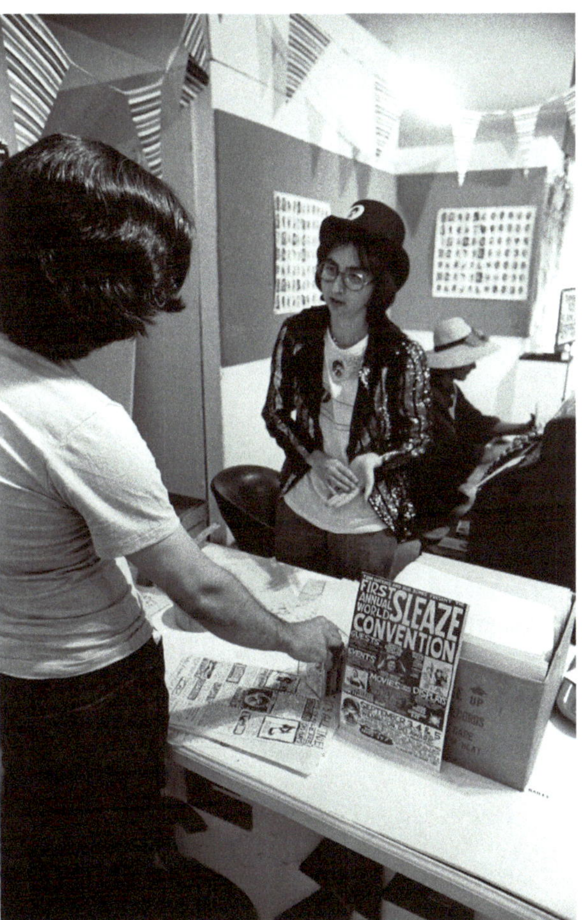


**PAT CROWE, *SLEEZE,*** SEPTEMBER 3, 1976

The only infraction worse than shoplifting was peeing in or on our building, curb, sidewalk, or doorways. The store was around the corner from the city's wino zone and those guys poured it into themselves from paper bags and poured it out at any time or possible angle.

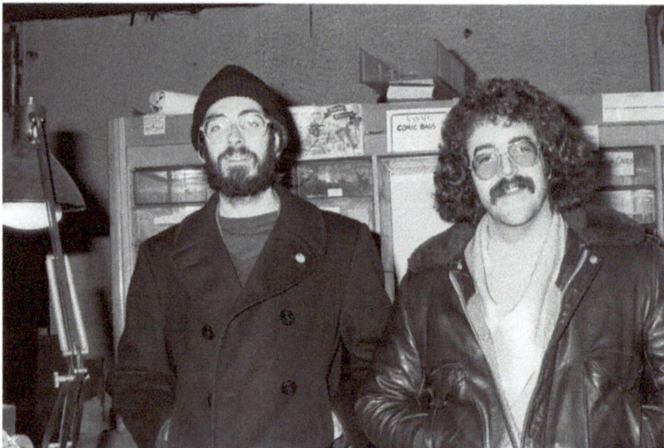

**JULIA GORTON, *TOM WATKINS AND CRAIG DAWSON IN XANADU COMICS AND COLLECTABLES*,** C. LATE 1970S

We tried uniform international warning signs: red circles with slashes through sprinkling silhouettes. No change. If a wino pissed in the hallway at the bottom of our stairs, Tom would send bowling balls down from the third-floor landing, bouncing at fearful trajectories. Craig used whatever was handy—electric pencil sharpeners, lunch boxes, or pepper spray—always selected according to the offender's age, height, weight, degree of intoxication, previous history of incontinence, and verbal explanation offered, if any. In court, one guy told the judge that he meant to urinate in the doorway next to ours. He was convicted because the judge understood that doorway was ours, as well.

Me? It depended on whether or not they seemed dangerous. I'd yell at the older wobbly ones, get them to turn out their pockets, and collect the change to send one of our little urchin volunteers off to buy cleaning supplies. Then, I'd make Foxy Grandpa mop it up, shake hands, and we'd be done.

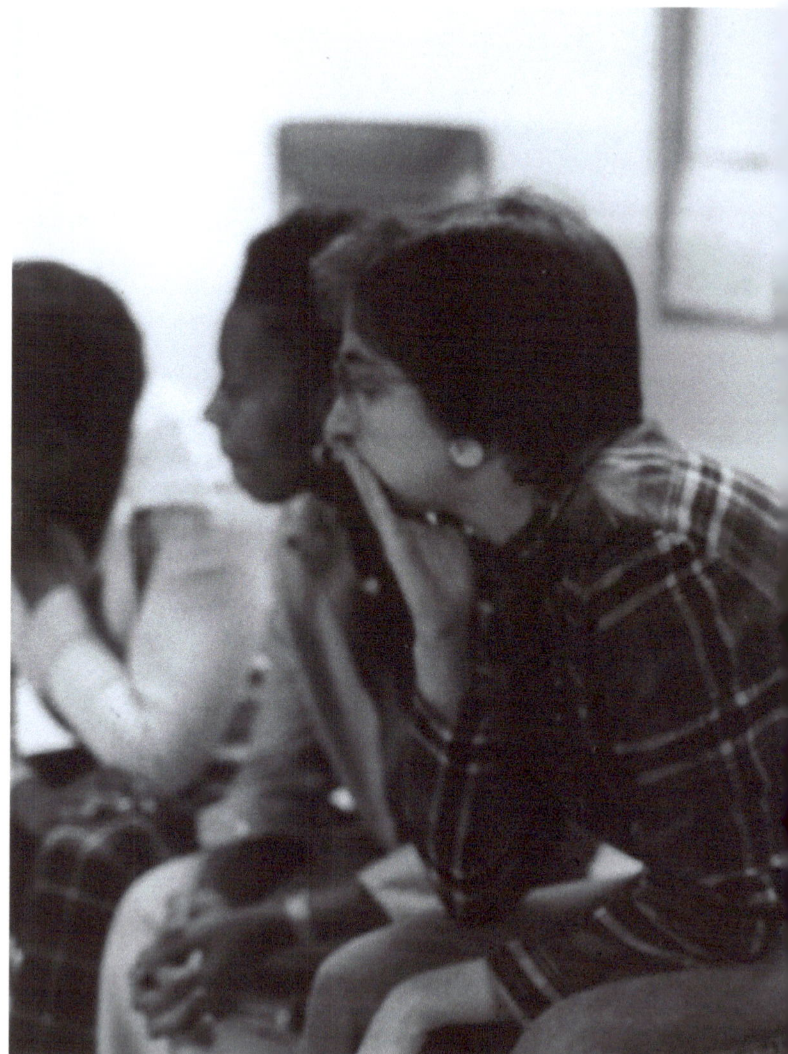

JOSEPHINE MOORE, EVOYNNE, JOYCE BRABNER, AND MARY PAGE EVANS IN WOMEN'S CORRECTIONAL INSTITUTE ARTS WORKSHOP, 1979

Artists are supposed to be happy living in neighborhoods too scary to visit, with winged rat pigeons overhead instead of track lighting, no hot water, plastic sheets instead of working heat, gun shots at night, and Rodolfo singing as Mimi climbs

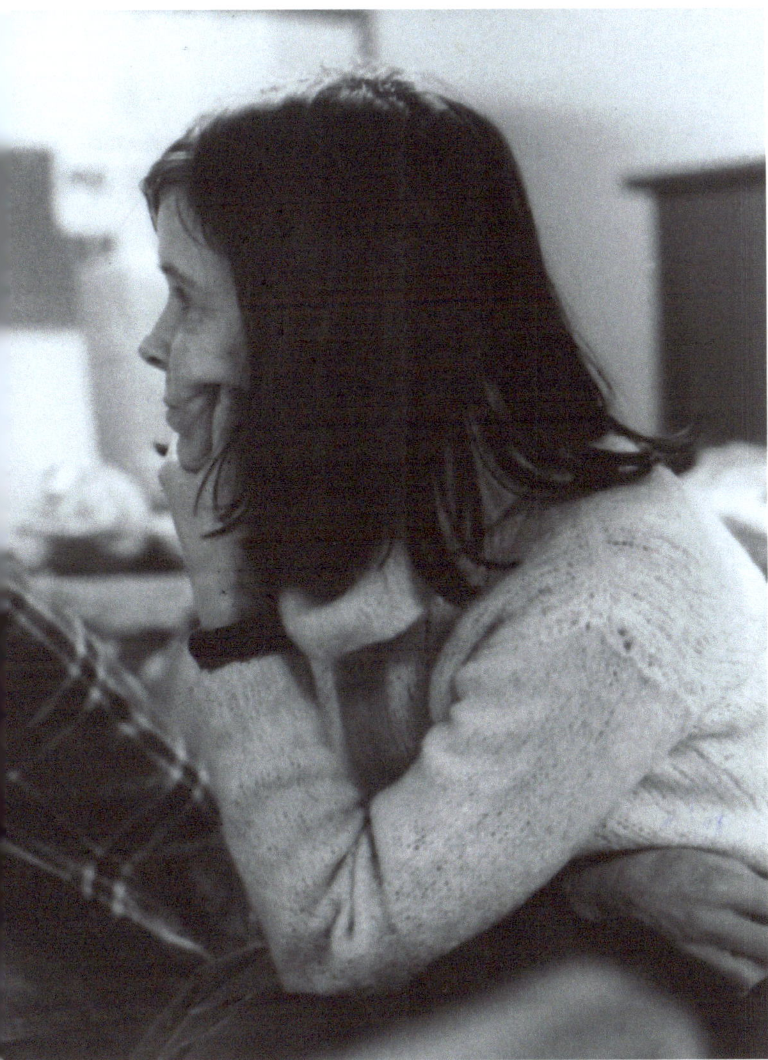

the stairs. No one warmed my *gelida manina*. I was a Shipley Street scarecrow in my place around the corner, across from both a dive bar and the Salvation Army. Tom was the 2 West Fifth scarecrow. We were ragbag dummy placeholders until urban renewal or zoning caught up with our landlords, who found having real live people likely to phone them at home in the wee hours—in case of break-ins or arson—more reliable than any installed alarm system.

1. One such project was a fan-designed, online role-playing game in which Harvey's character walks into the house, lies down on the sofa, and reads—for the entire game.
2. 2 West Fifth Street was also the address for the Women's Correctional Institute Arts Workshop, a prison support program I ran until its goals and purposes were absorbed into the Department of Corrections, who also hired me to do the same kind of work in the men's prison…
3. Rondo Hatton was a journalist who became a horror movie actor after he contracted acromegaly. The glandular disease so disfigured his face and hands that he could play characters like the villainous, stalking Creeper without makeup. Hatton was a lousy actor, and his flat intonation as he menaced a maiden ("Stop… that… screaming…") cracked us up.

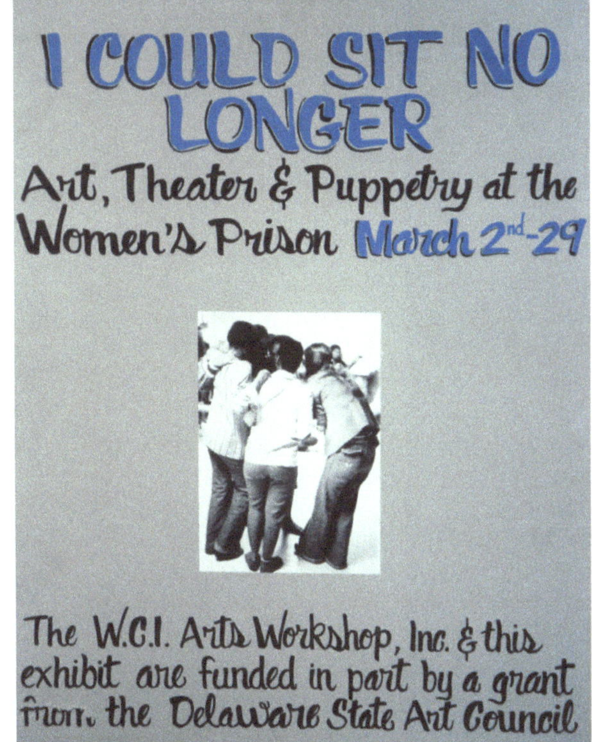


**JOYCE BRABNER, *I COULD SIT NO LONGER* POSTER,** 1979

# SUSAN ISAACS GALLERY

**J. Susan Isaacs**
*Curator and Art Historian*

Linda Brennan-Jones first suggested the idea of establishing a gallery to me in the summer of 1986. By that fall, we were partners in the L. B. Jones Gallery at 709 Tatnall Street in Wilmington. The building was a three-story brick townhouse, probably built in the late 19th or early 20th century, that had been renovated into a business space. It had flat fluorescent lighting and no kitchen. When we moved in, the third floor housed a fashion designer, but we fairly quickly took over the entire building.

Our early shows were eclectic, with many different media and styles. There were photographs by Connie Imboden and Carson Zullinger, paintings by John Giannotti, sculpture by John Schackerman, and prints by Randy Bolton and Shelley Thorstensen. It soon became clear that we needed to support the gallery with more than art sales, and thus I learned picture framing. I took this on with great zeal, even traveling to California to study with Paul Frederick, founder of the Picture Framing Academy and author of *The Framer's Answer Book*.

In the fall of 1988, I became the gallery's sole owner and changed its name to the Susan Isaacs Gallery. We also began to publish a newsletter, which moved through various titles, from *Newsletter* to *Perception* to *Minimal Perception*. My staff included artists Susan Benarcik and Amy Sterner Gould. A number of the artists who showed with the gallery helped out as well, the most regular of whom was Susan Rohrbach. We also installed offsite exhibitions at places like the Ristorante Carucci on Greenhill Avenue, the Hercules Building on Market Street, and, for about a year, photography shows in a gallery run by the University of Delaware on the Market Street Mall. At one point we even installed a large contemporary quilt show at both the gallery and the Hotel DuPont. We were highly involved with the initial years of Art on the Town, an idea brought to me by John Gatti, who was then with the Delaware State Arts Council. The Art Loop, as it became known, established collective art gallery receptions throughout the city as a way to encourage support of the Wilmington art scene.

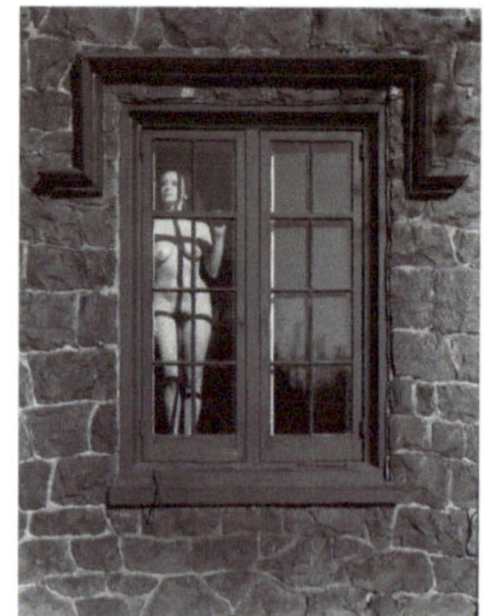

**CARSON ZULLINGER, *UNTITLED*,** 1987

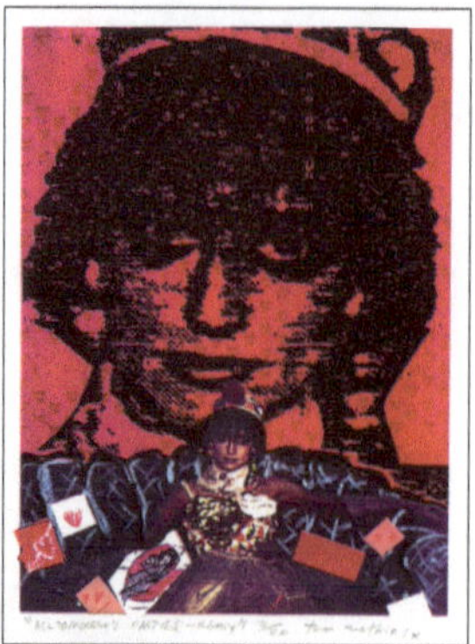

**TOM WATKINS, *ALL TOMORROW'S PARTIES–REMIX*,** 1989

During this time we showed regional and national artists working in all media, at different stages in their professional careers, but mostly in very contemporary styles. Among them were Teresa Barkley, Anna Massey Biggs, Charles Burwell, Paula Camenzind, Marjorie Egee, Olga Ganoudis, Sutton Hays, Catherine Fichtner Kirk, Keith Lewis, Steve Lewis, Henry Loustau, Sally Cooper March, Eo Omwake, Gerald Pogach, Judith Schwab, Tom Watkins, Ann Hopkins Wilson, and Phillia C. Yi.

In 1991, we moved to a true gallery space with an industrial gray tile floor and gallery lighting in the Bank of Delaware Center at 222 Delaware Avenue. But then, in the winter of 1992, the recession impacted Wilmington. We closed the gallery at the end of February of that year, but were gratified that the reception for our final exhibition, which included the work of Yolanda Chetwynd, Kyle (née Donna) Conway Ripp, and Norman Sasowsky, drew an overflow crowd.

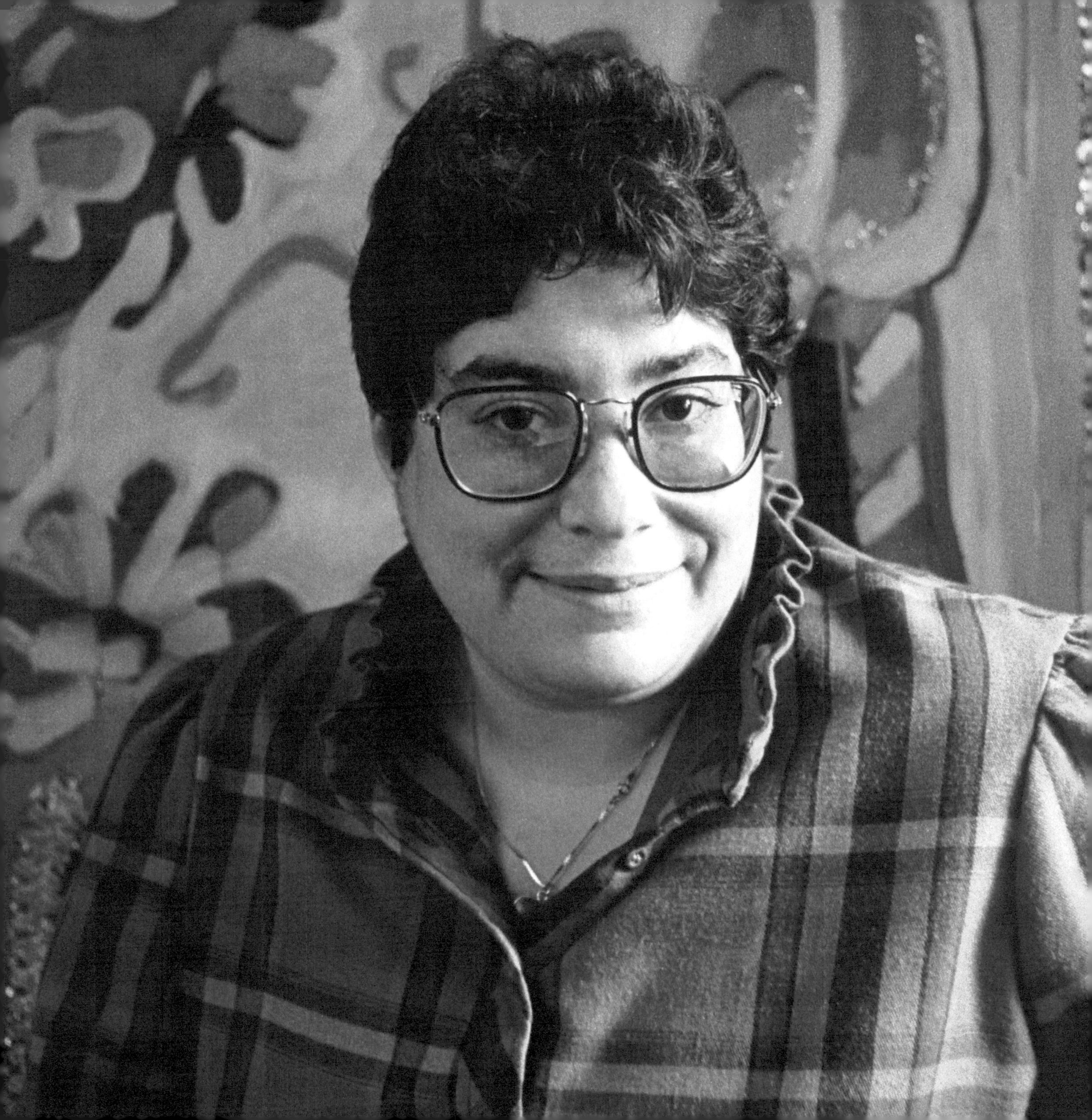

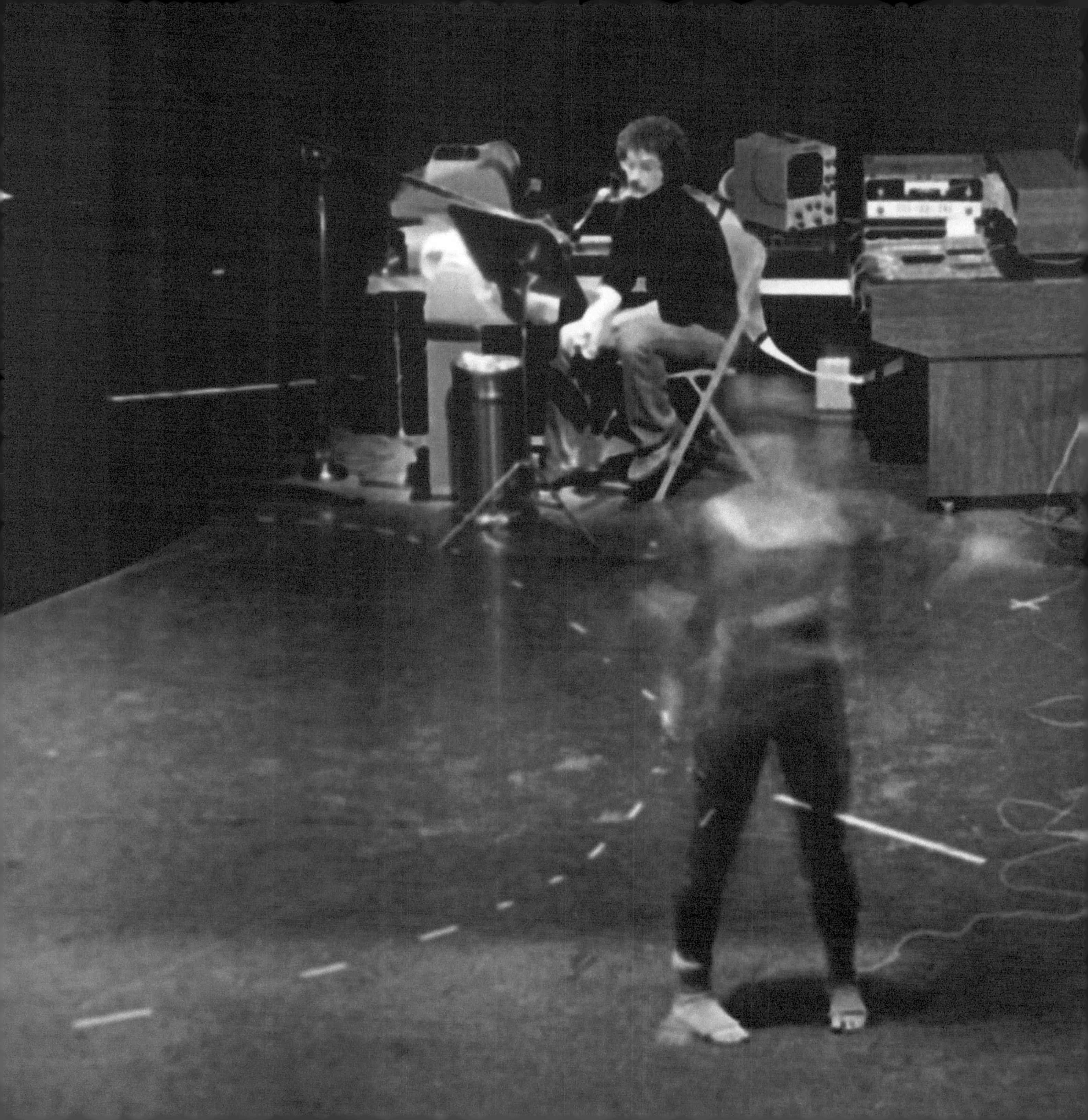

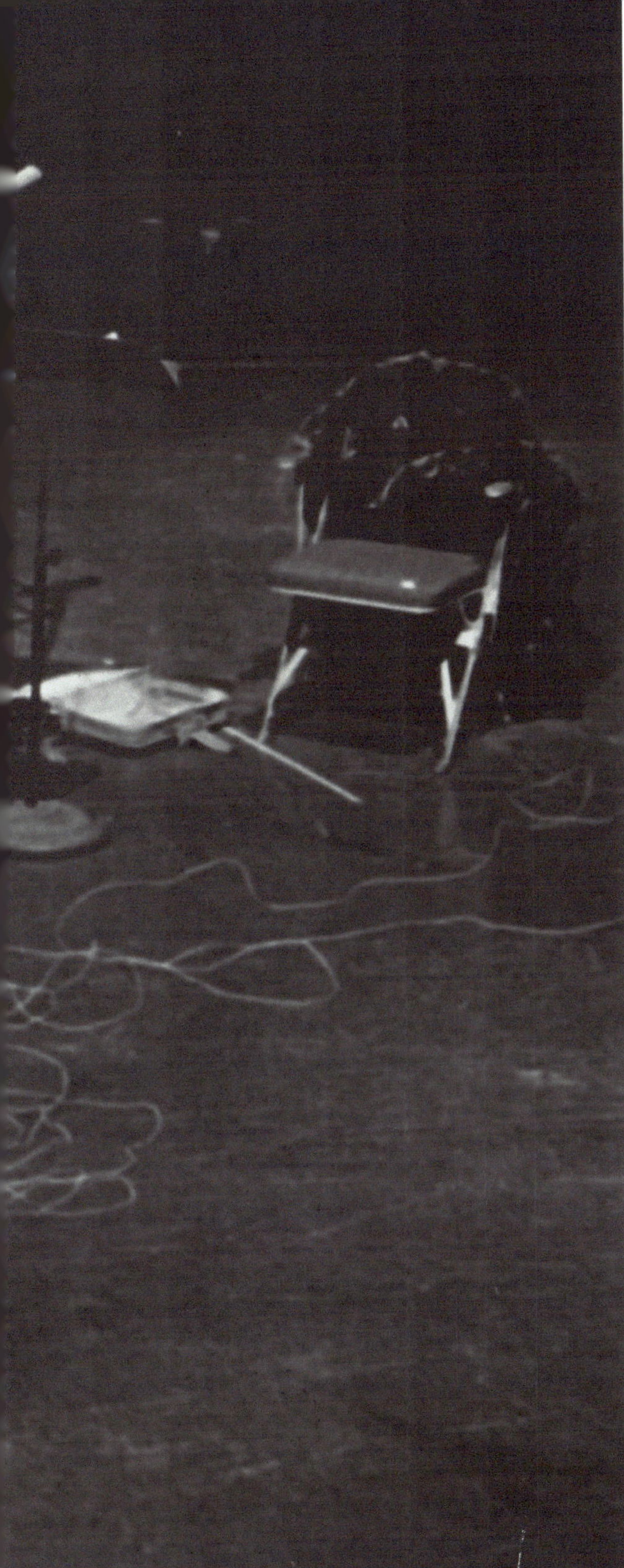

# DANCE AND NEW SPACE COMPANY

**Debra Loewen**
*Choreographer and Dancer*

In September 1974, I started teaching modern dance at the University of Delaware and working with a student performance ensemble called the New Space Company. Like other dancers and choreographers at the time, we were looking for alternatives that would depart from codified modern dance techniques, narrative form, emotional display, correlation with music, and the concert proscenium stage. We began to incorporate location in the creative process, along with task-based movements that could be performed by anyone.

Our inaugural presentation, *Outside/In*, featured two different performances, a week apart. Each dancer selected two locations—one outside, one inside—in which to develop choreography. On performance nights, the audience was transported by school bus from one site to another; they were asked to bring their own flashlights, which were used to light the dances. Performance sites included a soccer field, an enclosed room with stained-glass windows, an outdoor sound sculpture, and a grove of willows.

*Dance: At the Gym* (October 1975) consisted of ten dances performed continuously and simultaneously in ten different spaces within the two-story Hartshorn Women's Gym at the south end of campus. One dancer performed in candlelight reflected by the mirrored walls of the studio; another thrashed up and down the stairs, creating a cacophony by tossing hundreds of marbles against the walls. Showers blasted heat and steam as dancers scurried between the stalls. A woman sat still on a chair in the middle of a basement room, lit only by a streetlamp outside a window. Elsewhere a dancer moved within a mess of smelly leaves in the weight room, while a masked woman grappled with the equipment cage. The audience roamed from room to room, using a floor

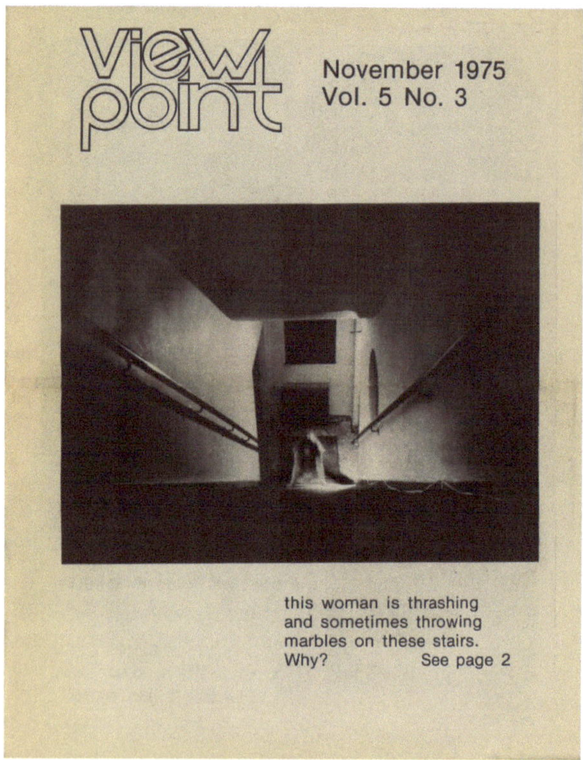


COVERAGE OF ***DANCE: AT THE GYM, VIEWPOINT,*** VOL. 5, NO.3, NOVEMBER 1975

plan of the building as a program guide. It was after this performance that we changed the group's name to the New Space Company.

*Altered Space* (May 1976) was held in Mitchell Hall and featured work by student filmmaker Jan Roberts, composer Joseph Pinzarrone, designer Dana Smith, and New York–based guest choreographer Batya Zamir. The audience entered through the doors at the back of the stage and, when the curtain opened, watched dancers appear and disappear in the auditorium seats. Then, in the far distance, doors opened to reveal a dance in process across the campus mall. Smith made "The Funicular Pantograph," an elaborate painting machine that dancers manipulated via a web of pulleys. Hung in front a wall of stretched muslin, the machine released paint via an attached mechanical relay apparatus, creating a painting in real time as the audience looked on.

*Moon* (October 1977) was an outdoor performance at Carpenter State Park Pond that coincided with the full moon. A collaboration with sculptor Rick Rothrock, the event featured a tower structure of lashed telephone poles

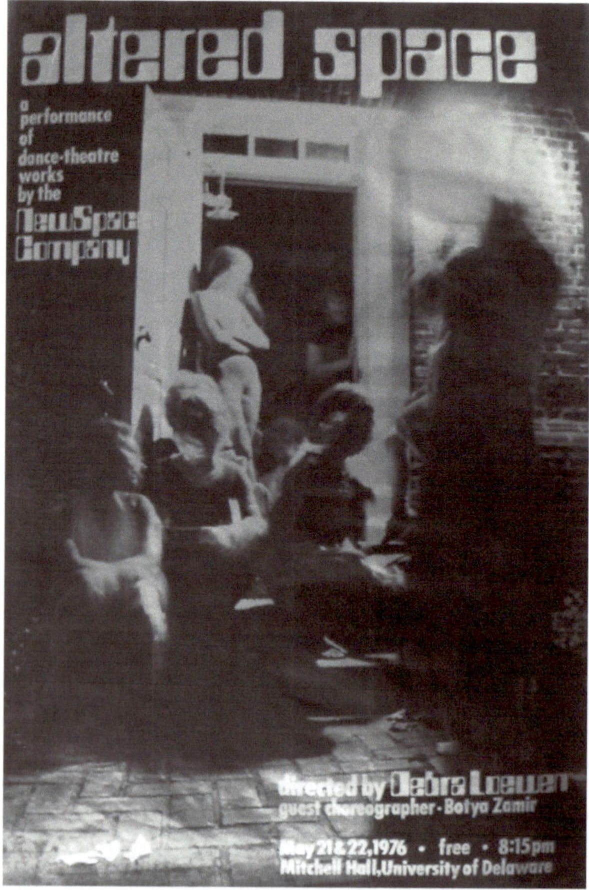


***ALTERED SPACE* POSTER,** 1976

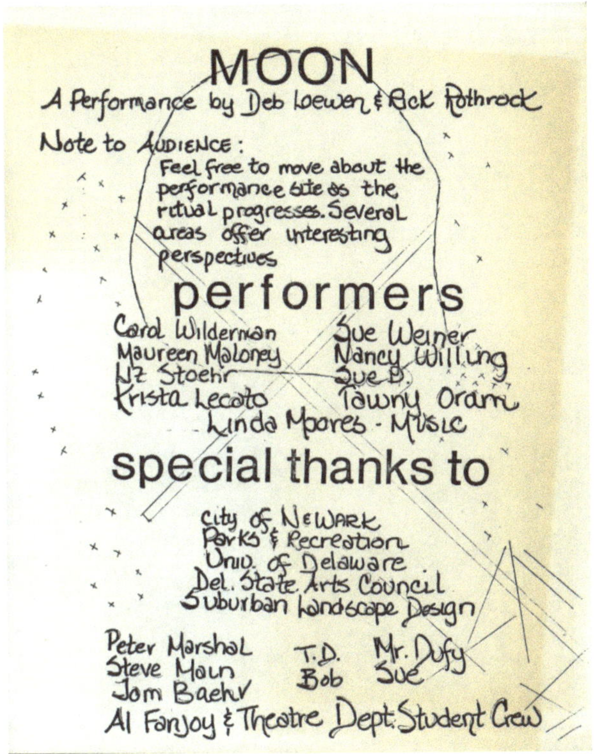


***MOON* POSTER,** 1977

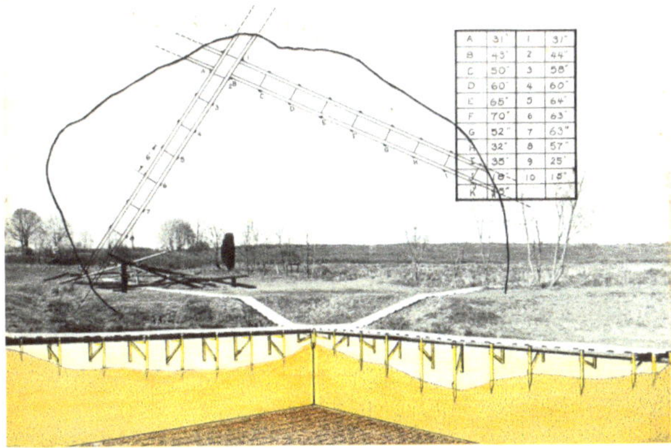

**RICK ROTHROCK, *UNTITLED*,** 1977

near the pond's edge. Crossing the pond were white painted skids on which the dancers moved and created sounds. The white X over the water glowed as the moon rose overhead. Performers were tucked into the woods, repeating sounds of the night, and the audience was encouraged to relocate. Dancers lit safety flares along the towering sculpture and climbed to perches high over the pond. Today such a performance would be labeled "site specific," but then it was simply considered a new way of dancing in new space.

# WAY BACK WHEN: THE BEGINNINGS OF THE DELAWARE THEATRE COMPANY

**Cleveland Morris**
*Artist, Co-Founder and former Artistic Director of the Delaware Theatre Company*

When the Off-Broadway hit *Godspell* was made into a movie in 1973, the creators added a new song, "Beautiful City." Its hippy-dippy lyrics ("We can build a beautiful city, yes we can, oh, yes we can") might seem naive now, but many of us believed in them at the time and envisioned using the arts to recreate cities like Wilmington, which had been torn apart by the riots and strife of the late 1960s.

By the time the Delaware Theatre Company was founded in 1978, Wilmington had bottomed out and was starting to climb out of the hole. The city had a hopeful mayor with an enlightened administration; organizations like the Greater Wilmington Development Council, funded by business leaders who had refused to abandon downtown; popular gathering spots like Artisans III on Market Street Mall; and a community of artists and arts advocates who dreamed of what might be.

The city's art scene also benefited from the financial support of the National Endowment for the Arts (NEA), which had been established by President Lyndon Johnson in 1965. Prior to the NEA's founding, national funding for the arts—when it existed at all—had been paltry, piecemeal, and precarious. But because the NEA mandate provided for direct distribution of funds to the states (in Delaware, via the indispensable Delaware State Arts Council), professional arts activities were no longer the exclusive domain of a handful of large metropolitan centers. By the late 1970s, regional theaters were popping up across the country. A couple of friends and I couldn't help but notice the conspicuous absence of such a theater in Delaware, and we set about changing that.

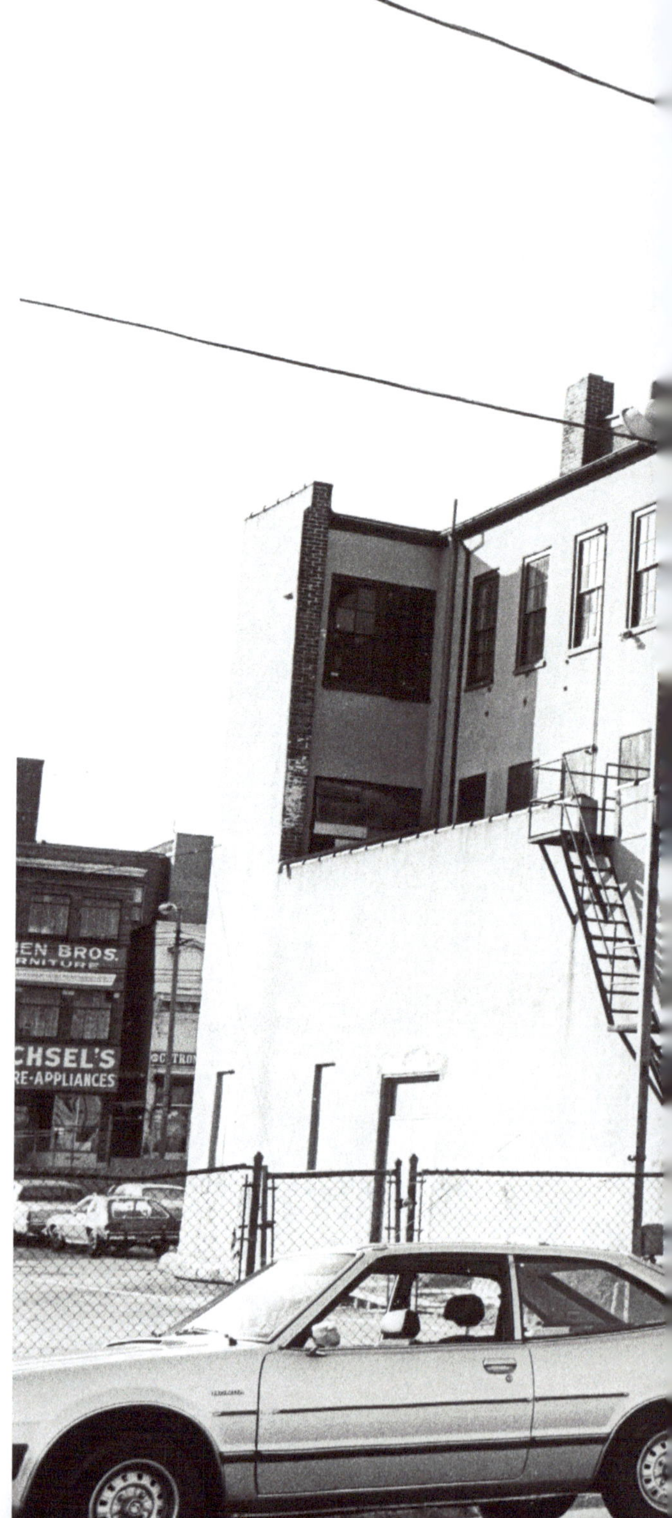

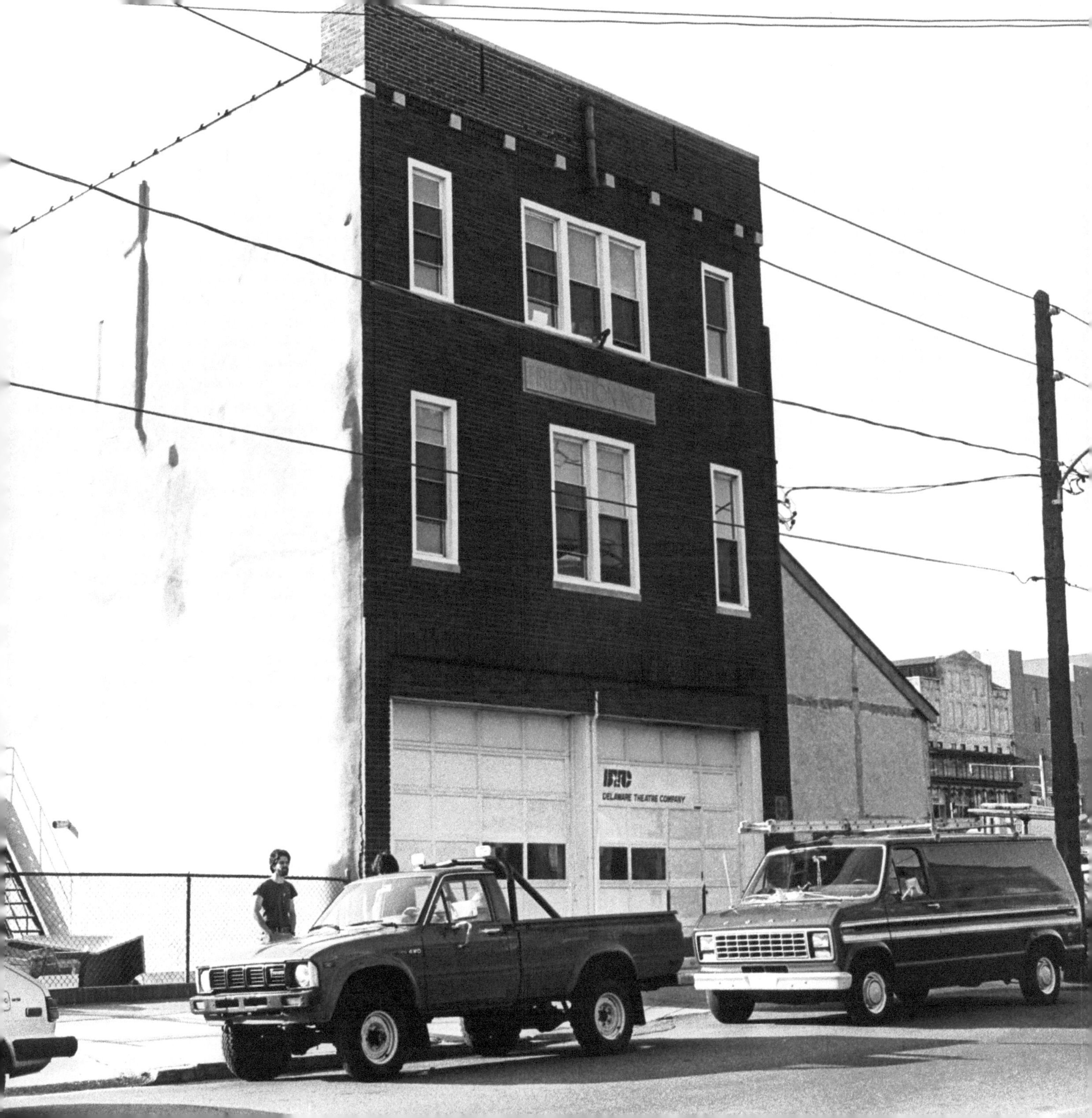
DELAWARE THEATRE COMPANY

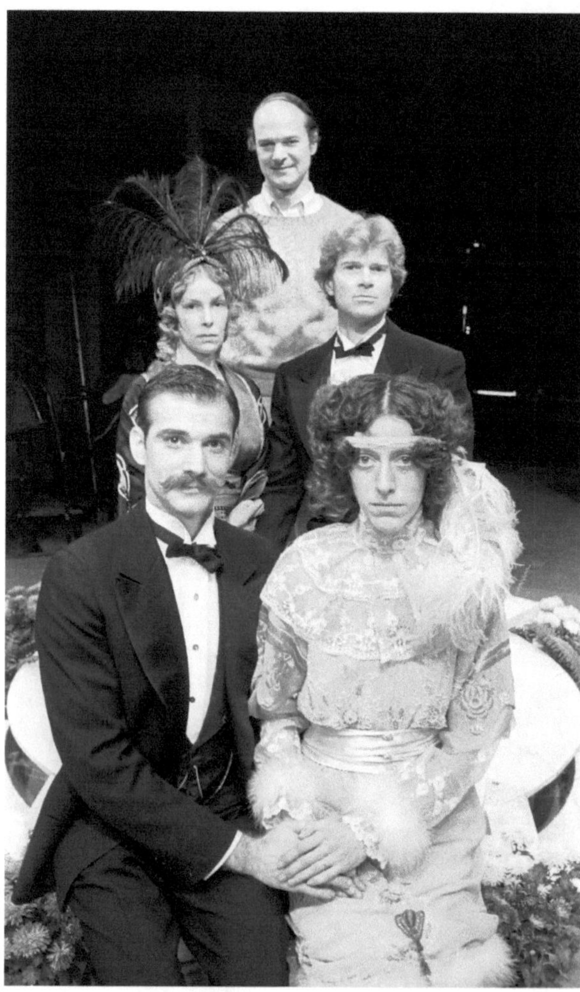

**FRED COMEGYS, *FIREHOUSE THEATER,*** DECEMBER 6–8, 1979

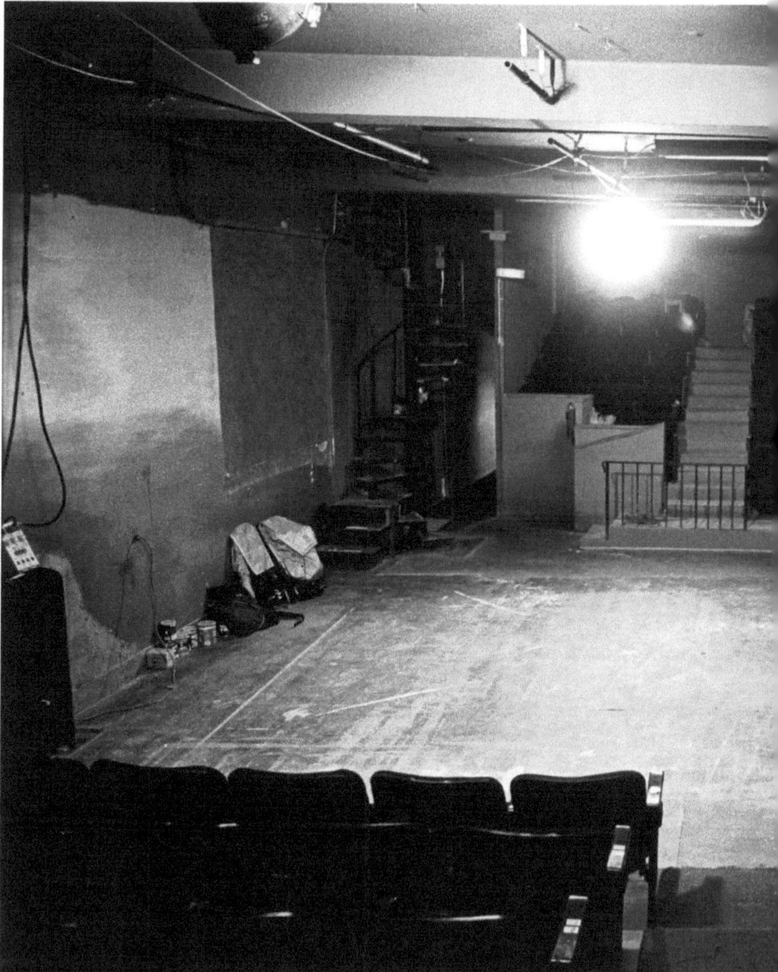

**LEO S. MATKINS, *DEL THEATRE CO,*** APRIL 19, 1982

Part of the identity of these new theaters (like their Off-Off-Broadway counterparts) was taking vacant properties and turning them into performance spaces. We weren't looking for "theatres" with curtains and proscenium arches; rather we wanted what Peter Brook, in his 1968 landmark manifesto, termed an "empty space." As soon as we set eyes on an abandoned firehouse at Third and French Streets, we knew we had found a home. It had everything: room for a scene shop, dressing rooms, a rehearsal space, offices, and an unconventional traverse stage (with the audience on two sides of the action and the players in the middle.) It was owned by the city, the rent would be $1 a year, and it had parking! After minor renovations funded by the city, individual donors, and sweat

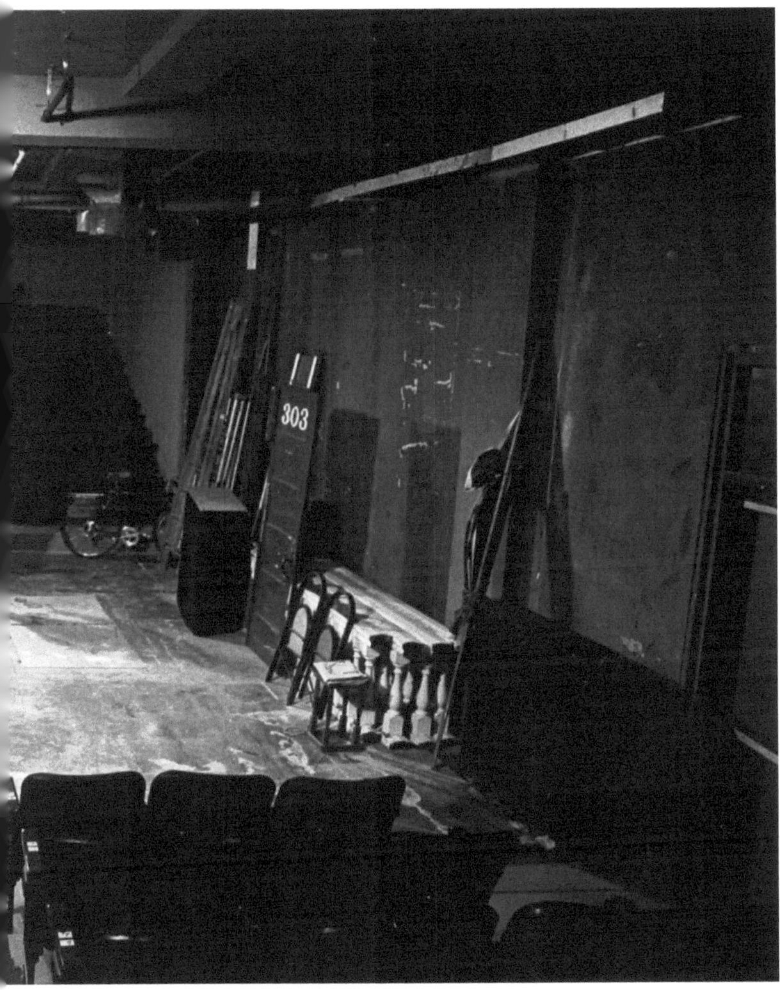


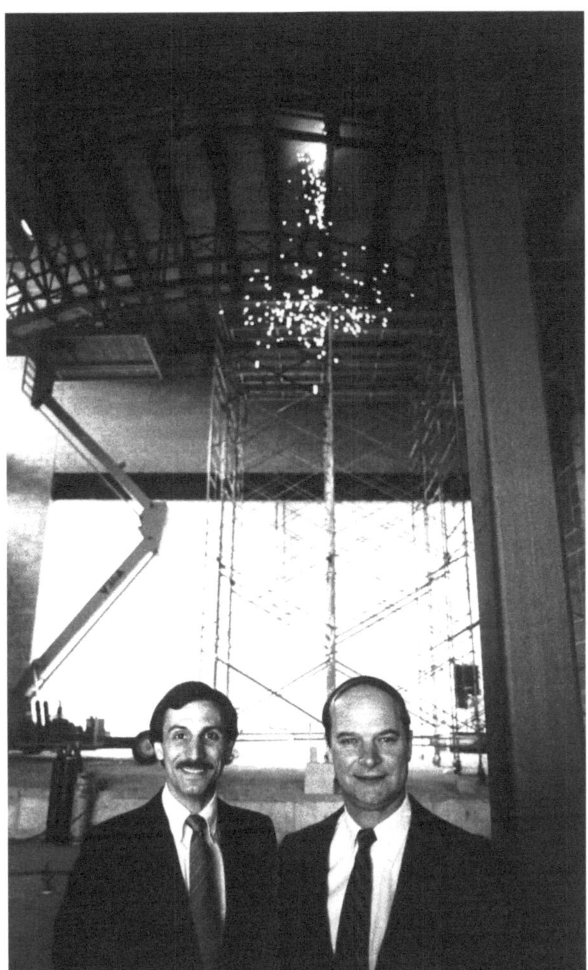

**FRED COMEGYS, *CLEVELAND MORRIS*,** APRIL 20, 1985

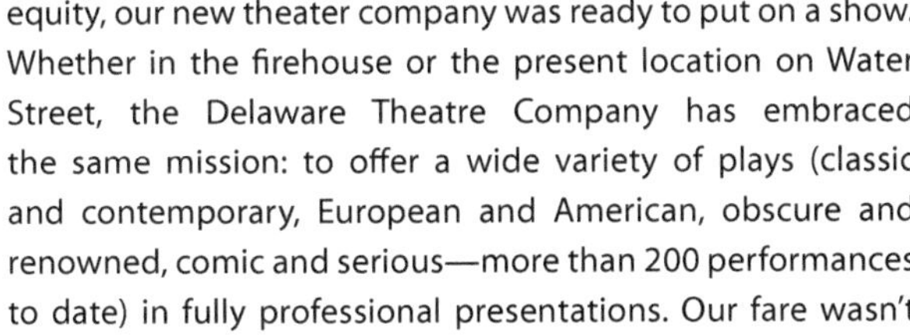

equity, our new theater company was ready to put on a show. Whether in the firehouse or the present location on Water Street, the Delaware Theatre Company has embraced the same mission: to offer a wide variety of plays (classic and contemporary, European and American, obscure and renowned, comic and serious—more than 200 performances to date) in fully professional presentations. Our fare wasn't intended to be a grab bag of "something for everyone," but rather an attempt to show that this ancient, powerful art form was capable of touching every human emotion. We felt that theater was about people coming together—in the same place, at the same time—as a communal whole. In other words, it was just like a city, just like Wilmington.

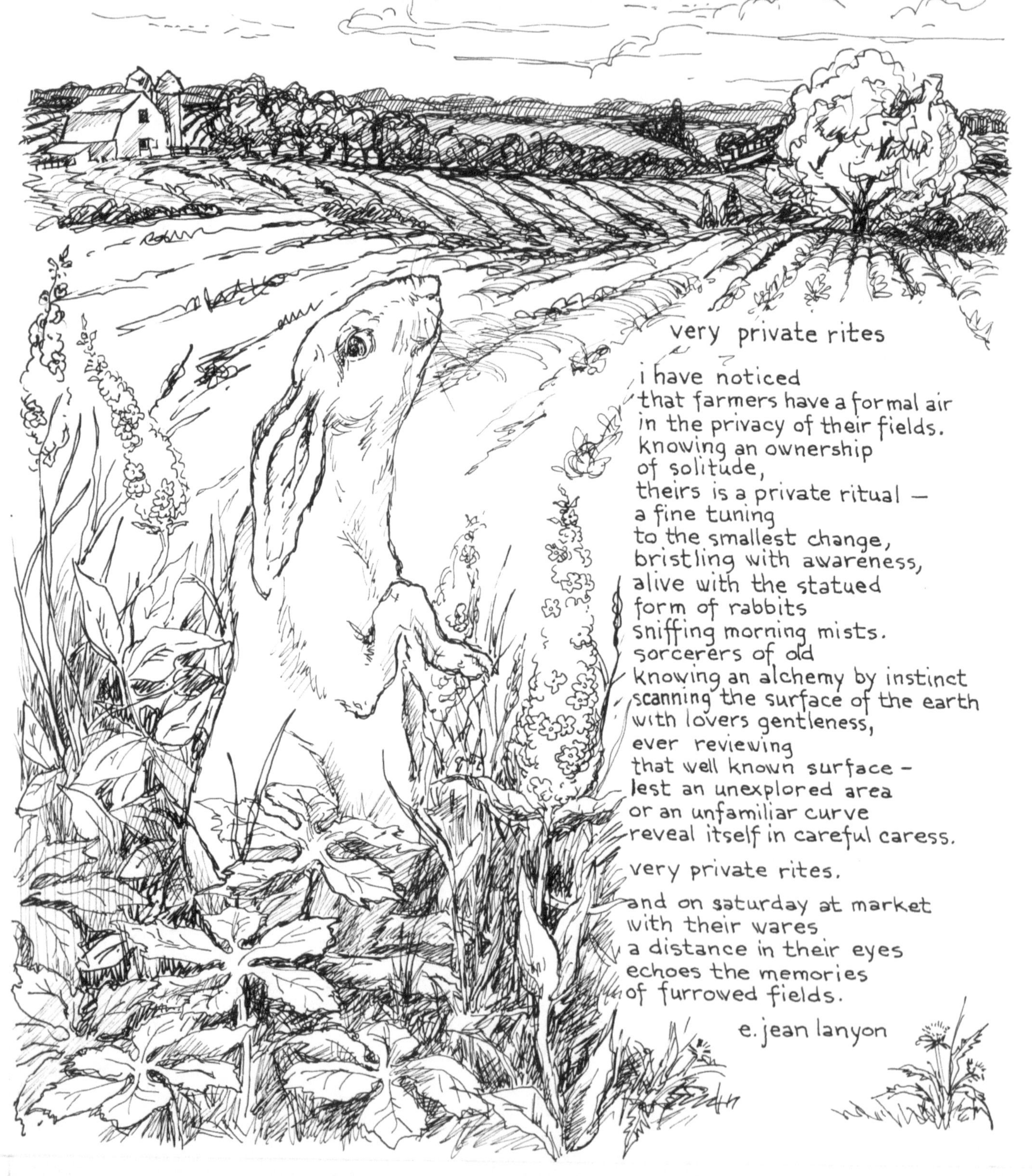

## very private rites

i have noticed
that farmers have a formal air
in the privacy of their fields.
knowing an ownership
of solitude,
theirs is a private ritual —
a fine tuning
to the smallest change,
bristling with awareness,
alive with the statued
form of rabbits
sniffing morning mists.
sorcerers of old
knowing an alchemy by instinct
scanning the surface of the earth
with lovers gentleness,
ever reviewing
that well known surface -
lest an unexplored area
or an unfamiliar curve
reveal itself in careful caress.

very private rites.

and on saturday at market
with their wares
a distance in their eyes
echoes the memories
of furrowed fields.

e. jean lanyon

**Steven Leech**
*Poet and Publisher*

Wilmington's literary community of the 1970s and 1980s had its roots in largely forgotten history. Delaware-based writers knew and shared influences with 19th-century giants such as Edgar Allan Poe and Mark Twain, both of whom spent time in nearby Philadelphia, and with 20th-century greats like Paul Laurence Dunbar, Hart Crane, F. Scott Fitzgerald, H. L. Mencken, and Edmund Wilson. For nearly two centuries, the work of local authors was published by such renowned firms as Harper, Boni & Liveright, Harcourt Brace, Scribner's, and Little, Brown.

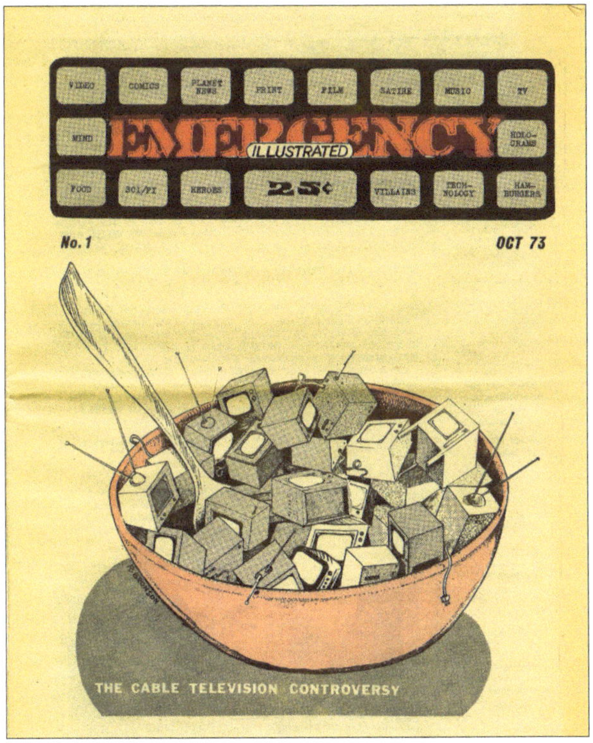

***EMERGENCY ILLUSTRATED,*** NO. 1, OCTOBER 1973

In the 1930s, success followed novelists Anne Parrish, Peyton and brother Charles Wertenbaker, who left Delaware, but eluded others, like John Biggs Jr., and Christopher Ward, who stayed. Local writers struggled to survive during the Great Depression, but found continuance in the latter part of the decade through the Federal Writers' Project, established by the Works Progress Administration (WPA) and the Wilmington Music and Poetry Circle.

While the WPA folded at the onset of World War II, the Wilmington Music and Poetry Circle carried the literary ball through the 1960s, publishing poetry anthologies at fairly regular intervals and lobbying successfully for the naming of Delaware's first poet laureate in 1947 (several subsequent poets laureate were also affiliated with the group). Internal squabbles contributed to the group changing its name to the Wilmington Poetry Society and Delaware Writers, and later to its separation into two factions: the Delaware Poetry Center, led by David Hudson, who had been Delaware poet laureate on two separate occasions, and First State Writers, founded by Jeannette Slocomb Edwards, another former Delaware poet laureate.

By the 1960s, the literary landscape in Delaware—particularly in Wilmington and surrounding towns—was changing, in large part because of a growing counterculture made from the maturing offspring of a well-educated post-war generation, coupled with the introduction of modern printing techniques. A new generation of local literati initially manifested itself under the aegis of the *Heterodoxical Voice*, a tabloid published between 1968 and 1970. While it focused on the antiwar and civil rights movements, the *Heterodoxical Voice* also published stories about cultural matters, as well as occasional poetry and short fiction.

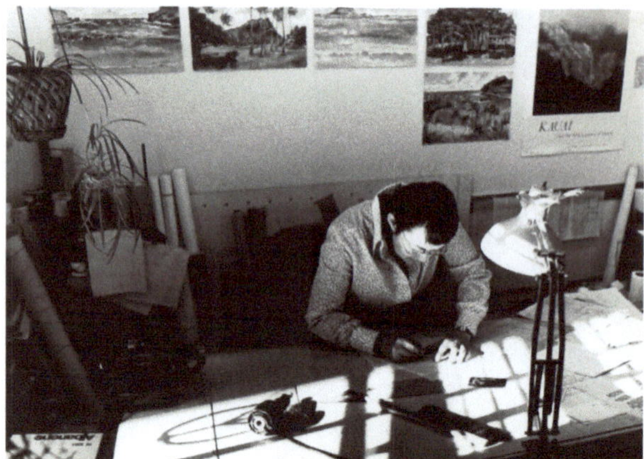

**MARY LOEWENSTEIN, *E. JEAN LANYON*,** C. 1977

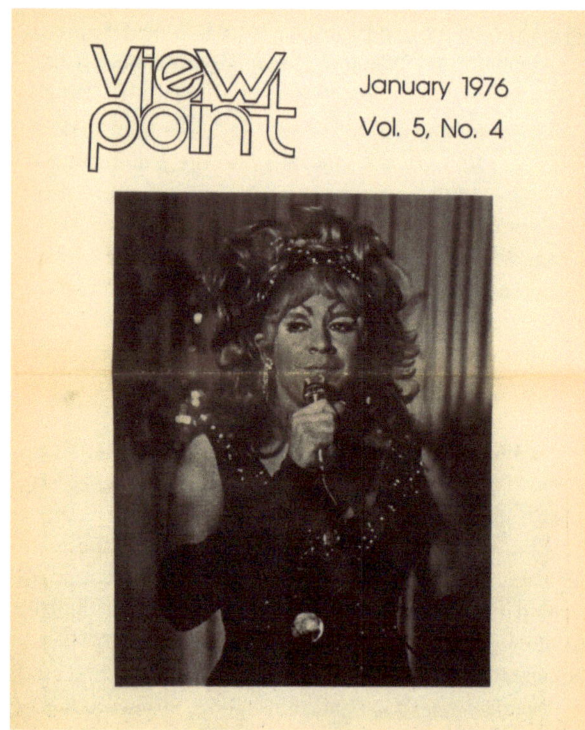


UNIVERSITY OF DELAWARE'S COSMOPOLITAN CLUB ***VIEWPOINT*** NEWSLETTER, VOL. 5, NO. 4, JANUARY 1976

After the *Heterodoxical Voice* folded, a number of publications emerged in the early 1970s to fill the breach. *New Directions for Women* reflected the country's emerging feminism. The *Delaware Spectator* and its successor, the *Delaware Star*, continued in the tradition of Wilmington's *Peoples' Pulse* by addressing civil rights and promoting the city's rich African American cultural history. The *Delaware Star* later became the weekly *Delaware Valley Star*, and, for a time, the Newark-based alternative tabloid *Tangent* was published both as a monthly insert in the *Star* and as an independent periodical. This coming together of communities within the print medium was an essential precursor to the integration of Wilmington's cultural movements in the 1980s.

Two other tabloids that emerged in the early 1970s contributed more directly to the cultural environment. *Emergency Illustrated* published its first issue in October 1973. *Viewpoint,* founded at about the same time, was published under the auspices of the University of Delaware's Cosmopolitan Club and largely limited in circulation to the campus and the surrounding Newark community. While *Viewpoint* offered articles on a wide range of issues, such as civil rights, feminism, and changes in a post-colonial Third World, it also included poetry, occasional fiction, cartoons, and graphic art in much the same manner as *Emergency Illustrated*. The two publications would foster associations among those who would be at the forefront of a new literary generation. It was through my role at *Viewpoint* that I met artist and poet e. jean lanyon. As it turned out, we would become leading figures in the new literary movement that grew out of the 1960s countercultural eruption.[1]

Both *Viewpoint* and *Emergency Illustrated* received crucial advertising revenue from Rob Jones, who in the early 1970s opened the Fifth Street Gallery on the second floor of the nearly derelict Queen Theater. The building's spacious rooms and large windows were ideal for displaying new work by up-and-coming local artists. Jones told me his intention in establishing the gallery was to challenge the monopoly of the Brandywine tradition on the local cultural landscape.

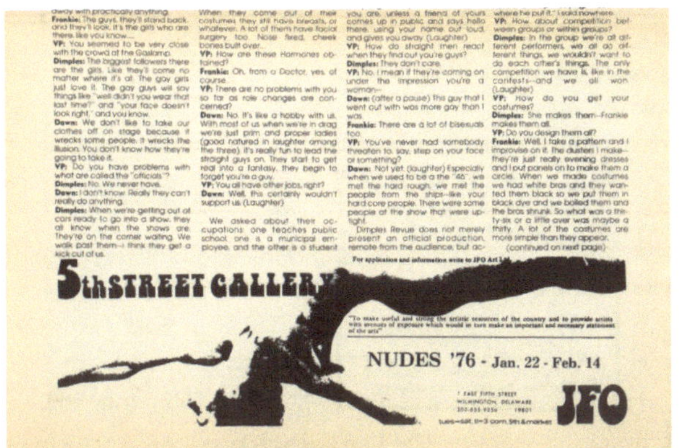

away with practically anything.

**Frankie:** The guys, they'll stand back and they'll look. It's the girls who are there, like you know....

**VP:** You seemed to be very close with the crowd at the Gaslamp.

**Dimples:** The biggest followers there are the girls. Like they'll come no matter where it's at. The gay girls just love it. The gay guys will say things like "well didn't you wear that last time?" and "your face doesn't look right," and you know.

**Dawn:** We don't like to take our clothes off on stage because it wrecks some people. It wrecks the illusion. You don't know how they're going to take it.

**VP:** Do you have problems with what are called the "officials"?

**Dimples:** No. We never have.

**Dawn:** I don't know. Really they can't really do anything.

**Dimples:** When we're getting out of cars ready to go into a show, they all know when the shows are. They're on the corner waiting. We walk past them—I think they get a kick out of us.

When they come out of their costumes they still have breasts, or whatever. A lot of them have facial surgery too. Nose fixed, cheek bones built over...

**VP:** How are these Hormones obtained?

**Frankie:** Oh, from a Doctor, yes, of course.

**VP:** There are no problems with you so far as role changes are concerned?

**Dawn:** No. It's like a hobby with us. With most of us when we're in drag we're just prim and proper ladies (good natured in laughter among the three). It's really fun to lead the straight guys on. They start to get real into a fantasy, they begin to forget you're a guy.

**VP:** You all have other jobs, right?

**Dawn:** Well, this certainly wouldn't support us. (Laughter)

We asked about their occupations: one teaches public school, one is a municipal employee, and the other is a student

you are, unless a friend of yours comes up in public and says hello there, using your name out loud, and gives you away. (Laughter)

**VP:** How do straight men react when they find out you're guys?

**Dimples:** They don't care.

**VP:** No, I mean if they're coming on under the impression you're a woman—

**Dawn:** (after a pause) This guy that I went out with was more gay than I was.

**Frankie:** There are a lot of bisexuals too.

**VP:** You've never had somebody threaten to, say, step on your face or something?

**Dawn:** Not yet. (laughter) Especially when we used to be a the "46", we met the hard tough, we met the people from the ships—like your hard core people. There were some people at the show that were uptight.

Dimples Revue does not merely present an official production, remote from the audience, but ac-

where he put it." I said nowhere.

**VP:** How about competition between groups or within groups?

**Dimples:** In the group we're all different performers, we all do different things, we wouldn't want to do each other's things. The only competition we have is, like in the contests—and we all won. (Laughter)

**VP:** How do you get your costumes?

**Dimples:** She makes them—Frankie makes them all.

**VP:** Do you design them all?

**Frankie:** Well, I take a pattern and I improvise on it. The dusters I make—they're just really evening dresses and I put panels on to make them a circle. When we made costumes we had white bras and they wanted them black so we put them in black dye and we boiled them and the bras shrunk. So what was a thirty-six or a little over was maybe a thirty. A lot of the costumes are more simple than they appear.

(continued on next page)



FIFTH STREET GALLERY ADVERTISEMENT, ***VIEWPOINT***, VOL. 5, NO. 4, JANUARY 1976

In addition to providing financial support, Jones occasionally offered story ideas. One such proposal was about what he called "the new underground" of emerging drag revues popping up around the region. Jones had contacted *Emergency Illustrated* first, but the publishers evidently got cold feet. He then offered it to *Viewpoint* and we took it on. We visited a couple of local drag shows, took photos, and followed up with interviews. In January 1976, *Viewpoint* published a multipage exposé that included a photo of a local drag queen on the cover. This happened on the very day that news broke that the University of Delaware had fired theater instructor Richard Aumiller for allegedly "promoting" a gay lifestyle in an article published by *The News Journal*.

In 1976, David Hudson published the anthology *A Bicentennial Salute: Delaware Poets, 1940–1976* under the auspices of the Delaware Poetry Center. The book included work by a number of Delaware poets, including many of the state's poet laureates. A sample of my own early writing could have been included had I signed my rights over to Hudson, but I decided against it. *Delaware Poets, 1940–1976* was as much a watershed tribute to a previous generation of Delaware poets as it was a marker between literary generations.

During the early and mid-1970s, local poets and authors began meeting to read and discuss their work at salon-type gatherings in private homes, chiefly those of Betty McCaughay (later Betty Tew) and Bob Davis. One regular participant was John Hickey, whom I met on the route 6 bus one rainy afternoon in 1977 when I was working in Wilmington as editor for the *Delaware Star*. The bus was crowded, but I found a seat next to Hickey. Across his lap was a large box, in which were the galleys and other graphic elements for a new publication he had titled *Dream Streets*. Hickey had chosen that name because, as a cab driver working the late shift in Philadelphia, he was often a bit sleep deprived, a state that gave the city's largely empty streets a dreamy quality.

Hickey knew I was the editor at the *Star* and asked me to recommend a place where he could get a good deal on printing for that first issue of *Dream Streets*. I gave him the contact information for our reasonably priced printer in New Jersey. A few months after our meeting on the bus, I learned that Hickey, who could be very particular, had had a disagreement with the printer regarding the final appearance of the issue. As a result, the printer threw out the entire press run, and ostensibly, Hickey along with them. But on the way out of the print shop, Hickey scooped up an armload of *Dream Streets* from the refuse bin. That armload constituted the first issue of *Dream Streets*.

In 1979, under editor Betty Tew, *Dream Streets* published its second issue in an 8 by 10 magazine format. *Dream Streets 3* was published in 1980, again in a magazine format, and this time with a cover design by e. jean lanyon. At 36 pages, it was the largest issue to date, large enough in fact to accommodate two editors: I took responsibility for the prose content, while lanyon arranged pages for poetry. *Dreamstreets* volumes four and five were multi-numbered—totaling six issues between 1982 and 1984—and returned to a tabloid format. The publication's title was changed to a single word, and because the group that had been behind the initiative, the Eschaton Writers, had begun to fade, an effort was made to bring in local poets and authors who had worked at other publications. Another intent of these volumes was to move beyond simply publishing literary works. The tabloid format enabled us to do a larger press run—and thus reach a wider audience—so *Dreamstreets* also became a vehicle for publicizing the many public readings that had begun to crop up in local libraries, bookstores, cafés, and taverns as well as publishing articles about the local literary community.

One of these public readings, first held in October 1983 at O'Friel's Irish Pub under the auspices of the pub's owner, Kevin Freel, turned into a recurring event: the Second Saturday Poetry Reading. After O'Friel's closed its doors, the event bounced around venues. For a time it found a home at Smokie's Restaurant near Fourth and Market Streets, then later settled at Polly Koster's 4w5 Café at Fifth and Shipley Streets.

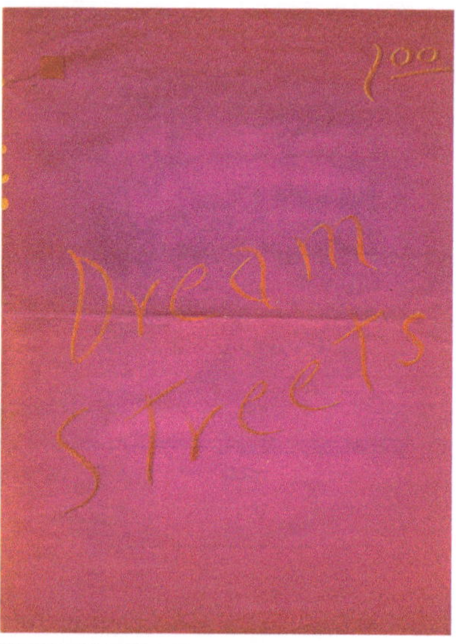


**JOHN HICKEY, *DREAM STREETS* COVER, NO. 1,** 1977

In 1984 *Dreamstreets* began using radio to promote the local literary scene. *Dreamstreets 6* was actually an audio edition of 13 half-hour programs broadcast on WXDR (now WVUD), the radio station at the University of Delaware. Over the next five years *Dreamstreets* was primarily a broadcast project. *Dreamstreets 6* was rebroadcast on a number of occasions, as were later variations, notably *Dreamstreets Premium*, which included longer prose fiction, plays, and extended programs by a single poet. Other variations were the shorter *Dreamstreets Poet of the Week* and *Dreamstreets Poem of the Week*, used mainly as drop-ins during the regular program schedule.

The 1980s ushered in a plethora of literary publications in addition to *Dreamstreets*. While the record of many of these is sketchy due to the failure to properly archive them, one deserves mention. *Goblets, a Magazine of Poetry and Art,* published and edited by Terry L. Persun and Jean Marie Junkus, was a chapbook-formatted periodical that featured local poetry, fiction, and graphic art. One edition included a short fiction piece by Charles Bukowski.

The focus of Wilmington's literary output, especially during the time when *Dreamstreets* had switched to radio, centered around Tom Watkins' Xanadu Comics and Collectables at Fifth and Shipley Streets (the same space that would later be occupied by Polly Koster's 4w5 Café). A number of short-lived but influential publications were launched during this time. One of these, *Expresso Tilt,* came out in 1984, and was produced and edited by Mike Walsh. Walsh produced one of the *Dreamstreets 6* programs entitled "Some Tips on Home Recording." He also wrote the book *Fallen Son* (Onyx, 1994) about Charles Cohen, who in 1988 murdered his parents near Wilmington, then went on the lam for two years.

Watkins' *Daily Plague* began as an insert in *Emergency Illustrated* before becoming an independent publication and later morphing into *Tom Watkins' X-Ray,* which was published between 1987 and 1988. *X-Ray* didn't feature literary art to the extent that *Expresso Tilt* had, but it did include articles on pop culture, cinema, and music. It drew the attention of like-minded people in Philadelphia, carrying advertising from that city. It also nurtured a relationship with Baltimore's new cultural community, particularly with John Waters' coterie of characters, including Edith Massey, who appeared in several of his films. *X-Ray* paid tribute to an earlier time by publishing, in its September–October 1987 issue, an article on the work of WPA-era Wilmington artist Bayard Berndt.

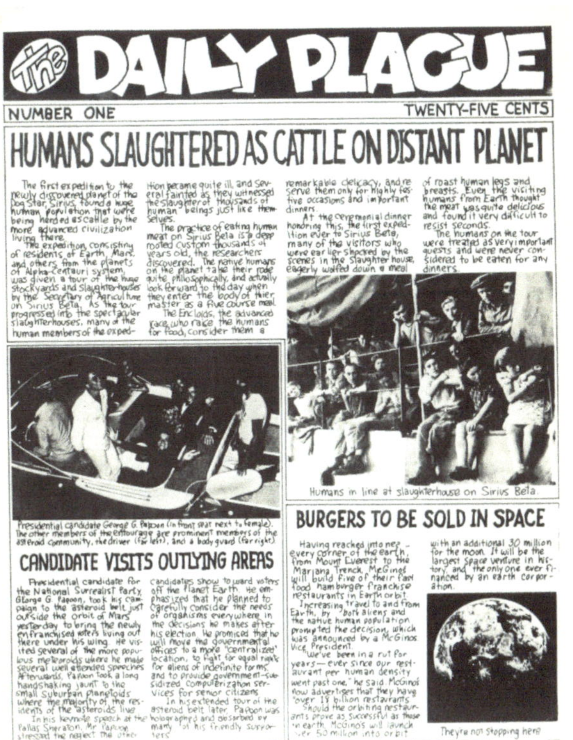

# The DAILY PLAGUE

NUMBER ONE | TWENTY-FIVE CENTS

## HUMANS SLAUGHTERED AS CATTLE ON DISTANT PLANET

The first expedition to the newly discovered planet of the Dog Star, Sirius, found a huge human population that were being herded as cattle by the more advanced civilization living there.

The expedition, consisting of residents of Earth, Mars, and others from the planets of Alpha-Centauri system, was given a tour of the huge stockyards and slaughterhouses by the Secretary of Agriculture on Sirius Beta. As the tour progressed into the spectacular slaughterhouses, many of the human members of the expedition became quite ill, and several fainted as they witnessed the slaughter of thousands of human beings just like themselves.

The practice of eating human meat on Sirius Beta is a deep rooted custom thousands of years old, the researchers discovered. The native humans on the planet take their role quite philosophically, and actually look forward to the day when they enter the body of thier master as a five course meal.

The Encloids, the advanced race, who raise the humans for food, consider them a remarkable delicacy, and reserve them only for highly festive occasions and important dinners.

At the ceremonial dinner honoring this, the first expedition ever to Sirius Beta, many of the visitors who were earlier shocked by the scenes in the slaughter house, eagerly wolfed down a meal of roast human legs and breasts. Even the visiting humans from Earth thought the meat was quite delicious and found it very difficult to resist seconds.

The humans on the tour were treated as very important guests and were never considered to be eaten for any dinners.

Humans in line at slaughterhouse on Sirius Beta.

Presidential candidate George G. Papoon (in front seat next to female). The other members of the entourage are prominent members of the asteroid community, the driver (far left), and a body guard (far right).

## CANDIDATE VISITS OUTLYING AREAS

Presidential candidate for the National Surrealist Party, George G. Papoon, took his campaign to the asteroid belt just outside the orbit of Mars yesterday to bring the newly enfranchised voters living out there under his wing. He visited several of the more populous meteoroids where he made several well attended speeches. Afterwards, Papoon took a long handshaking jaunt to the small suburban planetoids where the majority of the residents of the asteroids live.

In his keynote speech at the Pallas Sheraton, Mr Papoon stressed the neglect the other candidates show toward voters off the Planet Earth. He emphasized that he planned to carefully consider the needs of organisms everywhere in the decisions he makes after his election. He promised that he will move the governmental offices to a more "centralized" location, to fight for equal rights for aliens of indefinite forms, and to provide government-subsidized computerization services for senior citizens.

In his extended tour of the asteroid belt later, Papoon was holographed and absorbed by many of his friendly supporters.

## BURGERS TO BE SOLD IN SPACE

Having reached into nearly every corner of the earth, from Mount Everest to the Mariana Trench, McGinos will build five of their fast food hamburger franchise restaurants in Earth orbit.

Increasing travel to and from Earth, by both aliens and the native human population prompted the decision, which was announced by a McGinos Vice President.

"We've been in a rut for years — ever since our restaurant per human density went past one," he said. McGinos now advertises that they have "over 18 billion restaurants."

Should the orbiting restaurants prove as successful as those on earth, McGino's will launch over 50 million into orbit with an additional 30 million for the moon. It will be the largest space venture in history, and the only one ever financed by an earth corporation.

They're not stopping here

**TOM WATKINS, *THE DAILY PLAGUE*, NO. 1,** C. 1976

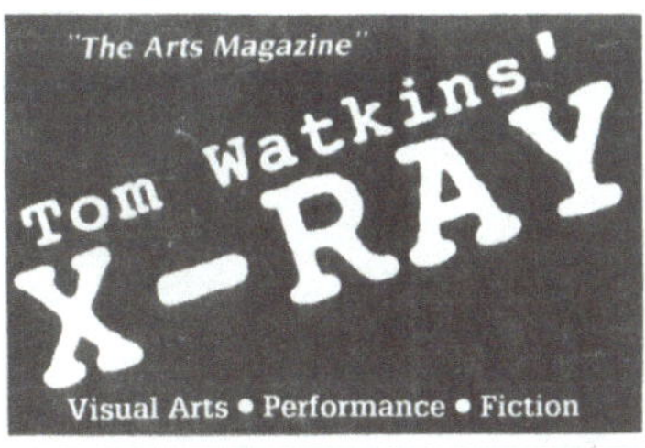


MAY, 1987 ■ FIRST ISSUE ■ FREE

This is a magazine with a purpose. X-RAY was conceived to satisfy several needs. The need for a consistent public journal covering the arts, the need for a publication that offers area writers, artists, photographers, and cartoonists a medium of expression free of the limiting specters of censorship and commercial timidity.

EDITORIAL
By Tom Watkins

On a personal basis, there's my *own* need to finally "do it right." I'd like to be able to write, draw, edit, and design work that meets *my* standards. I have a vision of a publication to which I'd like to contribute. No one else seems to want to publish such a magazine, so I've created my own. But this project isn't just for my own amusement, I'm counting on the support of contributors and readers who share this sense of frustration — and vision.

**X-RAY** has a unique philosophy. It was created as a tool to help define and create its own market. Seemingly disparate interests have been collected together under the same cover, in what promises to be an often unorthodox mix, at least for *this* area. The risky part of this undertaking lies more in what this magazine plans *not* to do, than in its actual contents.

**X-RAY** will cover "fine arts" and "mass media" with equal fervor. Any attempt to deny the hopeless entanglement of the two at this point is, at best, futile. But the arts coverage is going to deliberately avoid jargon, elitism, and the overbearing tone of cultural superiority that is often a subtext of contemporary criticism. In short, we're not playing by the rules, at least not the *unwritten* ones that say art (or Art) is only for *Those That Can Afford It* or *Have A Degree In Understanding What The Artist* ***Really*** *Meant.*

A lot of people won't like that. They also probably won't

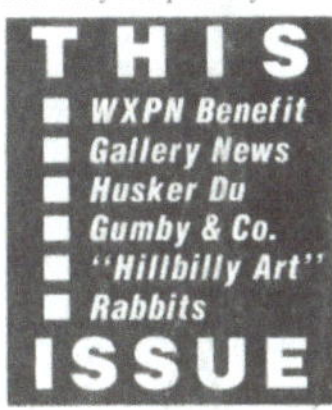


like seeing comic books, television commercials, and rock music reviewed and analyzed by the same base criteria as classical composers or gallery artists.

On the other hand, more than a few parties will be distressed to see no coverage of their favorite local rock band and/or their multi-million seller rock faves. Sorry, but several million people *can* be wrong. Or right for the wrong reasons.

***TOM WATKINS' X-RAY*, NO. 1,** MAY 1987

In 1989 *Dreamstreets* resumed print publication with *Dreamstreets 7*, which was dedicated to the memory of Rob Jones, who had died that year. *Dreamstreets* continued regular publication until 2006 with *Dreamstreets 50*, and included another broadcast issue, *Dreamstreets 26*, a series of 18 one-hour programs surveying Delaware's literary history from 19th-century poet and author John Lofland to Delaware's poet laureates and recent Second Saturday poets. *Dreamstreets 26* still airs intermittently on WVUD.

Wilmington's literary community of the 1970s and 1980s was not hampered by the internal squabbles that plagued the city's writers' groups immediately after World War II, nor was it hindered by the apathy and impulse to conform that were prevalent in the 1950s. Instead, it fostered sincere cooperation, good will, innovative ideas, and new perspectives. As a result, the literary community of this period left a legacy on which to build a continuing literary presence for the future.

1. My literary aspirations, dating to the late 1950s, included some minor association with David Hudson, whom my mother's family had known for years. I had shown Hudson some of my earliest poetry and he had encouraged me to continue writing. On the other hand, lanyon had a long association with Jeannette Slocomb Edwards, who harbored some animosity toward Hudson. It seemed fitting, yet obliquely symbolic, that lanyon and I would enjoy a growing literary relationship as part of a new generation of poets and authors.

# "OUT OF FRAME": THE NEWARK AND WILMINGTON ART SCENE, 1970S AND '80S

**Geo. Stewart**
*Artist, Filmmaker, and Radio Host*

When one is given the privilege to be his own Boswell, you can count on him standing in good light. How much of what I am about to relate is in any empirical sense "true," how much of it actually happened, I cannot attest. It is, however, how I remember it.

In the winter of 1971, the University of Delaware was experimenting for the first time with a six-week mini-semester of specialized study. I signed on for a course in filmmaking taught by Mark Marquisee and Jerry Millstein, having spent a good portion of my teenage years watching, shooting, and editing film. I had already made a 10-minute surrealist piece that featured just about every avant-garde technique I was aware of at that time, all set to the music of Pink Floyd's *Interstellar Overdrive*. Entitled *The Bride's Striped Bear by her Brothers Even*, my film was a reconceptualization of Marcel Duchamp's study in frozen movement done as a kinetic romp.

For the course I decided to make a film that had been gestating in my head for a while. With a few friends and fewer rolls of Super 8 film, I headed out one frightfully frigid morning to a handful of locations around Newark. The result was *A Small Gray Cloud is Killing the Garden*, a dour Maya Deren–inspired psychological exploration that reflected its title all too completely.

At around this time I went to a meeting for WHEN, a 10-watt campus radio station that could only be heard in campus dorm rooms or bleeding in over the university phone lines. It was the closest thing to onanism that the University would sanction. One February Saturday at midnight, Al Engberg, a friend from high school, joined me as co-host for the first

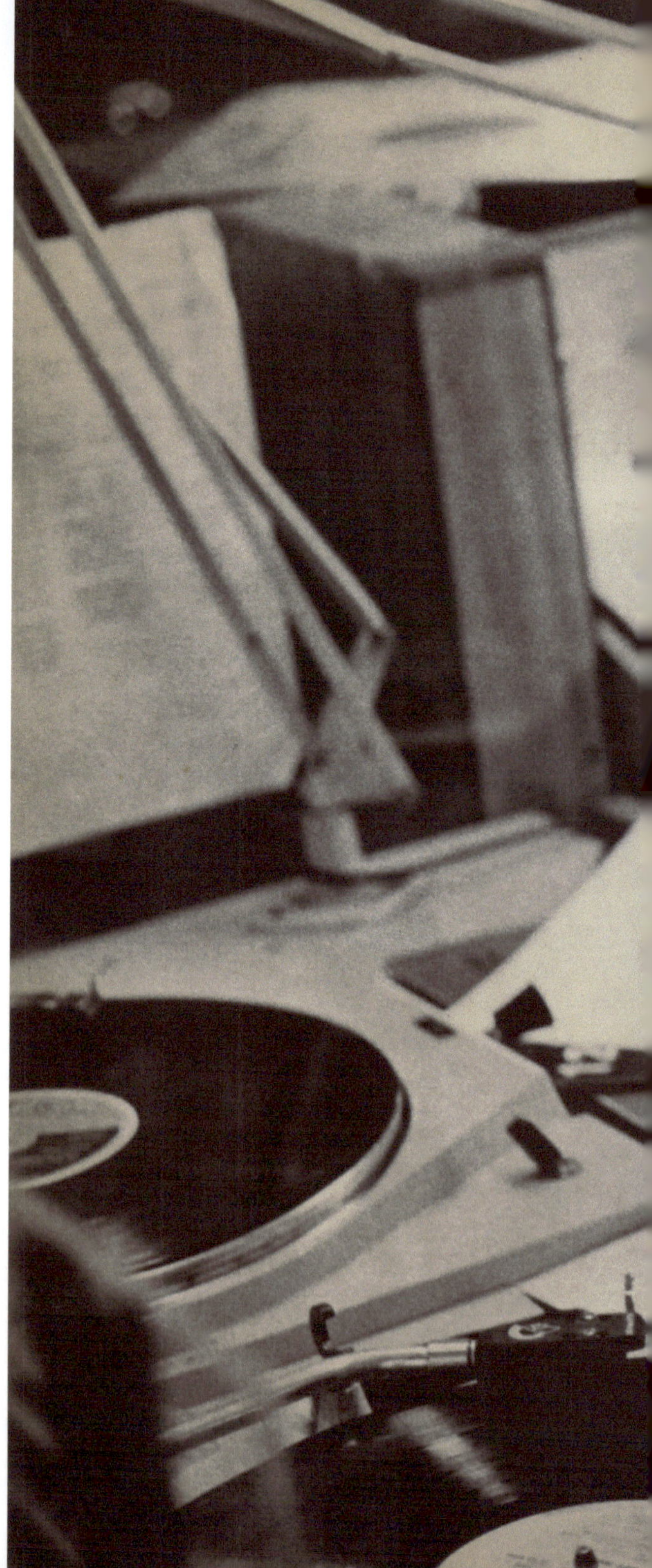

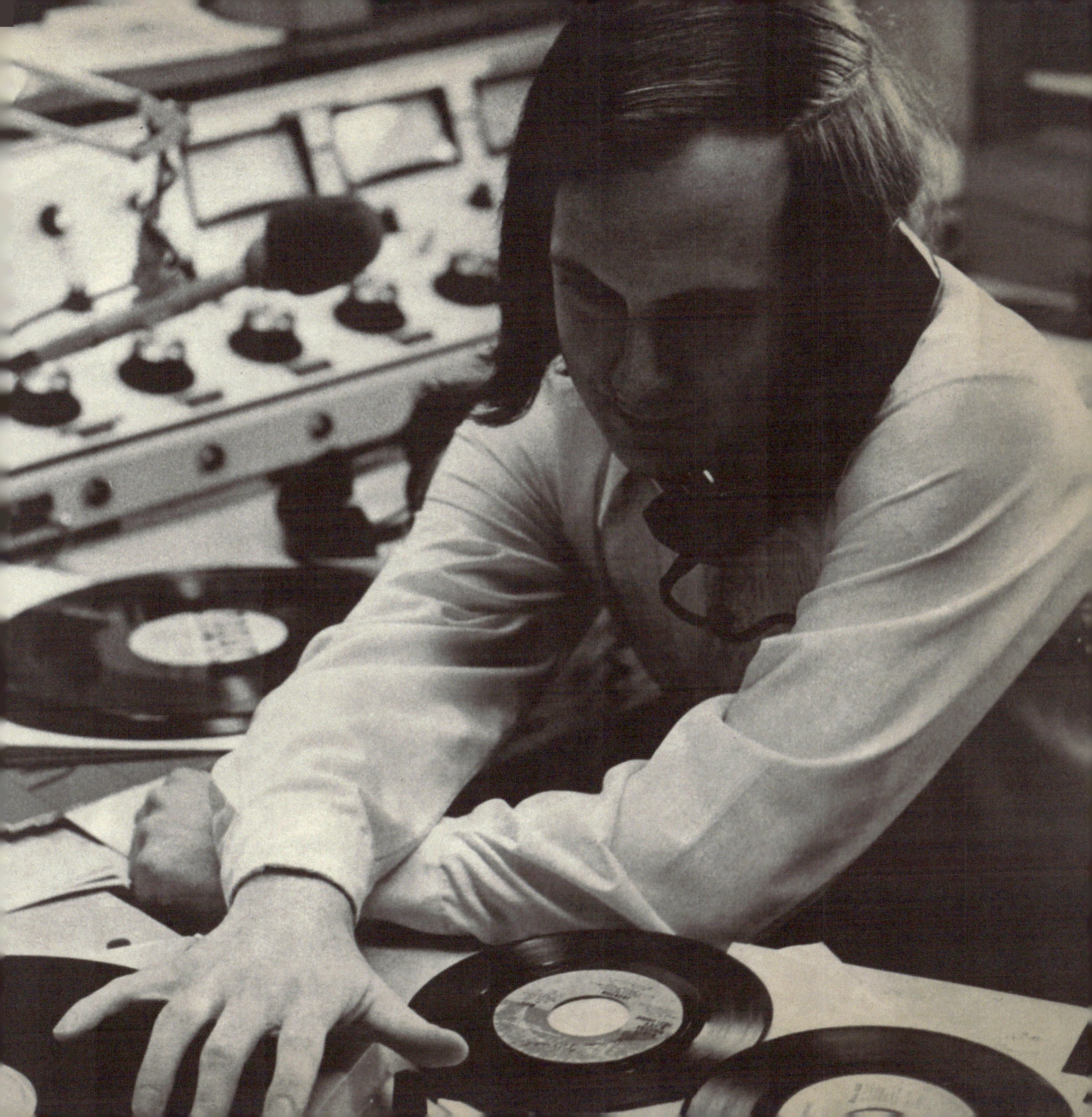

edition of *Side Two*, a name reflecting my commitment to the alternative music scene. For six hours every weekend we entertained ourselves with a mix of rare British imports, classics from the heyday of underground radio, and anything else that captured our fancy. Later that first night, as boredom set in, we held the first 45 Race, putting two copies of the same record on competing turntables and seeing which would finish first. Finally, as the shift was ending, we hung a microphone out the window and mixed in the sounds of the city behind the last few songs, climaxing when a street sweeper rumbled down the street and ran over a stray cat.

Gerald Barrett was an unassuming academic in the English Department from whom I received my first systematic education in film history and aesthetics. Later Barrett and Victor Spinski of the Sculpture Department taught a workshop in filmmaking, spurring another creative burst on my part.

My first project for the course was *The Andy Warhol Trilogy*, in which I appropriated silkscreen aesthetics. The soundtrack consisted of the first eight bars of the Velvet Underground's "Sister Ray," looped to replicate the mechanical repetition that was the cornerstone of Drela's mass production philosophy, especially the random elements it invariably introduced. Even though each film was less than three minutes long, the tedium of the single shot and the repetitious soundtrack tried the patience of many an audience, which was kind of the point.

The university had initiated a new Bachelor of Arts in Liberal Studies, an improvised curriculum that for me included music composition, theater, and other courses centering around Sophocles' *Oedipus Rex*. Out of that semester came electronic musique, a small collage, several illustrations, and a new respect for Mother's Day.

The most valuable line of study was Introduction to Art Criticism, which gave me the vocabulary and discipline to understand what I had been doing in my art, allowing me to become much more rigorous. I soon came to realize that while most artists intuitively make the right choices, it is usually left to the critics to explain why.

Musically the local scene was as diverse as you could hope for. The most exciting band to me was Dale Dallabrida's and Al Mascitti's All You Can Eat. I especially remember the extravaganza they put on at Mitchell Hall, a full-out production with the regular band augmented by a large horn section and too many drummers. Through a cascade of fog, someone with a handcart wheeled out a refrigerator containing the cryogenically preserved Kid Hollywood, looking for all the (other) world like a reprobate Ziggy Stardust. The show, the music, and the food fight afterward exhibited a sharp satiric edge that cut deep into the usual straw dogs of American consumerism. The music had sharp edges, a prog-rock version of the Mothers of Invention.

On the radio, *Side Two* continued to chug along. One night in 1973 I stumbled across a curious album called *Hustlers Convention* by Lightnin' Rod. Predating rap by years, it mixed braggadocio and sound effects over a funk beat heavy with bass in support of an intercity fantasy of sex, drugs, and violence that would only get nastier in less talented hands over the years. Soon punk and new age took center stage when by chance a friend from London dropped in with the Sex Pistols' first 45. Over the next few years, musical diversity exploded across the station's schedule with a slew of new shows devoted to everything from big band tunes to old cylinder recordings to Indian music. Carl Goldstein took to the air with his influential *Fire on the Mountain*. Jerry Grant and B. J. Lobermann began their soul program, *Hip City*. Dallabrida and Mascitti filled one late night spot with *White Noise/Window on the World*, a dangerous roundelay of insignificant news stories, random chatter, and running jokes mixed with madness by sound engineer Mike Moss. Adding to the absurdity was the musical background: the same side of a Time-Life record played over and over. John Cage would have been proud.

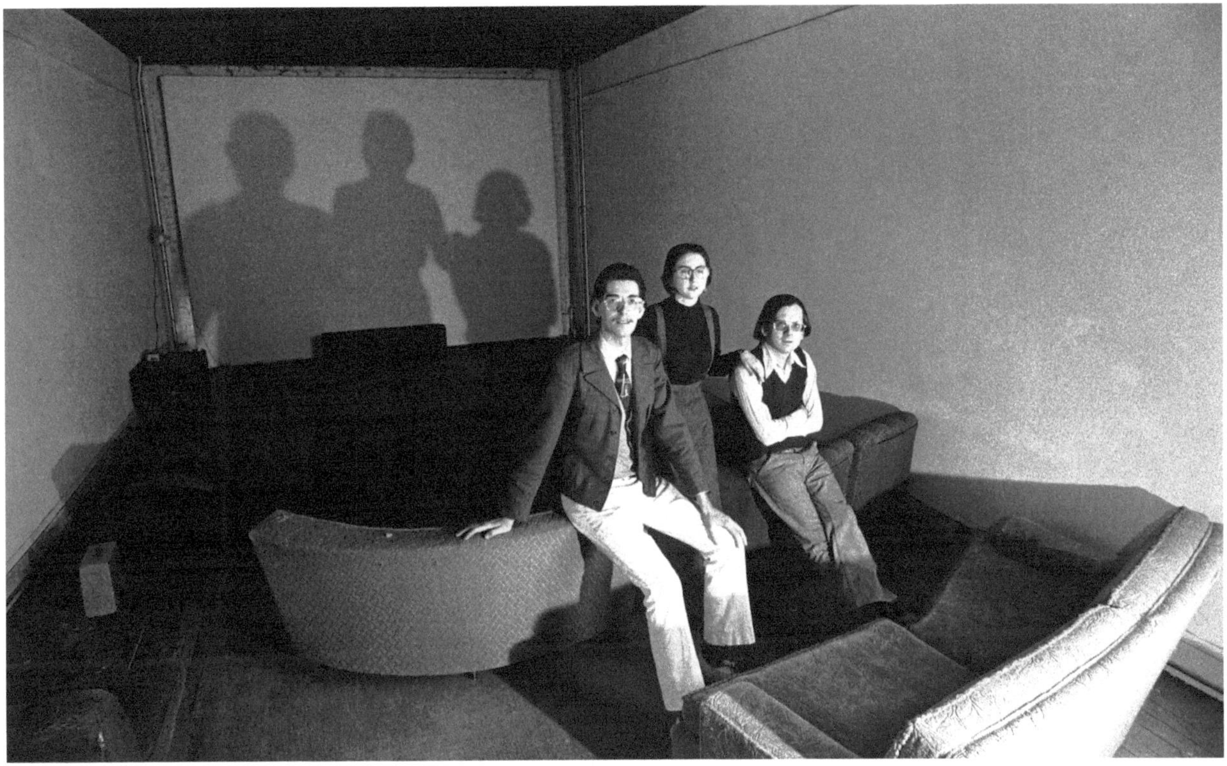

**RON DUBICK, *RONDO CENTER*,** MARCH 2, 1978

It was around this time that I began contributing comics and illustrations to various local underground newspapers. One, a borderless chronology of an evolving shadow, proved surprisingly popular around campus, hanging on many dorm room doors like the secret markings hobos would leave outside the homes of generous strangers. I was inspired by Duchamp to create several readymades that summer, only one of which, *The Oculus Contained*, survives. I also drew a portfolio entitled *Horror House*, a graphic novel called *The Doomsday Book*, and *Lachrymose Lake*, which captures a future state through present details.

One time I was given carte blanche to use the university TV studio, so I decided to explore the textual possibilities inherent in analog television. I shot a series of gliding glass balls enclosed in a miniature funhouse of mirrors using a debeamed camera, which smeared the image. Another camera reshot that feed off a monitor, accentuating the rasters. The resulting video, *Thoth*, named in honor of the Egyptian god who invented writing, was performed live. The score was by Delaware musician Woz (Paul Woznicki).

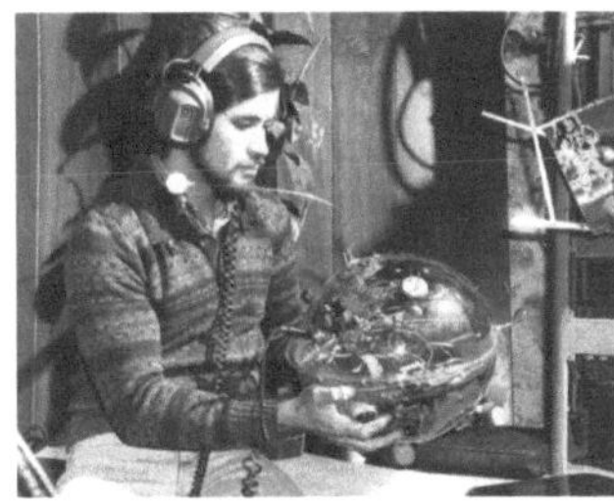

**BENJAMIN B. WOZNICKI, *PAUL WOZNICKI WITH ROBOT*,** C. 1978

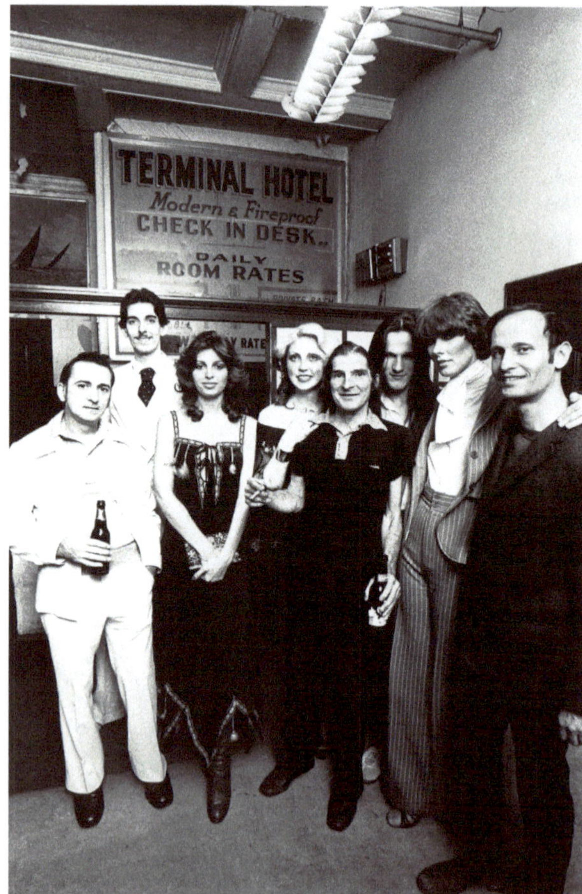


**LEO S. MATKINS, *TERMINAL HOTEL PARTY,*** APRIL 14, 1977

Unable to stretch my college career any further, I found myself in Wilmington, part of an unsuccessful attempt at revitalizing the decaying city. Tom Watkins, Joyce Brabner, Craig Dawson, and I were part of an arts collective called the Rondo Center, whose various parts included Tom's studio apartment, a cinematheque, and the Xanadu Comics store. The four-story brick building sat on the corner of Fifth and Shipley Streets that housed a newspaper in an earlier century.

The Rondo Center overlooked Market Street—barely visible through the huge, grimy windows—and was dumpster-furnished with a few mismatched chairs, a couch, and some well-worn pillows on the floor. It was named after Rondo Hatton, an obscure 1940s character actor who suffered from a rare, disfiguring disease that left the once handsome man with a countenance ready for cheap horror films. Tom and I booked most of the events at the Rondo Center, a casually scheduled series of programs that was eclectic in the extreme.

Hatton also served as the mascot for Tom's biggest undertaking, the 1976 Sleaze Convention. The event brought the nascent New York punk scene to Wilmington in the form of

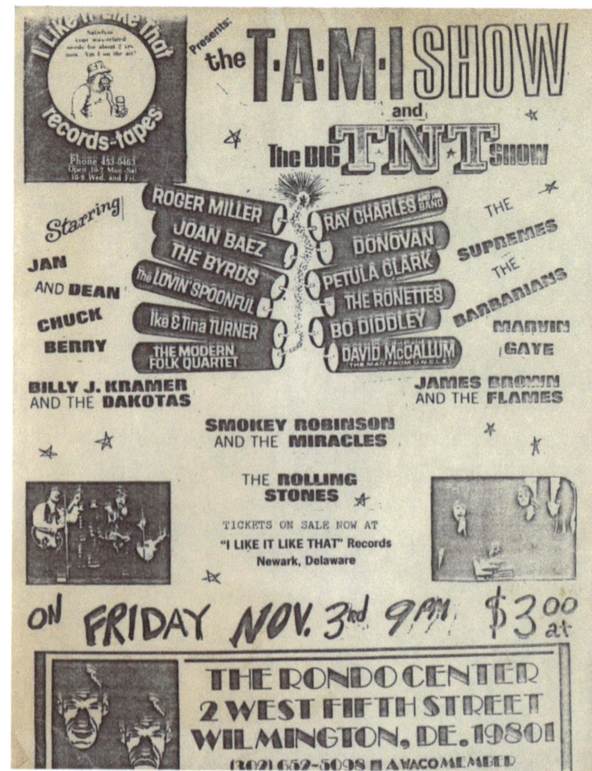


***THE T.A.M.I SHOW AND THE BIG T.N.T. SHOW* POSTER,** C. 1977

John Holmstrom and Legs McNeil, the publishers of *Punk* magazine, who walked in and immediately vomited on the studio floor. Soon-to-be superstar Debbie Harry also came, having just left the Stilettos for a new band named in her honor, Blondie. She gave me a copy of their first 45, *X Offender*, which debuted on *Side Two* that weekend. Sparing much expense, our guests stayed at the Terminal Hotel, named not only for its location near the train station, but also for the health of many of its habitués.

Later that spring Edie "The Egg Lady" Massey, John Waters' second-most-famous star, came to town for a visit. Tom somehow convinced the city fathers that such a famous personage was a natural to lead the Wilmington Easter Parade down Market Street. It even made the papers: Edie dressed elegantly with a basket of spring flowers on one arm, a giant bunny on the other.

During its brief existence, the Rondo Center exposed the local cognoscenti to a mixed bag of delights. I was behind the booking of a 1938 film called *The Goldwyn Follies*; Tom booked Waters' *Desperate Living*. I Like It Like That Records sponsored the most financially successful program, a double bill of the *T.A.M.I. Show* and the *Big T.N.T. Show*, featuring the most important acts of 1964, including Chuck Berry, Smokey Robinson, Lesley Gore, the Beach Boys, James Brown, and the Rolling Stones. It packed the house.

A patron of the arts lent us a half-inch video deck, which allowed me to explore an area of communication theory that always intrigued me: the boundary between entropy and redundancy in a message. In *Gen X* (a term of no cultural significance at the time), I recorded a one-minute station break and duplicated it over and over, going down ten generations. Each dub degraded the message further until it eventually descended into incoherence. I then spliced them in reverse order, physically, with scissors and scotch tape. When played back, the audio was the first to emerge from the electronic miasma, due to the greater predictability of its structure. The picture revealed itself several generations later.

I was honored when sculptor Rick Rothrock asked me to document one of his art projects, a series of steel chocolate Toblerone boxes that were finished by C-4. I mirrored his process in *Dynamite Art*. A diptych video, *Heat*, followed shortly thereafter.

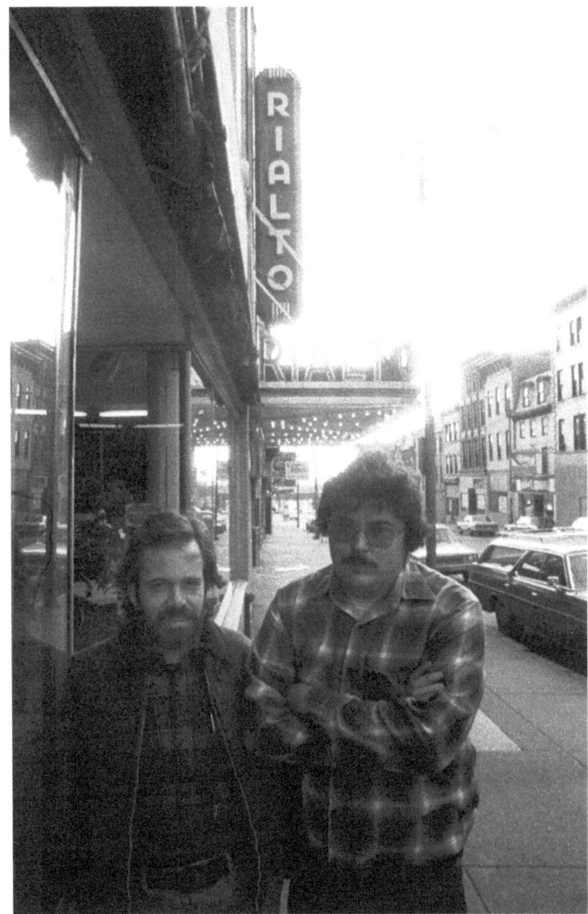


**PAT CROWE, *RIALTO THEATER*,** MARCH 1981

By 1978, the Rondo Center was gone and I had moved back to Newark. Barry Solan contacted me about a new enterprise of his, a repertory cinema. For the next half decade nearly every important movie played the State Theatre in a parade of double bills that changed two or three times a week, with more at midnight on the weekends. In the deceptive glow of the State's early success, Solan tried the same sort of programming in Wilmington, at the Rialto down on Second and Market Streets. Despite assurances that there was plenty of free parking near the theater, not enough suburbanites were willing to chance it and the Rialto closed within a year.

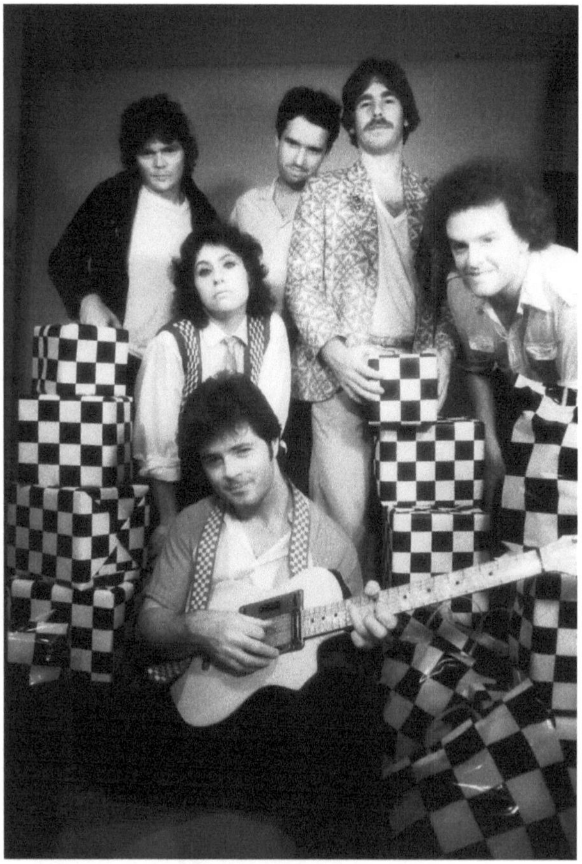

**ELIZABETH BOTWRIGHT BECKER, *THE COMMOTIONS*,** C. 1981

Giving the State some solvency was a weekly showing of *The Rocky Horror Picture Show*. Of course *Rocky Horror* was more than a midnight movie; it was an interactive, multimedia experience, the logical extension of everything the Theater of the Ridiculous had long been preaching. Many nights those red lips wouldn't pucker until way past 1:00 a.m., after a full bill that began with a live band and shorts like Meatloaf singing "Paradise by the Dashboard Light," in the middle of which sportscaster Phil Rizzuto supplied color commentary of the backseat action. That was the cue for the audience to put on their mitts and play a game of catch.

It had been decades since anyone had played the stage of the State, so we decided to let it revive its days as a vaudeville house by booking live music every so often, a move devoid of any fiduciary logic. Barry brought in Rick Danko and Paul Butterfield. Muddy Waters also appeared one night. I brought in John Cale. All lost money, but the ex-Velvet lost the least, only because he was the cheapest.

The theater also presented us with an opportunity to showcase local talent, like the Voltages, Honour Society, and the M.I.B.s. (These acts would also drop in on *Side Two* and play live. I liked the show's casual air, much like Arthur Godfrey had on his morning show. I purposely left the studio door open and invited pretty much anyone who happened down the hall to join the party.) Jerry Grant, who had recently formed a band named The Commotions with family and friends, played well-selected classics and their own originals. George Thorogood and the Delaware Destroyers played there several times, always putting on a high-energy show.

Tommy Conwell performed with his band the Young Rumblers, who exceeded him in musicianship and matched him in crowd-pleasing antics; Conwell once emerged from a coffin to walk across the top of the theater seats while

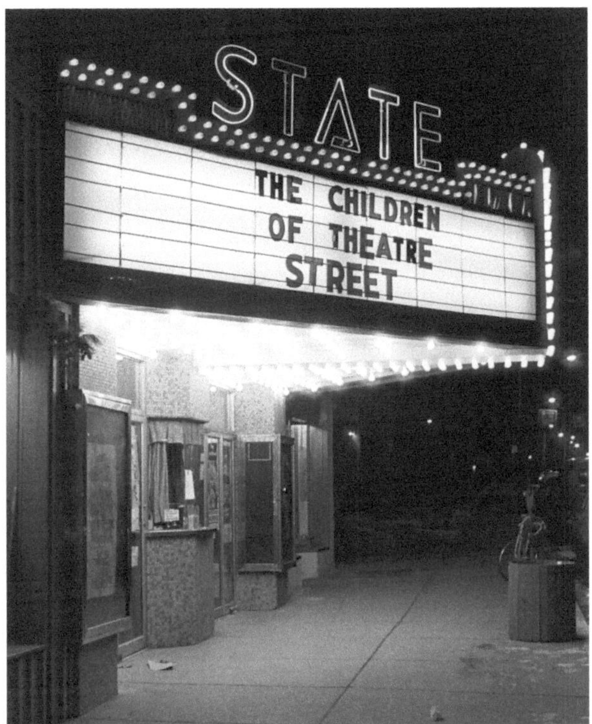


**TREY WHITE, *STATE THEATRE*,** C. 1981

blasting away on his guitar. The first time he played the State it was as the drummer in Bob Ross' band, the Christian Sniper. A well-respected guitar maker, Bob had made one for himself, a clear-body Plexiglas Flying V that looked really cool but weighed a ton. Bob was booked to open the weekly showing of *The Rocky Horror Picture Show*. There were the hoped-for boos when I announced that we would first be showing a short documentary about the clubbing of rich women so seals could have nice coats. That was the projectionist's cue to start running the avant-garde nightmare *Un Chien Andalou*. As the director took a straight razor across an aristocratic woman's eye, Bob let out with a god-awful guitar run that would frighten even Cerberus into submission. The screen rose to reveal Bob decked out in a Girl Scout uniform eating popcorn from a Stayfree box, Tommy attacking his drums, and Phil Hutchenson vamping on his Farfisa before launching into a high-energy instrumental. Bob was almost run out of town.

Barry would also book people on the spur of the moment. Once when Edie the Egg Lady was in town, Barry slipped her a few bucks to get on stage and lip-sync to her recording of "Big Girls Don't Cry." It was a nice gesture on Barry's part, but then he didn't have to help strap Edie into her black vinyl dominatrix costume. I did.

The rise of the video store was the death knell for the State. Interest in "serious" cinema was in decline. I went off to the Big Apple for a spell to work at the Museum of Broadcasting (now the Paley Center for Media). Barry moved on in 1986 to better financial success with a chain of video stores under various names at various times. The State's projectors struck their last carbon rod shortly thereafter. One Sunday morning, while everyone was asleep, the building was knocked down. Few noticed; fewer cared.

Ars Gratia Artis. Ars Longa, Vita Brevis. Cave, Gaberbocchum moneo tibi, nate cavendum!

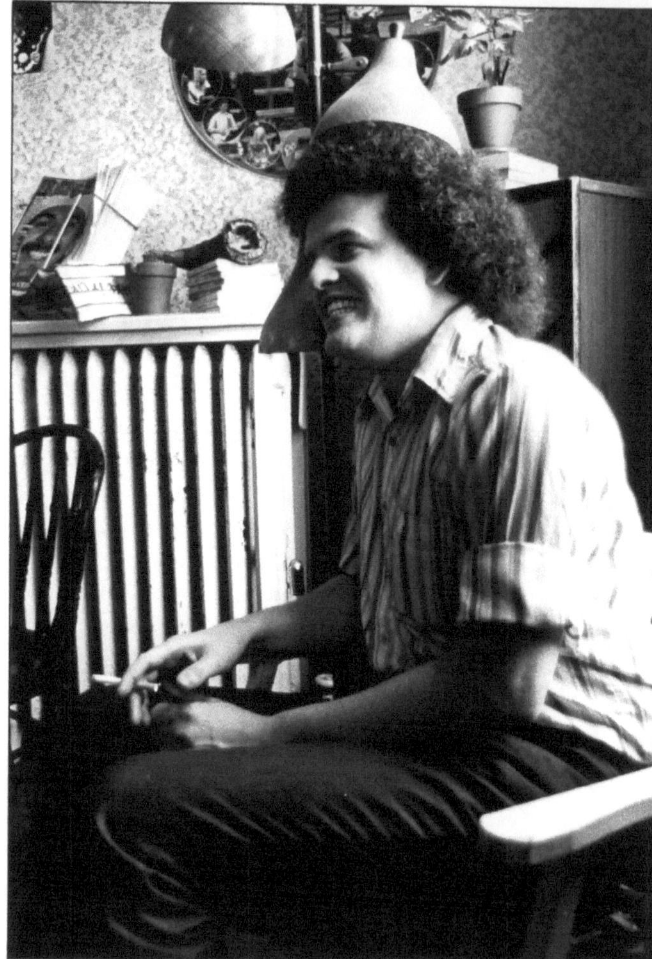

Jerry Grant

Newark's okay.
I like Newark. I like a small town.
I have no desire to go to New York or Colorado.
I get restless once in a while but there's a lot of stuff to do in Newark.
(not counting restaurants)
Newark is your basic, gaudy, late 50's - early 60's main street with all it's gaudy signs.
It's friendly, pretty clean, nice.
Nothing really profound to say about Newark: it's not a profound town.
I'm part owner of a record store called "I Like It Like That"
and I work in the bookstore across the street called "David's Bookshelf."
I've been in Newark 5 years. 4 years? It seems like
a long time and I DON'T remember when Main Street
was two-way.
(I like the Kirkwood Highway)

**Jerry Grant**
*Musician and Politician*

At the dawn of the 1970s, Wilmington's record retailing scene reflected the changes that had been taking place in the music business nationwide for nearly a decade. In the mid-1960s, 33 1/3 RPM albums had begun to replace the 45 RPM single as the Beatles invaded America and teenagers demanded the "long-playing" format. Previously the province of older classical and jazz aficionados, albums held more than 20 minutes of music on each side, allowing performers to record longer tracks that exceeded the unofficial AM radio station limit of three minutes. As a result, listeners began to abandon Delaware AM favorites like WAMS and WFIL in favor of "underground" stations like WMMR-FM and WDAS-FM that played the new, longer tracks. The underground radio scene contained a healthy dose of political and cultural commentary, aided by the popularity of what we today delicately call "recreational drug use." The change in broadcasting the music was reflected in how the music was sold. Eventually the record buying experience wasn't complete without incense and rolling papers available under the counter. Much had changed since the previous decade when youngsters could purchase a couple of 45s at Hoy's 5 & 10 cent store while picking up a live baby turtle at the cash register to take home as a pet. Back then retailers assumed that neither the life of the turtle or the musical appeal of rock-and-roll would last very long.

The Wilmington–Newark corridor was home to many record stores, from independent shops to national chains. Wilmington Dry Goods on Market Street was a cubbyhole with an impossibly low ceiling, but the store's tightly packed racks carried every charting pop and soul 45, as well as an unmatched array of gospel, blues, jazz, and pop LPs. Owner Milton A. Pomerantz, known as "Mister P" (or "MAP" to those who knew him only by his monogrammed shirts), sang the praises of each customer's purchase, regardless of genre—he was either a man of wide-ranging musical tastes or a salesman who knew how to encourage repeat customers. The store's closure in the mid-1970s sounded the death knell for many of Wilmington's other destination retail shops.

Wonderland on Main Street in Newark was the prototypical 1970s record store, carrying what would come to be called "classic rock"—Jimi Hendrix, the Grateful Dead, progressive rock, and British blues—on vinyl LP, 8-track, and cassette. Employees were friendly and knowledgeable, and the whole store had a hippie vibe, enhanced by the extensive selection of drug paraphernalia at the counter. Wonderland still exists today, under different management, as a record store and recording studio.

Bert's Tape Factory, which opened on Concord Pike in 1972, obviously intended to sell the latest technology. It was a great little store for blues, jazz, and rock, available on tapes and LPs. If you shopped in the afternoon, you might be offered a glass of wine. As the 1980s wound down, you may also have been subjected to high-volume political discussions.

In 1976, around the time the punk movement was being born, a quirky operation called the Lazy J Record Ranch on Newark's Main Street came under new ownership and was renamed I Like It Like That Records. ILILT carried rock, soul, and punk LPs and 45s, and featured a large selection of used LPs, drawing collectors from in and out of Delaware. George Thorogood and the Destroyers performed at least two surprise afternoon shows there. If you passed by after closing time, you might have heard one of several local bands who used the store as a rehearsal space.

Jeremiah's Record Exchange, on Philadelphia Pike, opened in the early 1980s and became the place to go for imported British LPs. The store also carried many live albums that were unavailable through the usual music distribution channels.

National and regional chains were also part of the record buyers' milieu. Philadelphia's Record Museum on Market Street provided competition for Wilmington Dry Goods as did Woolworth's, which offered packages of three oldie 45s for 69 cents. The 45s were wrapped so the buyer could see the two outside selections, but the flip sides and the middle single were a mystery, adding an element of chance to the record buying experience. Sears, a sentimental favorite of many North Wilmington music lovers, offered an LP selection that was a cut above the usual department store fare. Rolling Thunder Records, north of Wilmington, opened in the late 1980s as a Deadhead-oriented music store, serving a subculture that has been historically strong in Delaware.

By this time, the LP was being supplanted by the compact disc, which used the digital audio technology that in 20 years would cause the local record retailer to suffer the same fate as the village blacksmith.

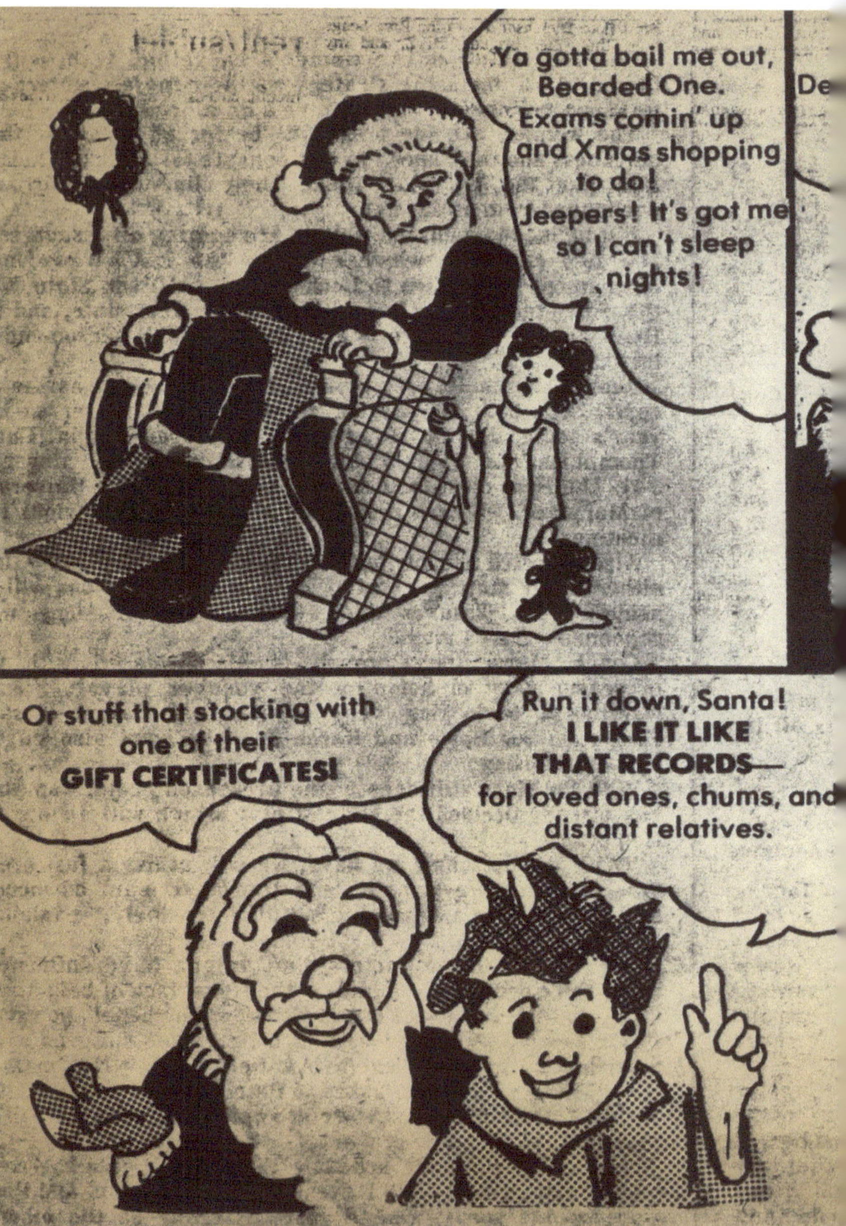


**GEO. STEWART, I LIKE IT LIKE THAT ADVERTISEMENT,** 1976

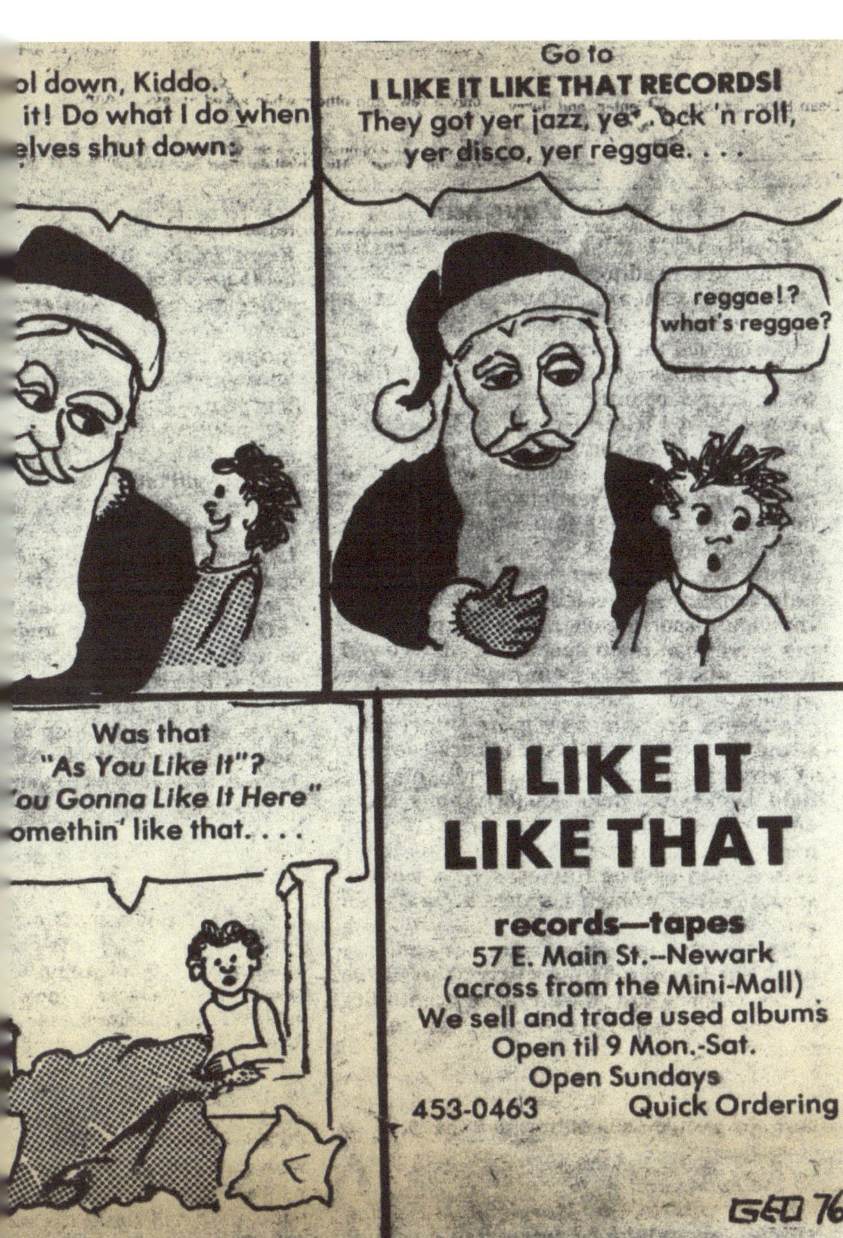
ol down, Kiddo.
it! Do what I do when
elves shut down:
Go to
I LIKE IT LIKE THAT RECORDS!
They got yer jazz, ye ock 'n roll,
yer disco, yer reggae. . . .
reggae!?
what's reggae?
Was that
"As You Like It"?
'ou Gonna Like It Here"
omethin' like that. . . .
I LIKE IT
LIKE THAT
records—tapes
57 E. Main St.--Newark
(across from the Mini-Mall)
We sell and trade used albums
Open til 9 Mon.-Sat.
Open Sundays
453-0463
Quick Ordering
GEO 76

## Leonard Perlson
*Gallerist*

On May 17, 1984, 15 enigmatic figures appeared on the corrugated steel canopy above the disused meatpacking plant that housed my gallery, in what was then one of Manhattan's most derelict areas. This installation was the creation of Rob Jones, an artist, gallery owner, and entrepreneur from Wilmington.

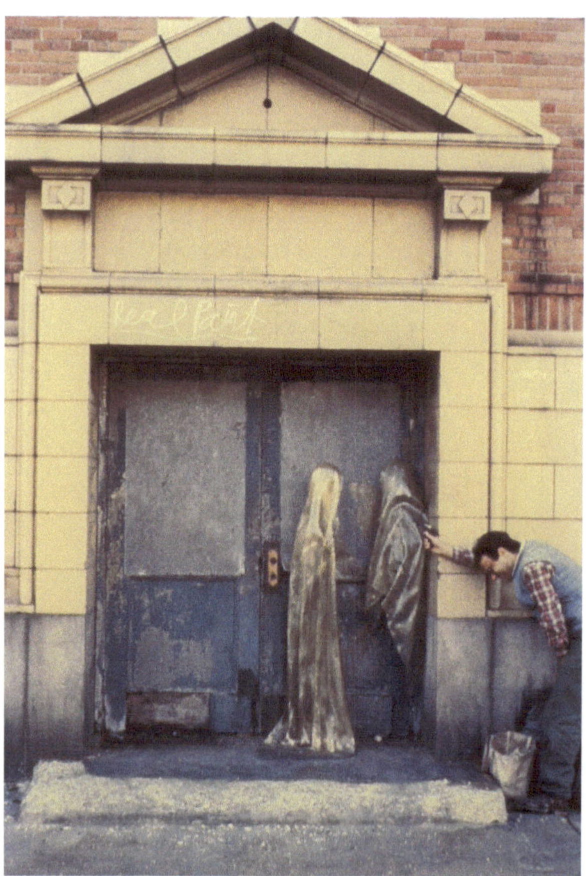

**UNKNOWN PHOTOGRAPHER, *PIER 34 FRONT DOOR*,** AUGUST 1983

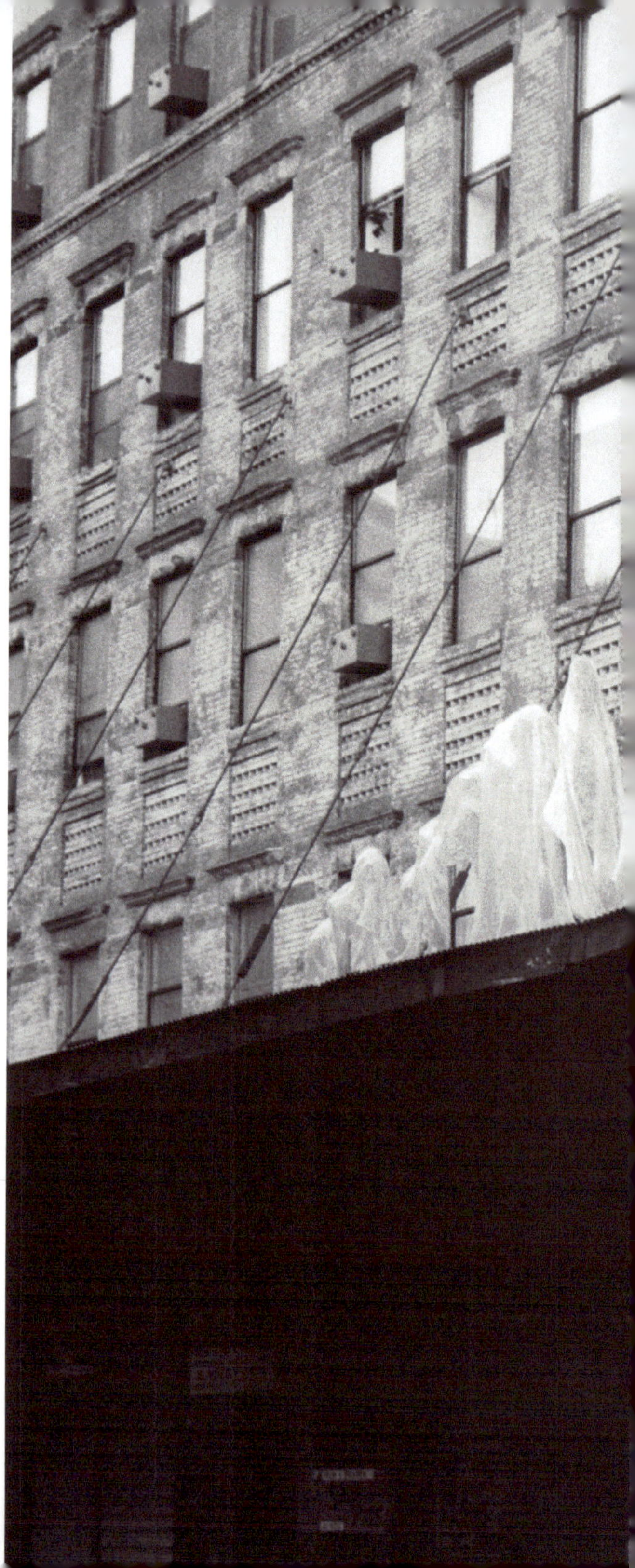

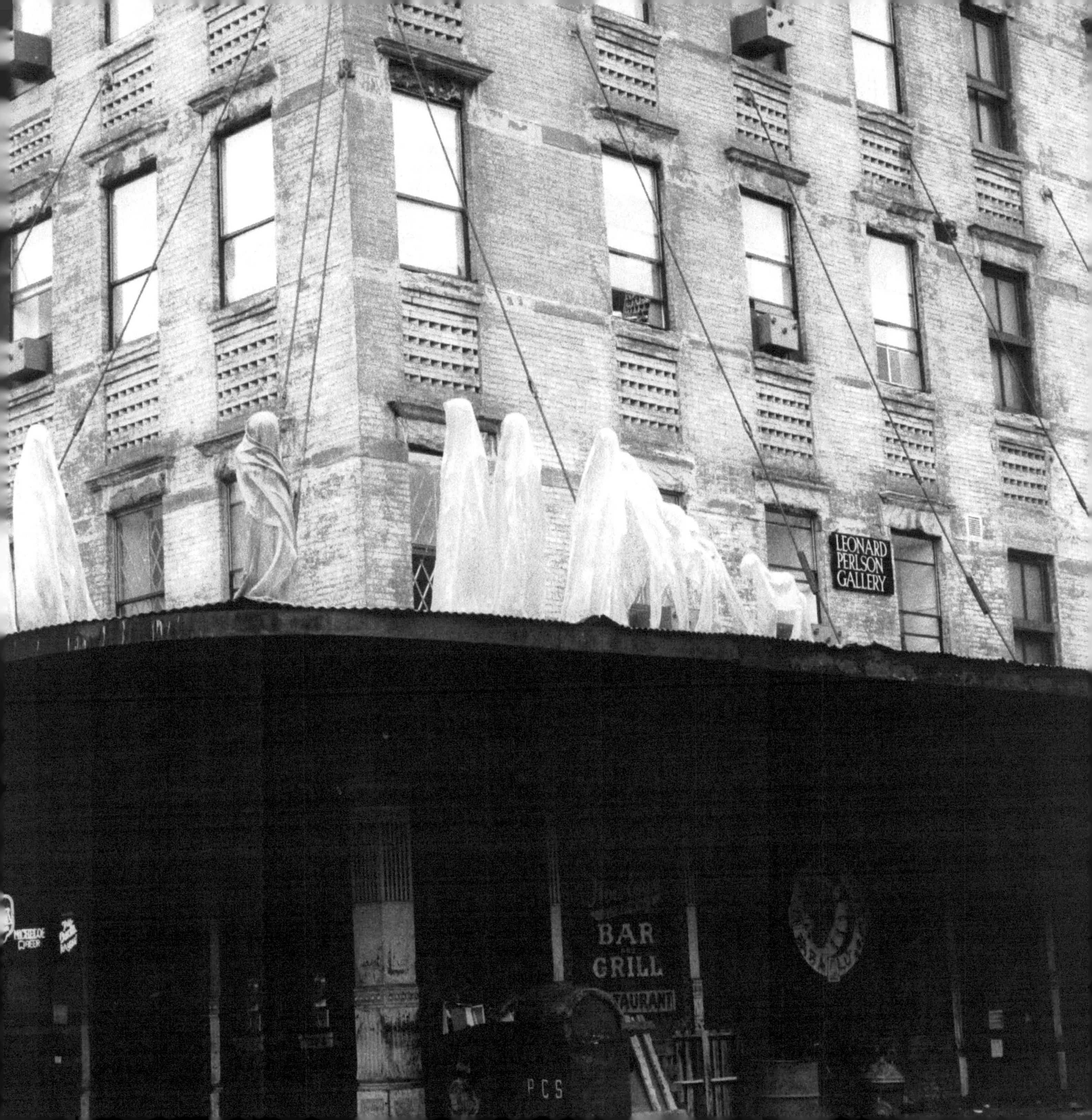
LEONARD PERLSON GALLERY
BAR
GRILL
PCS

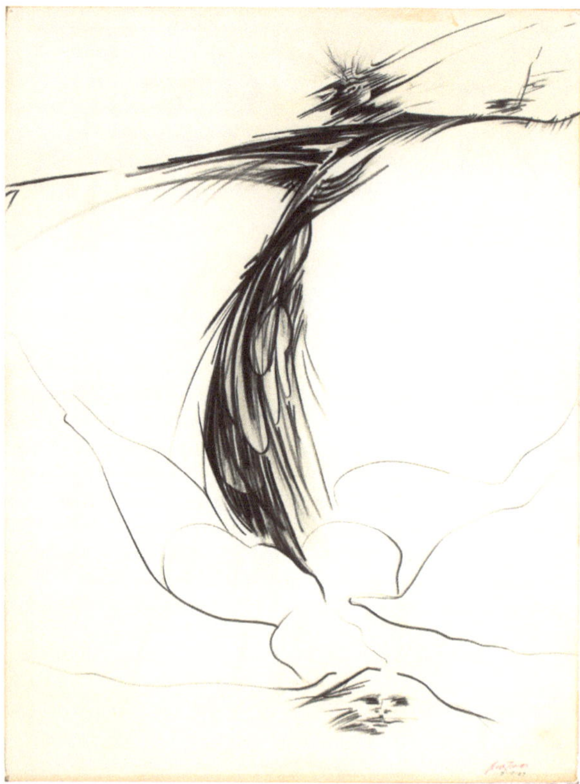

**ROBERT JONES, *UNTITLED*,** 1983

Jones made the figures by draping polyurethane-coated fiberglass over a dress mannequin (which he named "Beulah") and allowing it to set. He then removed the mannequin, leaving behind a fiberglass shell that looked like flowing drapery over an invisible body. He fixed the resulting sculptures to the rusting canopy, strategically positioning them under the soft glow of various incandescent streetlights. The forms—along with the dripping of the polyurethane resin, which suggested tears—put one in mind of shrouds.

As time passed, the sculptures suffered the effects of weather and of the exhaust fumes from passing trucks. The grime added to the color palette; the resin "tears" began to look like dripping fat, the drapery like sinew, hide, or cartilage. Thus Jones' figures came to evoke the hanging carcasses that had once waited to be butchered and polywrapped in the building.

Jones was no stranger to art-based gentrification. His opening of the Fifth Street Gallery in Wilmington had given him firsthand insight into the destruction of distressed neighborhoods and the subsequent rebuilding process. Metaphorically, his "shrouds" highlighted the space between

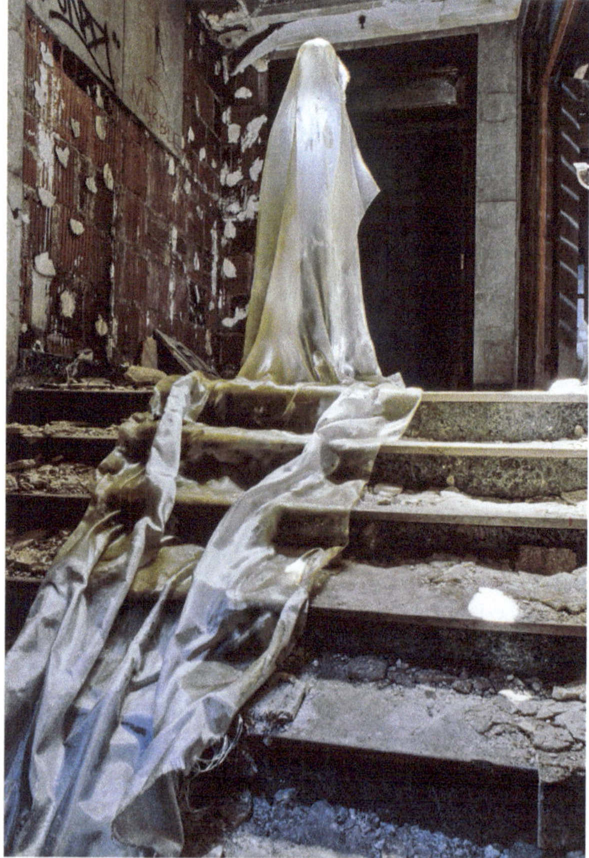

**ANDREAS STERZING, *PIER34-24 ROB JONES*,** 1983

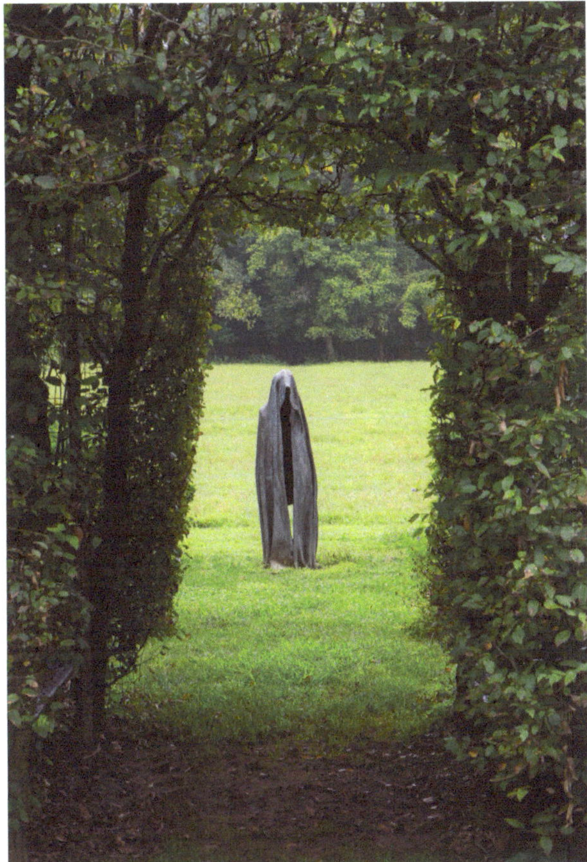

**ROBERT JONES, *SHROUD*,** 1984

life and death and, in this particular case, the void between a neighborhood's past and present.

Coinciding with Jones's sculptural epitaph to the meat market was the zenith of the AIDS epidemic. In the early 1980s, the area was home to several after-hours clubs. Revelers making their way home at dawn were caught off guard by the shrouds. The specter of AIDS was clearly beginning to influence artists.

As with most site-specific, ephemeral work, documentation is all that remains of this installation. Jones's photographer, Ellen Skye, ensured that the drama of the tableau he had created was effectively conveyed.

Jones was very much an artist of his time, in both his choice of materials and his subjects. His work had much in common with the pioneering polyester resin experiments of Eva Hesse and Lynda Benglis. He infused his art with his concerns about urban renewal, AIDS, and underground nightlife in the city and thus, contributed to the urban art scene of the 1980s.

# NOTES ON THE IMAGES

Unless otherwise indicated, images are copyright of the artist. Additional acknowledgment is as follows:

**Cover:** Julia Gorton, *Wilmington, Market Street* (detail), c. 1976. Digital C print, 9 1/2 x 14 inches. Collection of the artist. © Julia Gorton.

**Pages 2–3:** Kevin McLaughlin, *Southern Approaches,* 1984. Oil on canvas, 38 x 60 inches. Collection of Thomas C. Shea, Jr. © (2015) Kevin McLaughlin.

**Pages 4–5:** wowe (Wolfgang Wesener), Robert Jones in Raoul's, c. 1986. Digital print, 8 x 10 inches. Collection of the Jones Family.

**Page 6:** E. JEAN LANYON, *Viewpoint* cover, vol. 2, no. 2, November 1972. Ink on paper, 13 3/4 x 9 7/8 inches. Collection of the artist. © E. JEAN LANYON. Photograph by Carson Zullinger.

**Pages 8-9:** Stephen Tanis, *The Steiner Sisters* (detail), 1977. Oil on canvas, 54 x 47 1/4 inches. Collection of the artist. © Stephen Tanis. Photograph by Carson Zullinger.

**Page 10:** James E. Newton, *Homage to Frederick Douglass*, 1972. Collagraph, 17 5/8 x 13 1/4 inches. Collection of the artist. © James E. Newton. Photograph by Carson Zullinger.

**Pages 12–13:** Fred Comegys, *"Love Your Neighbor," Wilmington Train Station*, 1972. Digital print, 12 15/16 x 19 1/2 inches. Delaware Art Museum, Gift of the artist and Stuart M. Grant, 2011. © *The News Journal.*

**Pages 14–15:** Fred Comegys, *Wilmington Riots, 500 Block of Washington Street*, 1968. Digital print, 12 7/8 x 19 1/2 inches. Delaware Art Museum, Gift of the artist and Stuart M. Grant, 2011. © *The News Journal.*

**Page 16, left to right:** Pat Crowe, *Art Van*, April 17, 1972. Courtesy of the Delaware Historical Society. © *The News Journal.* | Ron Dubick, *Art Mitchell Dance*, October 17, 1972. Courtesy of the Delaware Historical Society. © *The News Journal.* Just three years after the founding of Dance Theatre of Harlem, Arthur Mitchell visited Wilmington under Delaware State Arts Council funding for a three-day residency in Wilmington High School. The company had performed earlier that spring at the Delaware Art Museum.

**Page 17, top to bottom:** Fred Comegys, *Market Street Mall Groundbreaking*, July 16, 1974. Courtesy of the Delaware Historical Society. © *The News Journal.* | Pat Crowe, *Grand Theater Ceremonies*, July 1, 1974. Courtesy of the Delaware Historical Society. © *The News Journal.* The launch of the Grand Opera House renovation project began on July 1, 1974 when Mayor Thomas Maloney climbed a fire engine ladder to paint the Masonic eye on the central pediment of the façade.

**Page 18, left to right:** Installation view of Robert Jones' *A Natural Environmental Foam Phenomenon* (March 12–31, 1973) at the Haas Gallery of Art, Bloomsburg University. Courtesy of the Jones Family. | Robert Jones, *Fiberglas Nude*, 1970. Fiberglass, 40 x 22 inches. Collection unknown. Courtesy of the Jones Family. © Artist's Estate. Jones' *Fiberglas Nude* was included in the Delaware Art Museum's *59th Annual Delaware Show* (June 8–July 29, 1973).

**Page 19, counterclockwise from middle-left:** Ron Dubick, *Rob Jones Artist*, January 10, 1975. Courtesy of the Delaware Historical Society. © *The News Journal*. Jones' solo exhibition, *Delaware Art Museum Presents, Rob Jones: Black Wilmington*, was on view January 13–February 9, 1975. | Ron Dubick, *Rob Jones Artist*, January 10, 1975. Courtesy of the Delaware Historical Society. © *The News Journal.* The creation of the polyurethane foam forms for *Black Wilmington* took place in the Delaware Art Museum gallery. | Glenn Crawford, *Downtown Gallery*, May 1, 1974. © *The News Journal.* Fifth Street Gallery's inaugural exhibition of *News Journal* photographers. | Ron Dubick, *Rob Jones*, April 19, 1977. Courtesy of the Delaware Historical Society.

**Page 20, counter-clockwise from top-left:** Fred Comegys, *Julio Acuna–Artist*, October 22, 1975. Courtesy of the Delaware Historical Society. © *The News Journal.* | Installation view of Nick Snook's *Vehicular Sculptures* (May 14–June 2, 1974) at Fifth Street Gallery. | Bill Ballenberg, *Sculptures on Mall*, June 12, 1978. Courtesy of the Delaware Historical Society. © *The News Journal. Sundial–1978* was co-sponsored by Delaware Trust and the City of Wilmington. | Fred Comegys, *5th St Gallery–Party*, May 22, 1976. Courtesy of the Delaware Historical Society. © *The News Journal.* Paradise Party performer at Fifth Street Gallery. | Pat Crowe, *Sleeze*, September 3, 1976. Courtesy of the Delaware Historical Society. © *The News Journal.* Edie "The Egg Lady" Massey enthroned during the Sleaze Convention at Fifth Street Gallery.

**Page 21, clockwise from top-left:** Ron Dubick, *Tom Watkins*, April 19, 1977. Courtesy of the Delaware Historical Society. © *The News Journal.* Tom Watkins in front of his Citysights/Citysounds mural, *Stasis* (1976). | *Citysights/Citysounds* (Wilmington, DE: City of Wilmington, 1976). Collection of Norma Calabro. Photograph by Carson Zullinger. | *People*

*Are The Key* mural, 1975–76. *Citysights/Citysounds* (Wilmington, DE: City of Wilmington, 1976). Collection of Norma Calabro. Photograph by Carson Zullinger.

**Page 22, counterclockwise from middle-left:** Norma Calabro, *The City Child*, 1975. *Citysights/Citysounds* (Wilmington, DE: City of Wilmington, 1976). Collection of Norma Calabro. Photograph by Carson Zullinger. | Raymond Kopcho, *The Storefront Merchants*, 1975. *Citysights/Citysounds* (Wilmington, DE: City of Wilmington, 1976). Collection of Norma Calabro. Photograph by Carson Zullinger. | Donaghey Brown, *Tom Stiltz*, January 25, 1976. Courtesy of the Delaware Historical Society. © *The News Journal*. Tom Stiltz's *The Urban Worker* (1975) on view in Wilmington's Public Building.

**Page 23, counterclockwise from bottom-left:** Jack Buxbaum, *Untitled*, 1976. Gelatin silver print, 6 1/4 x 6 1/4 inches. Bicentenial Metroscope Collection housed at the Delaware Art Museum. © Jack Buxbaum. | Thomas Sherman, *Untitled*, 1976. Gelatin silver print, 7 3/4 x 9 inches. Delaware Art Museum. © Thomas Sherman. | Pat Crowe, *Metroscope*, August 13, 1976. Courtesy of the Delaware Historical Society. © *The News Journal*. Bicentennial Metroscope photographs installed in DART buses. | Tony Calabro, *Charles L. Wyrick, Jr., director, Delaware Art Museum, in Contemporary Gallery*, 1976, in *Wilmington Awake*, 1977. Gelatin silver print, 5 1/2 x 8 1/8 inches. Bicentennial Metroscope Collection housed at the Delaware Art Museum. © Tony Calabro. | Norma Calabro, *Wilmington Parade*, 1976. Gelatin silver print, 6 5/8 x 10 inches. Bicentennial Metroscope Collection housed at the Delaware Art Museum. © Norma Calabro.

**Page 24, counterclockwise from top-left:** Fred Comegys, *Kids–Art Reach X-ibit*, April 10, 1978. Courtesy of the Delaware Historical Society. © *The News Journal*. An ArtReach participatory exhibition, *Rhythm & Blues & Reds, A Visual Concert* (April 1978), at City/County Building. | Installation view of Rick Rothrock's *Wilmington Green*, 1978. Collection of Rick Rothrock. | Alan Sonfist installed in an animal cage for *The ArtSquad Goes to the Zoo* (October 1978). Collection of Rick Rothrock.

**Page 25:** *Homage to Winter* (March 1979) on view in Willingtown Square. Collection of Rick Rothrock.

**Page 26, counterclockwise from top-middle:** Dan Teis, *40 x 40 Blue*, 1985. Mixed media on canvas, 40 x 40 inches. Collection of Wesley and Harriet Memeger. © Estate of Dan Teis. Photograph by Carson Zullinger. | Tom Bostelle, *Woman Dressing*, 1973. Oil on canvas mounted on wood panel, 66 x 48 inches. Delaware Art Museum, Gift of Mr. and Mrs. William H. Boucher, 1975. © Estate of Tom Bostelle. Photograph by Carson Zullinger. | Mary Page Evans, *The Yellow Table*, c. 1971. Oil on canvas, 30 x 20 inches. Collection of the artist. © Mary Page Evans. Photograph by Carson Zullinger.

**Page 27, counterclockwise from middle-left:** Leo S. Matkins, *Opening Opera Gallery*, September 18, 1977. Courtesy of the Delaware Historical Society. © *The News Journal*. Sewell C. Biggs at the opening of his Grand Gallery in the Grand Opera House on Market Street. | Ron Dubick, *Artisans III*, December 6, 1977. Courtesy of the Delaware Historical Society. © *The News Journal*. Artisans III opened on Market Street Mall between Seventh and Eighth Streets as a collaboration between three businesses—Carol Balick and Marilyn Huthmacher's Amerind Artisans, Fred Carspecken's Carspecken-Scott Gallery, and Judy McCabe's Blooming Arts. | Mitch Lyons, *Untitled*, 1980s. Clay monoprint, 27 x 25 inches. Delaware Art Museum, Gift of the artist, 2012. © Mitch Lyons. Photograph by Carson Zullinger. | Graham Dougherty, *Float*, 1986. Oil on canvas, 42 x 54 inches. Delaware Art Museum, Louisa du Pont Copeland Memorial Fund, 1986. © Graham Dougherty. Photograph by Carson Zullinger.

**Page 28:** Fred Comegys, *Snead sculpture*, June 3–8, 1985. Courtesy of the Delaware Historical Society. © *The News Journal*. Ric Snead in front of his 1985 sculpture, *PROA* at Fourth and Shipley Streets.

**Page 31:** Donaghey Brown, *Artist of the Year* (detail), November 19, 1975. Courtesy of the Delaware Historical Society. © *The News Journal*. James E. Newton with his 1974 collagraph, *Madonna and Child*.

**Page 32:** James E. Newton, *The Pill*, 1972. Collagraph, 37 1/8 x 29 inches. Collection of the artist. © James E. Newton. Photograph by Carson Zullinger. *The Pill* was included in the 1980 *Delaware African American Art Exhibition*.

**Page 33, left to right:** Percy Eugene Ricks, *Black Samson of Brandywine*, c. 1989. Oil on canvas, 32 x 32 inches. Private collection. Courtesy of James E. Newton. © Percy Eugene Ricks. Photograph by Carson Zullinger. *Black Samson of Brandywine* is based on Paul Laurence Dunbar's poem of the same name. | Simmie Knox, *A Place: Suspended*, 1970. Acrylic and enamel on canvas, diptych, 61 3/4 x 143 inches overall. Courtesy, The Kreeger Museum, Washington, DC © Simmie Knox.

**Pages 34–35:** Joe Moss, *Sun and Sound*, 1975. Fiberglass and carbon steel, 78 inch diameter. Collection of the artist. © Joe Moss. *Sun and Sound* was installed in *Sculpture 75* at the Philadelphia Museum of Art, in the artist's summer 1977 exhibition in the George Read House garden in New Castle, Delaware, in 1979 at the Dover campus of Delaware Technical Community College, and at the Blossom Music Center in Cleveland in 1982.

**Page 36, clockwise from top-left:** Julio daCunha, *Entanglements II*, 1975. Oil on canvas, 33 3/4 x 40 inches. Delaware Art Museum, Gift of Sewell C. Biggs, 1975. © Julio daCunha. Photograph by Carson Zullinger. *Entanglements II* was included in the artist's solo exhibition, *The Entanglements* (October 1975), at Fifth Street Gallery. The show travelled to Pleiades Gallery in New York the following month. | Larry Holmes, *Alligator Painting #6*, 1984. Oil on canvas, 72 x 60 inches. Collection of the artist. © Larry Holmes. Photograph by Carson Zullinger. *Alligator Painting #6* was included in *Paintings by Larry Holmes* (September 12–October 28, 1984) at the Delaware Art Museum. | Robert Larry Straight, *P-115*, 1979–81. Oil, encaustic, canvas, wood, and fiberglass, 38 1/2 x 78 x 4 1/2 inches. Courtesy of Schmidt-Dean Gallery, Philadelphia, Pennsylvania. © Robert Larry Straight, 2015. Photograph by Carson Zullinger.

**Page 37, top to bottom:** John Weiss, *THE WEDDING THAT MEASURED ITSELF*, 1974. Gelatin silver print, 6 1/2 x 10 inches. Collection of the artist. © John Weiss. Photograph by Carson Zullinger. | Frederick Sommer and John Weiss at the opening of *Venus, Jupiter, and Mars: Frederick Sommer Photographs* (April 27–June 8, 1980). Delaware Art Museum, Institutional Archives.

**Pages 38–39:** Installation view of *19th Contemporary Crafts Exhibition* (November 9–30, 1975). Delaware Art Museum, Institutional Archives.

**Page 40, clockwise from to-left:** Vera E. Kaminski, *Androgyne*, 1976. Dyed, hand-spun silk, 7 x 6 1/2 x 3 inches. Collection of the artist. © 1976 Vera E. Kaminski. This delicate fiber work was included in the artist's *Webs & Whispers* (May 11–June 3, 1978) at Fifth Street Gallery. | Victor Spinski, *Sludge Trashcan*, 1986. Ceramic, 14 x 12 x 12 inches. Collection of Sally Van Orden. © Sally Van Orden Spinski. Photograph by Carson Zullinger. | Installation view of *Helen Mason: Form and Spirit* (May 20–June 19, 1988) at the Delaware Art Museum. Delaware Art Museum, Institutional Archives.

**Page 41, left to right:** Terence Roberts, *Teresa Barkley and former Wilmington Mayor William T. McLaughlin*, 1987. Collection of the artist. © Terence Roberts. Teresa Barkley's 1987 quilt, *The Wilmington Stamp*, can be seen in the background of this publicity photograph for the October 1987 issue of *Delaware Today*. | Ceramicist Charles Nalle established a studio and warehouse in downtown Wilmington at 111 Orange Street in 1982 to produce his Parvenu Tableware line. Collection of Charles Nalle.

**Page 42:** Flash Rosenberg, *Hello, I'm Susan Rosenberg.* (detail), 1979. Gelatin silver print, 11 x 14 inches. Collection of the artist. © Flash Rosenberg. Photograph by Carson Zullinger.

**Page 44, top to bottom:** Flash Rosenberg, *Now it's over. No, it's not over*, 1981. Six gelatin silver prints, each 8 1/2 x 6 1/2 inches. Collection of the artist. © Flash Rosenberg. Photograph by Carson Zullinger. Rosamond "Roz" DuPont and Bernard Flech serve as models. | Flash Rosenberg, *Dance Around the Town*, 1976–77. Chronapaque polyester print, 11 x 14 inches. Collection of the artist. © Flash Rosenberg.

**Page 45, counterclockwise from top-left:** Opening reception of the photography exhibition, *Six Shooters* (March 12–April 1, 1978) at Fifth Street Gallery. Exhibiting artist Flash Rosenberg (right) stands with her Rosenberg's *Art Gum Machine*, filled with *SueVenirs* (in deference to Sue Rosenberg). Each vending machine buddle holds a contact sheet photograph matted onto a miniature mat board. Dayle Severns (left) has just purchased a photo bubble by inserting two quarters into the machine. Collection of Flash Rosenberg. Photograph by Morton David Rosenberg. | Ron Dubick, *Byron Shurtleff*, March 19, 1976. Courtesy of the Delaware Historical Society. © *The News Journal.* Artist and installation view of *Color Songs* (March 18–April 10, 1976) at Fifth Street Gallery.| Exhibition poster for *Metroscope: Photographs* (January 7–February 20, 1977) at the Delaware Art Museum. Collection of Flash Rosenberg. Photograph by Carson Zullinger.

**Pages 46–47, left to right:** Rick Rothrock, *Wilmington Green* poster, 1978. Poster, 12 13/16 x 17 1/8 inches. Collection of the artist. © Rick Rothrock. Photograph by Carson Zullinger. | Rick Rothrock, *Spring Ritual*, 1977. Collection of the artist. © Rick Rothrock.

**Page 48, left to right:** ArtSquad artists, *The ArtSquad Goes to the Zoo* poster, 1978. Poster, 17 x 11 inches. Collection of Rick Rothrock. Photograph by Carson Zullinger. | Various artists, *Arts Alive* poster, 1981. Poster, 11 x 8 1/2 inches. Collection of Rick Rothrock. Photograph by Carson Zullinger.

**Page 49:** Leo S. Matkins, *DCCA New Museum*, May 13, 1984. Courtesy of the Delaware Historical Society. © *The News Journal.* Delaware

Center for the Contemporary Arts in the Waterworks Building at 103 East 16th Street.

**Page 50:** Carson Zullinger, *Untitled* (detail), 1981. Color photograph, 14 15/16 x 18 3/4 inches. Delaware Art Museum, Louisa du Pont Copeland Memorial Fund, 1981. © Carson Zullinger.

**Page 51, top to bottom:** Fred Comegys, *Dart Art*, September 20, 1977. Courtesy of the Delaware Historical Society. © *The News Journal.* ArtReach Exhibitions Assistant David Tonnesen and Technical Assistant Carson Zullinger hang photographs inside a DART bus. | Leo S. Matkins, *Gallery Show,* September 26, 1982. Courtesy of the Delaware Historical Society. © *The News Journal.* DCCA's first employee, Roseanna Capaldi Richards, and Carson Zullinger installing artwork at 224 French Street.

**Pages 52–53, left to right:** Tom Watkins, *Sleaze Digest,* no. 1, 1976. Color photocopy, 8 1/2 x 5 1/2 inches. Collection of Jerry Grant. © Tom Watkins. Photograph by Carson Zullinger. | Anne Eder, *Fences* (detail), not dated. Color photocopy with chain link fence frame, 47 x 35 3/4 x 3 inches. Collection of Patt Panzer and Carson Zullinger. © Anne Eder. Photograph by Carson Zullinger.

**Page 54, left to right:** Tom Watkins, *Xanadu Pleasure Dome*, 1981. Black and white photocopy, 8 x 5 1/4 inches. Collection of Julia Gorton. © Tom Watkins. Photograph by Carson Zullinger. | Bill Lynch and Tom Watkins, *Sleaze Convention* poster, 1976. India ink and white ink with pasted Photostat photographs on graph paper, 11 1/2 x 18 inches. Collection of Bill Lynch. © Tom Watkins. Photograph by Carson Zullinger.

**Page 55:** Tom Watkins, *Untitled*, 1983. Color photocopy, 15 x 8 1/2 inches. Collection of Paul Woznicki. © Tom Watkins. Photograph by Carson Zullinger.

**Page 56, top to bottom:** Anne Eder, *Mermaids*, 1984. Color photocopy, 16 x 9 5/8 inches. Collection of the artist. © Anne Eder. Photograph by Carson Zullinger. | Anne Eder, *She Hears Voices (even though the speakers are gone),* 1987. Color photocopy, 11 x 14 inches. Collection of the artist. © Anne Eder.

**Page 57, left to right:** Anne Eder, *Jehanne Sur Le Bucher* from *Joan of Arc Trilogy*, 1985–86. Mixed media, 11 x 14 inches. Collection of the artist. © Anne Eder. | Tom Watkins, *Waitresses from Outer Space* doll, 1984. Color photocopy on fabric, 13 x 5 x 1 inches. Collection of Anne Eder. © Tom Watkins. Photograph by Carson Zullinger.

**Page 58, left to right:** Anne Eder modeling *Xerographic Clothing Line*, 1985–86. Collection of Anne Eder. | Postcard for show at *Neither/Nor Gallery, New York Exhibition*, February 1985. Collection of Anne Eder.

**Page 59, left to right:** Anne Eder outside Tom Watkins' *Gallery X* at 65 West Seventh Street, Wilmington, DE, c. 1985–86. Collection of Anne Eder. | Tom Watkins, *Hot Blonde*, 1990. Color photocopy, 15 3/8 x 8 7/8 inches. Collection of Anne Eder. © Tom Watkins. Photograph by Carson Zullinger.

**Page 60:** Julia Gorton, *Joyce Brabner*, 1977. Photograph, 8 x 8 inches. Collection of the artist. © Julia Gorton.

**Page 61:** Pat Crowe, *Sleeze*, September 3, 1976. Courtesy of the Delaware Historical Society. © *The News Journal.* Joyce Brabner selling tickets to the Sleaze Convention.

**Pages 62–63, left to right:** Julia Gorton, *Tom Watkins and Craig Dawson in Xanadu Comics and Collectables*, c. late 1970s. Photograph, 13 x 19 inches. Collection of the artist. © Julia Gordon. | Josephine Moore, Evoynne, Joyce Brabner, and Mary Page Evans in Women's Correctional Institute Arts Workshop, 1979. Collection of E. JEAN LANYON. | Joyce Brabner, *I Could Sit No Longer* poster, 1979. Collection of E. JEAN LANYON. © Joyce Brabner. *I Could Sit No Longer* was a March 1979 exhibition held in the State Office Building Mezzanine gallery of the arts, theater, and puppetry program of the Women's Correctional Institute Arts Workshop.

**Page 64, top to bottom:** Carson Zullinger, *Untitled*, 1987. Gelatin silver print, 18 5/8 x 14 inches. Collection of the artist. © Carson Zullinger. | Tom Watkins, *All Tomorrow's Parties–Remix*, 1989. Color photocopy, 13 7/8 x 10 inches. Collection of Anne Eder. © Tom Watkins. Photograph by Carson Zullinger.

**Page 65:** Unknown photographer, *Susan Isaacs*, January 1984. Courtesy of the Delaware Historical Society. © *The News Journal.*

**Pages 66–67:** Unknown photographer. Deb Loewen and Joseph Pinzarrone perform *Electronic Dance No. One*, 1975. Collection of Deb Loewen.

**Page 68, left to right:** Coverage of *Dance: At the Gym*. University of Delaware's Cosmopolitan Club *Viewpoint* newsletter, vol. 5 no. 3, November 1975. Collection of Deb Loewen. Photograph by Carson Zullinger. | *Altered Space* poster, 1976. Collection of Deb Loewen. © Deb Loewen.

**Page 69, top to bottom:** *Moon* poster, 1977. Collection of Deb Loewen. | Rick Rothrock, *Untitled*, 1977. Gelatin silver print with ink drawing, 13 1/2 x 19 1/4 inches. Courtesy of the artist. © Rick Rothrock. Photograph by Carson Zullinger. The lashed telephone poles and skids for *Moon* can be seen in Rick Rothrock's sketch.

**Pages 70–71:** Leo S. Matkins, *Del Theatre Co*, April 19, 1982. Courtesy of the Delaware Historical Society. © *The News Journal.*

**Pages 72–73:** Fred Comegys, *Firehouse Theater*, December 6–8, 1979. Courtesy of the Delaware Historical Society. © *The News Journal.* Cleveland Morris with the cast of George Bernard Shaw's play, *Overruled*, the first public performance of the Delaware Theatre Company (December 7–9, 1979). | Leo S. Matkins, *Del Theatre Co*, April 19, 1982. Courtesy of the Delaware Historical Society. © *The News Journal.* | Fred Comegys, *Cleveland Morris*, April 20, 1985. Courtesy of the Delaware Historical Society. © *The News Journal.* Managing Director, Dennis Luzak and Cleveland Morris at the construction site of the Water Street location of the Delaware Theatre Company.

**Page 74:** E. JEAN LANYON, *Tangent* cover (detail), June 1981. Ink on paper, 13 1/4 x 8 1/2 inches. Collection of the artist. © E. JEAN LANYON. Photograph by Carson Zullinger.

**Page 75:** *Emergency Illustrated*, no. 1, October 1973. Newspaper, 15 3/4 x 14 15/16 inches. Special Collections, University of Delaware Library, Newark, Delaware. Photograph by Carson Zullinger.

**Page 76, top to bottom:** Mary Loewenstein, *e. jean lanyon*, c. 1977. Collection of e. jean lanyon. In addition to being an artist and serving as Delaware's poet laureate from 1979–2001, e. jean lanyon worked as a draftsperson at the University of Delaware in the 1970s. | University of Delaware's Cosmopolitan Club *Viewpoint* newsletter, vol. 5, no. 4, January 1976. Magazine, 15 x 11 1/2 inches. Collection of Steven Leech. Photograph by Carson Zullinger.

**Page 77:** Fifth Street Gallery advertisement, University of Delaware's Cosmopolitan Club *Viewpoint* newsletter, vol. 5, no. 4, p. 2, January 1976. Collection of Steven Leech. Photograph by Carson Zullinger.

**Page 78:** John Hickey, *Dream Streets* cover, no. 1, 1977. Archive of Dreamstreets, Special Collections, University of Delaware Library, Newark, Delaware. Photograph by Carson Zullinger.

**Page 79, left to right:** Tom Watkins, *The Daily Plague*, no. 1, c. 1976. Magazine, 11 x 8 1/2 inches. Collection of Steven Leech. Photograph by Carson Zullinger. | *Tom Watkins' X-Ray*, vol. 1, no. 1, May 1987. Magazine, 10 13/16 x 8 5/8 inches. Collection of Paul Woznicki. © Tom Watkins. Photograph by Carson Zullinger.

**Pages 80–81:** Debbie Cohn, *Geo. Stewart*, c. 1979. Photograph, 8 x 10 inches. Collection of Geo. Stewart.

**Page 83, top to bottom:** Ron Dubick, *Rondo Center*, March 2, 1978. Courtesy of the Delaware Historical Society. © *The News Journal.* Tom Watkins, Joyce Brabner, and Geo. Stewart in the Rondo Center. | Benjamin B. Woznicki, *Paul Woznicki with robot*, c. 1978. Collection of Paul Woznicki.

**Page 84, left to right:** Leo S. Matkins, *Terminal Hotel Party*, April 14, 1977. Courtesy of the Delaware Historical Society. © *The News Journal.* | *The T.A.M.I Show and The Big T.N.T. Show Poster*, c. 1977. Collection of Jerry Grant.

**Page 85:** Pat Crowe, *Rialto Theater*, March 1981. Courtesy of the Delaware Historical Society. © *The News Journal.* Al Malmfelt and Barry Solan in front of the Rialto Theater.

**Page 86:** Elizabeth Botwright Becker, *The Commotions*, c. 1981. Collection of Jerry Grant.

**Page 87:** Trey White, *State Theatre*, c. 1981. 35mm Kodak Tri-X film. Collection of the artist. © Trey White.

**Page 88:** Flash Rosenberg, *Listening Photographs: Jerry Grant*, 1976. Gelatin silver print, 14 x 11 1/8 inches. Collection of the artist. © Flash Rosenberg. Photograph by Carson Zullinger.

**Pages 90–91:** Geo. Stewart, I Like It Like That advertisement, 1976. Collection of the artist. © Geo. Stewart.

**Pages 92–93, left to right:** Unknown photographer, *Pier 34 Front Door,* August 1983. Collection of Leonard Perlson. Robert Jones installed shrouds throughout Pier 34—one of several abandoned docks on the Hudson River used by artists during the 1970s and 1980s—during the summer and fall of 1983; two were positioned at a front entrance. | Ellen Skye, *Shrouds*, 1984/2014. Archival pigment print, 7 1/2 x 11 inches. Collection of the artist. © Ellen Skye. Robert Jones' May 17–June 15, 1984 installation on the awning of the Leonard Perlson Gallery at 430 West 14th Street in Manhattan.

**Page 94, left to right:** Robert Jones, *Untitled*, 1983. Graphite on paper, 30 1/4 x 22 1/2 inches. Collection of Wendy Jones Donahoe. © Artist's Estate. Photograph by Carson Zullinger. Drawings and "notations" of the Anvil Dance Club were also included in the 1984 show at the Leonard Perlson Gallery. | Andreas Sterzing, *Pier34-24 Rob Jones*, 1983. Collection of the artist. © Andreas Sterzing. One of Robert Jones' shrouds inside Pier 34.

**Page 95:** Robert Jones, *Shroud*, 1984. Bronze. Collection of George A. Weymouth. © Artist's estate. Photograph by Carson Zullinger. Five shrouds were acquired by George A. Weymouth and installed along a garden path at his home, Big Bend, in Chadds Ford, Pennsylvania; one was subsequently cast in bronze.

www.ingramcontent.com/pod-product-compliance
Lightning Source LLC
LaVergne TN
LVHW070132110826
845147LV00002B/238

* 9 7 8 0 9 9 6 0 6 7 6 2 1 *